# THE EVERYTHING® Project Management Book

## 2ND EDITION

Dear Reader,

It is a difficult task to write a complete guide to project management because it is a profession that continues to grow and evolve, but I wanted to write a book to get you started. Use this book to learn great habits to help build your project management prowess. This book is a culmination of the lessons from those that taught me and was written for those searching for knowledge and those who teach project management. There is much more to project management than you can fit in many volumes, but the knowledge contained in this book will give you direction as you search for and find your project management style. Be wary of books or people that teach that there is only one way or one methodology to manage projects. The first rule of project management is that there are few rules. Project managers become great based on their experiences, so get out there and create yours. Good luck!

Rick A. Morris, PMP

# Welcome to the EVERYTHING® Series!

These handy, accessible books give you all you need to tackle a difficult project, gain a new hobby, comprehend a fascinating topic, prepare for an exam, or even brush up on something you learned back in school but have since forgotten.

You can choose to read an *Everything*® book from cover to cover or just pick out the information you want from our four useful boxes: e-questions, e-facts, e-alerts, e-ssentials. We give you everything you need to know on the subject, but throw in a lot of fun stuff along the way, too.

We now have more than 400 *Everything*® books in print, spanning such wide-ranging categories as weddings, pregnancy, cooking, music instruction, foreign language, crafts, pets, New Age, and so much more. When you're done reading them all, you can finally say you know *Everything*®!

## QUESTIONS?
Answers to
common questions

## FACTS
Important snippets
of information

## ALERTS!
Urgent
warnings

## ESSENTIALS
Quick
handy tips

**DIRECTOR OF INNOVATION** Paula Munier

**EDITORIAL DIRECTOR** Laura M. Daly

**EXECUTIVE EDITOR, SERIES BOOKS** Brielle K. Matson

**ASSOCIATE COPY CHIEF** Sheila Zwiebel

**ACQUISITIONS EDITOR** Lisa Laing

**DEVELOPMENT EDITOR** Katie McDonough

**PRODUCTION EDITOR** Casey Ebert

Visit the entire Everything® series at *www.everything.com*

# THE
# EVERYTHING®
# PROJECT MANAGEMENT BOOK

## 2ND EDITION

Tackle any project with confidence
and get it done on time

Rick A. Morris, PMP

avon, massachusetts

*I would like to dedicate this book to my family:*
*My wife Stephanie, daughter Ramsey, and son Remo.*
*If it were not for them, none of this would be possible.*

An Everything® Series Book.
Everything® and everything.com® are registered trademarks of F+W Media, Inc.

Published by Adams Media, a division of F+W Media, Inc.
57 Littlefield Street, Avon, MA 02322 U.S.A.
*www.adamsmedia.com*

ISBN 10: 1-59869-635-1
ISBN: 13: 978-1-59869-635-6

Printed in the United States of America.

J  I  H  G  F  E  D  C

**Library of Congress Cataloging-in-Publication Data**
is available from the publisher.

This publication is designed to provide accurate and authoritative information with regard to the subject matter covered. It is sold with the understanding that the publisher is not engaged in rendering legal, accounting, or other professional advice. If legal advice or other expert assistance is required, the services of a competent professional person should be sought.

—From a *Declaration of Principles* jointly adopted by a Committee of the American Bar Association and a Committee of Publishers and Associations

Many of the designations used by manufacturers and sellers to distinguish their products are claimed as trademarks. Where those designations appear in this book and Adams Media was aware of a trademark claim, the designations have been printed with initial capital letters.

*This book is available at quantity discounts for bulk purchases.*
*For information, please call 1-800-289-0963.*

# Contents

**Top Ten Mistakes New Project Managers Make / x**

**Introduction / xi**

**1 What Is Project Management? / 1**
So, You Have a Project **2** • Where Do Projects Come From? **3** • The Sponsor and the Stakeholders **4** • Let's Talk Project Management **5** • Is the Big Picture Big Enough? **8** • Has It Ever Been Done? **12** • Going Where No One Has Gone Before **14** • We Don't Have Time to Plan! **15**

**2 Setting the Wheels in Motion / 17**
Clear Vision **18** • Old Ways Versus New Ways **18** • Competition **19** • Are You Ready to Roll? **20** • Do Your Homework **21** • Three Common Mistakes **24** • Prioritize **27** • Selecting the Right Project **28**

**3 The Project Life Cycle / 29**
Understanding the Project Phases **30** • Initiating **30** • Planning **31** • Executing **32** • Controlling **33** • Closing **33** • Project Methodologies **33** • Methodologies Versus Life Cycles **34**

**4 Project Initiation: You Have to Start Somewhere / 35**
Turn Vision into a Plan **36** • Creating the Playbook (Project Charter) **36** • Everyone on the Same Page? **38** • Decisions and Assumptions **39** • Defining Specific Objectives **40** • Defining Key Resources **41**

**5 Project Planning / 43**
Myths about Project Plans **44** • It's Not Just a Task List **44** • The Plans That Make the Plan **46** • The Sum of the Parts **47** • Garnering Acceptance **51** • Selling the Plan **52** • Project Baselines **53**

**6**

**Project Execution / 55**

Track, Report, Change, Plan, Track **56** • Getting the Right Answers **56** • Sending the Right Message **57** • Progress, Progress, Progress **58** • Let Your Plans Ebb and Flow **59** • Showing the Real Date **59**

**7**

**Project Controlling / 61**

Making the Right Adjustments **62** • The Cycle Within the Cycle **63** • Ask All of the Questions **64** • How to Communicate Change **65** • Measuring Against the Baseline **67** • Determining When to Panic **67**

**8**

**Project Closing / 69**

What Is the Definition of Done? **70** • The Last 2 Percent **70** • Lessons Learned **71** • Closure Documentation **72** • The Handoff **73** • The Sign Off **75** • Disassembling the Team **76** • How Do You Feel? **77** • Down the Road **80**

**9**

**Assembling the Best Project Team / 81**

Your Team's Core Members **82** • Selecting Your Project Team **82** • R-E-S-P-E-C-T **86** • Where to Find Team Members **87** • Getting It Down on Paper **90** • Determining Availability **93** • Ancillary Roles **94** • Who Has the Authority? **94** • Building Commitment **96** • Finding the Right Mix **97**

**10**

**Effective Project Leadership / 101**

Team Huddle **102** • What Kind of Leader Are You? **102** • The Importance of Consistency **104** • First-Rate Teams **105** • Senior Management Reporting **107**

**11**

**Creating the Schedule / 109**

In the Beginning **110** • The Network Diagram **110** • Verify Your Estimates **116** • Absolute Completion Date **117** • Cut Yourself Some Slack **118** • Various Projects, Various Methods **119** • The Famous Gantt Chart **119** • Task Schedule or Matrix **120** • Anticipating Pitfalls **122** • And the Calendar Says . . . **123**

**12**

**The All-Important Budget / 125**

Ready, Set, Budget **126** • Affecting the Bottom Line **129** • Let the Budget Work for You **132** • And the Project Goes On **134** • A Juggling Act **136** • Budget Busters **137**

**13** **Monitoring Progress / 139**

Why Monitor? **140** • How Often to Monitor **141** • Performance Periods **145** • Monitoring at the Individual Level **147** • Three Steps Forward, Two Steps Back **151** • Monitoring Expenditures **152** • Project Evolution **155** • Monitoring Yourself **156** • Tools for Monitoring Your Project **158** • Monitoring Intangibles **159**

**14** **The PMO: Project Management Office / 163**

What Is a PMO? **164** • Types of PMOs **164** • Responsibilities of the PMO **165** • Standards for Project Managers **166** • The Collective Group **167** • Give Me a "P," Give Me an "M," Give Me an "O!" **168**

**15** **Project Management Software / 169**

Using Software to Facilitate Your Project **170** • Software Shopping **171** • Popular Favorites **173** • Other Software Products **175** • High-End Users **180** • Enterprise Project Management Systems **180**

**16** **Risk Management / 183**

The Nature of Risk **184** • Types of Project Risks **185** • Assessing Risks **186** • Dealing with Risks **187** • Prioritizing Risks **191** • Monitoring Every Step of the Way **192** • Worth Your While **197** • Risk Interactions and Magnification **198** • Common Project Problems **202**

**17** **Communications Management / 205**

Who's on First? **206** • Communication Paths **207** • I Have to Plan My Communications Too? **207** • Types of Communication Documents **208** • Formal, Informal, Written, Verbal, and Everything Else **211** • Communications Matrix **212** • Ensuring Communication **212** • Communicating on All Levels **213**

**18** **Conflict Resolution and Handling Various Personalities / 215**

Cooperative Resolution **216** • Identifying Key Characters **217** • Assessing the Conflict Situation **218** • Methods of Conflict Resolution **219** • Taking the Initiative **225** • Other Factors to Keep in Mind **227** • Handling Various Personalities **228** • Other Characters **229** • The Art of Negotiating **232**

**19**

**Motivational Skills / 235**

What Motivates Us? **236** • Motivational Theories **236** • Lighting Their Fire **239** • Motivational Seminars **241** • It's the Little Things **242** • Bridging the Gap **243** • What Will It Take? **244** • Keeping Yourself Motivated **245**

**20**

**What Happens If My Plans Fail? / 247**

The Inevitable Project Roadblock **248** • Why Plans Fail **248** • How to Course Correct **249** • How to Garner New Support **250** • Where Did All of My Resources Go? **251** • This Project Has No Risk, Because It HAS to Finish on Time! **252**

**21**

**Finishing the Project and Evaluating the Results / 253**

The End Is Near **254** • Final Phase Responsibilities **256** • Postproject Evaluations **259** • Setting Up the Next One **262** • What Did You Learn? **263** • Now What? **265**

**22**

**Project Training and Certifications / 267**

Project Management Institute (PMI) **268** • Certified Associate in Project Management (CAPM) **268** • Project Management Professional (PMP) **269** • Other Certifications **270** • Other Training **272** • Local Involvement **273**

**23**

**Tales from the Other Side: Pitfalls to Avoid / 275**

The Ego **276** • The Procrastinator **276** • The Noncommunicator **277** • The Hoarder **277** • The Blamer **278** • The Traitor **278** • The Apathy Machine **279** • The Yes Person **280** • Closing Thoughts **280**

**Appendix A: Glossary / 282**

**Appendix B: Resources / 284**

**Index / 287**

# Acknowledgments

First, I would like to thank my family: my beautiful wife, Stephanie, my daughter Ramsey, and my son Remo. They teach me more about life than I could ever hope to experience. I would also like to thank my team at Highmark Technology: Mark, Blake, Terry, Morgan, Candler, and we will still claim Tony.

I would also like to thank individuals that I consider my mentors: Cary Blaes, Don Delashaw, and Dan Bailey. A special thank you goes to the team that was built at AmSouth Bank. You guys taught me more about myself and project management than anyone else ever has. To anyone whom I have forgotten, thank you to you as well.

# Top Ten Mistakes
# New Project Managers Make

1. They are afraid to present the real status of a project. They would rather spin positive information than reveal negative information.

2. They let themselves be bullied by team members not wanting to plan or document.

3. They are afraid to ask for what the project needs (more money, resources, or time).

4. They don't see the value in following a methodology until the project goes wrong.

5. They fail to properly account for risk.

6. They don't motivate their teams to get the best from them every day.

7. They don't use proper scheduling tools, making it impossible to truly understand if they are ahead of or behind schedule.

8. They create documents because they are supposed to, not because they understand why they should be done.

9. They do not develop the resources into a team; they let the team come together without a leader.

10. They think that if they plan properly, then nothing will go wrong with the project.

# Introduction

▶ LIKE A WELL-WRITTEN STORY, a successful project has a beginning, middle, and end. It all starts with the so-called idea phase, when someone or several people decide to begin a project. The middle phase is that lengthy stretch beginning with lists, plans, and strategies and ending with the completion of the plan. Hopefully, the plan leads to a completed project that all team members can take pride in having accomplished.

Some people are not even aware that they are project managers. Picking up eight ten-year-old children, getting them into your car, and driving them to soccer practice is a project. Pulling together 200 volunteers and cleaning up the neighborhood is a project. Setting up a new branch office for your company is a project.

What these examples have in common is the planning, scheduling, budgeting, problem solving, and time constraints that go into it. Those are the common denominators; there is also a separate goal for each and every project.

How can project management skills help you? Would you like to accomplish your project goals within the time frame and budget allotted? How often have we seen the old black-and-white film clips of early airplane prototypes falling apart upon take off or going in circles and never leaving the ground? The good project manager gets the plane in the air safely, without spending excessive time or money.

A computer is a tremendous asset to managing projects. Software programs, discussed later in the book, can help organize and facilitate even the most complex projects and make project management that much easier. Technology and modern corporate project managers go hand in hand (literally), as their laptop and cell phone are rarely far from their grasp.

That said, software and technology cannot replace learning, planning, proper execution, people skills, decision making, and hard work. As the old saying goes, "If it came in a box, everyone would have one."

There have always been successful projects without technology. The Wright Brothers did get that plane to fly, Lindbergh landed safely after crossing the ocean, and despite the Depression, the Empire State Building rose to great heights. Let's not forget the Egyptian Pyramids, which were built with no Gantt charts, no flowcharts, and probably no online brainstorming sessions. Ancient structures around the world and inventions throughout the centuries are the result of completed projects, all managed in some manner and most fraught with setbacks and rethinking along the way. Even unsuccessful projects have had positive outcomes. After all, Columbus didn't set out to discover America, did he?

Everyone is involved in projects at many levels, from school projects to personal projects to business projects. At some point, everyone also becomes a project manager. Did you schedule and lead a scout troop on a hike? Organize the company picnic? There is no set budget, time frame, or number of people involved that constitutes a project.

As you're reading this book, look for projects all around you. You'll probably be able to write down about five you've been involved in, if you sit back and think about it for a while. As you read, think back on those projects that you've taken part in. Did they go wrong for one of several reasons mentioned in the book? What you learn in these pages will help you stay on track with your future projects—whatever forms they may take. Good luck!

# CHAPTER 1

# What Is Project Management?

People are faced with numerous projects throughout the course of life. Building a new home, raising a family, planting a garden, or deciding which refrigerator to buy are all types of projects. Project management is the process and techniques to follow when you are doing something you have never done before or trying to improve something you have done before. Our lives are made up of a variety of projects, and how we go about managing the chaos of change can make us successful in our business and our personal lives.

## *So, You Have a Project*

To manage a project, you first need to understand what constitutes a project. After all, if you're in charge you should have a firm grasp of what you are in charge of. Let's take a look at some of the key components of a project:

- **A project needs a specific goal.** You don't just get together, do some work, and see what happens. Well, maybe you do, but that is why project management is needed!
- **A project has a time frame.** Projects have a beginning and an end, they do not continue endlessly.
- **A project has a final outcome or result.** For better or for worse, each project produces results.
- **A project has a budget and requires resources.** Resources may include skilled individuals, reference materials, special equipment, information systems, or other tools of the trade.
- **A project requires a plan of action defining what needs to be done, when, and by whom.** Plans, procedures, schedules, software programs, and various systems for tracking the work that is being done may all be necessary to keep your project on course.
- **Projects can be evaluated on their own.** Apart from other tasks and chores you may perform at your job or in your daily routine, a project stands on its own to be evaluated by one person or by many people. Political campaigns are, in essence, projects put before many people—the voters.

As a project manager, you need to put all of the pieces together. Call it a puzzle, a battle plan, a mission, or whatever—you are the person who is responsible for the end result. It is up to you, as project manager, to see that the project is completed on time and on budget and achieves the anticipated results.

Good project managers are able to look at the big picture. They know what needs to be done and can assemble and motivate a team to complete the vision. They can also determine the shortcomings—or potential shortcomings—that must be dealt with to keep a project on track. A project manager may also determine that a project is simply impossible to complete.

Successful professional project managers can make a great deal of money by pulling together all of the pieces of the project puzzle for large-scale, often complicated, undertakings. Even if you're not planning on a career in project management, these skills will be helpful in many aspects of your business and personal life.

**FACT**

A project is defined as a unique undertaking that has a definitive beginning and end. Many projects can support a similar goal, creating a program or a group of related projects. President Kennedy had the vision of landing on the moon. A program made up of many projects, each with a unique intended result, was created to achieve his vision.

## *Where Do Projects Come From?*

You may select projects or have them selected for you. Personal projects are usually done at your own discretion, allowing you to select the projects you undertake. This might include planning a vacation or remodeling your home. A business project may also be self-initiated. For example, if you own your own business or you simply decide your workload is slow, you can take the next two weeks to rearrange your office for maximum efficiency.

A project at work, however, is often the result of your boss or supervisor selecting you to head up a specific assignment. In some instances, you may have made a suggestion about how to run the company more efficiently. For example, maybe you proposed a better way to handle sales strategies and you find yourself on the verge of a project. In other instances, the company simply needed someone to handle a task and, tag—you're it.

Another type of project arises out of a common need. This could be a community need or a project to meet the growing needs of a particular group. Organizations, associations, and various charitable groups are constantly engaged in planning and carrying out projects that benefit others. A severe storm might elicit the need for a community effort to clean up and restore a neighborhood. You might volunteer your time and abilities to oversee a fund-raising project initiated by your daughter's school.

There are also projects that fall in your lap. Your daughter is getting married, and you're the only one who can plan the wedding. Your boss assigned Fred Flintstone to plan the upcoming company picnic, but Fred suddenly quit the company and ran off with Wilma to Rock Vegas. Guess who's in charge now?

No matter how the project comes to you, you will still need to have a specific end result in sight. That clear goal is what you will work toward. You will also need to plan and set a schedule, stay within your budget, and utilize your resources—whether the project consists of your two children helping you build a patio or a team of twenty-five so-called experts helping you develop a formula that prevents wrinkles. The size, cost, and manpower will vary, but the basics of assessing the project requirements, setting the wheels in motion, and having the resources to get to your desired conclusion on time are still the same.

## The Sponsor and the Stakeholders

The way in which you came to be project leader will affect some of the variables. A self-generated project makes you the sponsor of the project: The impetus for the project came from you. At work, however, the sponsor of the project is ultimately responsible for the end result. This could be your immediate superior, the company president, owner, or perhaps a top executive. He will often be responsible for the financial backing and may select key team members as well as experts and advisors. The sponsor or individual(s) requesting the project may very often set the time frame as well. An organization or a group may sponsor a project, meaning that they set the budget and time frame. You then act as project manager.

The more adaptable you are to working under various systems, the more valuable you can become as a project manager. Recognize the needs of the sponsor of the project and become familiar with the parameters that are in place. Some project managers work well within any type of constraints, while others need more flexibility.

Beyond the sponsor are stakeholders who will also have an interest, personal or financial, in the end result. The more stakeholders involved, the more you need to appease a variety of people. If you've made your home office more efficient through remodeling, you are the primary stakeholder. The other stakeholders are your clients, who will benefit from your increased ability to complete work more quickly.

Any party interested in or affected by the outcome of the project is a stakeholder. This will also include project members who are responsible for the work they contribute to the project. Stakeholders may contribute ideas on a regular basis, be involved in a hands-on manner, or not be involved in the actual work of the project at all. Stakeholders may be the community at large. Everyone in the city who will be using the new bridge is not necessarily working on it, but they will all benefit from the ease with which they will be able to drive to work once the bridge is completed. You'll read more about the stakeholders later in the book.

## Let's Talk Project Management

Okay, so now you have a general idea of what constitutes a project and how it might come to land in your hands. But what exactly is project management and why is the term so popular today?

The producer of a television show has a project: twenty-six episodes in one season to be taped within an allotted budget and time frame. The producer is therefore responsible for pulling together the cast and crew; arranging for a sound studio, sets, and other locations; selecting theme music; and identifying all of the elements that go into making the program a reality. From finding the writers to watching his or her name roll by on the closing credits, the producer is managing the project. No matter what the size of the project, or scope, all of the players need to be in place, on the same page, and progress must be accounted for. As project manager, you are the captain of the ship, but just until the project is over. Remember, projects are specific, not open ended or ongoing like your daily job. An open-ended work situation is not a project.

## What Makes Up the Project?

Project management means organizing, running, and bringing a project to its conclusion. It includes the following:

- Defining the goal of the project
- Determining the results you expect to be accomplished
- Working within a budget
- Setting up a schedule
- Selecting your team and establishing individual roles
- Making sure the tools and technology are in place
- Monitoring ongoing progress
- Maintaining team morale
- Dealing with problems that arise
- Keeping stakeholders abreast of your progress
- Bringing the project to completion
- Assessing what went right and what went wrong

Take a look at this example:

| | |
|---|---|
| *Project:* | Moving into a new home. |
| *Time frame:* | March 15th through July 31st |

- *Defining the goal of the project:* To move out of one home and move into another.
- *Determining the results you expect to be accomplished:* Everything is in its place and accounted for in the new home.
- *Working within a budget:* There is $5,000 allotted for the movers, moving supplies, required touchups in the old home, and new items for the new home.
- *Setting up a schedule:* The move date is a fixed date. Time must be allotted prior to the move date to ensure that everything is packed and ready to be moved. Time will be allotted to make the move as well as unpack everything. Even though the move is on a specific date, the schedule will account for time before and after the actual move date. There is also scheduling of the power, cable, telephone, changing billing addresses, etc.

- *Selecting your team:* The team may include just you or a few friends to assist or a moving company. The size (and scope) of the move can determine the best makeup of teams.
- *Establishing the roles of each individual:* Who is in charge of coordinating the utilities? Who will stay with the movers? Who is going to pack up the kitchen?
- *Monitoring ongoing progress:* Keep track of what is left to be done. Establish a checklist of companies to notify of the move and monitor how many are left. Establish targets for which room will be packed up when.
- *Dealing with problems that arise:* I have packed all of the utensils and now have nothing to eat dinner with!
- *Bringing the project to completion:* The move occurs.
- *Assessing what went right and what went wrong:* I promise I will never move again! But if I do, I will not use the moving company who just broke all of my china.

A rough example indeed, but you get the idea. As project manager, you know what is expected of you.

## Project Management Today

Although projects can be found dating back hundreds and thousands of years, project management has become a buzzword in the modern business world. Improved technology has allowed and enabled a vast increase in the number of projects to be completed in the workplace. Projects that would once have taken months to complete now take weeks, and new projects follow on their heels. The latest software makes tracking multiple projects easier, and training courses in project management demonstrate new tricks of the trade. The booming economy of the late 1990s made it feasible, from an economic standpoint, for companies to engage in more new endeavors than ever before. New products, new locations, and enhanced services were all the byproducts of the increase in projects.

While a recession could mean a dip in big business projects, there will always be a need to complete projects successfully. If nothing else, project management can teach you how to see the big picture and organize all the smaller components of any significant task you undertake.

## Is the Big Picture Big Enough?

As noted previously, projects can begin in many ways. You might trip over a carton while entering your garage and decide that it's time for a major garage sale to clean up all the junk in there. Poof! You have a project: organize and hold a garage sale. Your boss might come into your office complaining that vacuum sales are down and that you need to create a better product that knocks out the competition before the end of the fiscal quarter. Poof! You have a project: get a team together and create the ultimate vacuum cleaner!

Seasons and holidays often inspire projects. For example, many retail businesses choose January to do their inventories, when things are relatively quiet. In your personal life, you may use the summer break from school to plan your family's vacation or hold an annual garage sale.

The first question should be whether the project is feasible. That is, can the project be done, or is it impossible? Is the big picture big enough? If the electronic wiring of the school isn't ready for modern technology and the cost of rewiring the school is $4,000, the project won't work on a $3,000 budget. There are other initial concerns to consider before you commit yourself to a project. For example:

- **Do you need the approval of someone else (including legal or community approval) before you embark on and complete a project?** A documentary about the Grand Canyon will not happen if the filmmakers do not attain a shooting permit. Likewise, you may need the go-ahead from senior executives before you decide to reallocate the parking spaces in the company parking lot. Zoning permits, construction licenses, and numerous external factors need to be considered before embarking on a project.
- **Are the resources available?** A company softball team may be hard to form in a company with only six people. Before you organize the team, you need to determine if you can get the manpower, the funds,

the tools, the equipment, and other important elements while staying within the budget. Often you can use ingenuity, but sometimes the odds are stacked against you. A construction project will not work if the only cranes in town are all in use the week that you are looking to rent one. This isn't to say you can't be ingenious and have a crane imported from another area, or have the project altered so you'll need the crane a week later, when one is available. However, if this will not work because of your budget, you may be in trouble.

It's always worth looking at the big picture and determining if there are any major issues before proceeding.

## Do a Feasibility Study

While it's impossible to predict obstacles that will arise once the project is under way, it's a good idea to take some time to make an overall assessment of the needs of the project and how they correlate to the budget and time frame before you decide to start. A feasibility study takes into account the variables of the project, including budget, resources, and time constraints, and determines the likelihood that it can be done. Take a long, hard look at a feasibility study and don't continue with the project if you determine that it simply can't be done.

## Evaluate the Cost

Another factor that will influence your decision to begin your project is whether or not you feel that the project will be cost effective. Will the benefits you hope to gain be worth the price you will pay to get there? This is more than just a financial question. After all, if you are taking time away from your kids' homework so they can help you complete the family project of building a patio, aren't you doing more harm than good? There are always tradeoffs.

## Weigh the Positives and Negatives

A positive outcome to a project is the desired result. This could come in the form of more customers, more business, less turnover, less stress, higher morale, or perhaps even more rewarding results, such as toys for underprivileged children. Personal goals might mean a more comfortable living environment or a higher value for your home should you plan to sell it. Projects can have numerous desired outcomes; some are personal, while others are career based or business oriented.

**FACT**

Sometimes a project's benefits are not measured in dollars. Your health, stress level, and the needs of your family may be at the root of your decision to move forward with a project. A simple list of pros and cons might be your cost analysis when deciding whether to take that family vacation.

Cost-benefit analysis is the formal method used by many companies to determine the value of the project. The individuals or the company sponsoring a project use detailed methods to determine all the factors involved to calculate whether or not the benefits outweigh the costs (financial, manpower, time, etc.). While a company has to evaluate this process (usually, this has been done before the project lands in your lap), you need to do your own version of cost analysis on your projects.

In a small business, you'll need to determine whether the project will be more costly than it's worth. Adding a new computerized system to an office may cause a slowdown or even bring the current workload to a standstill. If, however, you are running a small retail business that relies on selling goods and you are doing well (and have a successful method of keeping inventory), you may not need to lay out the money or take the time to train your staff to run the new computer. Don't embark on a project because everyone else is forging ahead into the high-tech world.

Keep in mind that cost analysis is not a black-and-white concept; you need not say yea or nay, but can throw in a "maybe if we . . ." response. More often than not, the stakeholders can reach a compromise. You may decide to get a smaller, less expensive computer system for the store and only train three people to use it. You may decide that leaving your business for two weeks during the summer might not be a good idea, so your two-week vacation in August might become a one-week vacation.

Compromise is good. And it is often a necessity when getting a project off the ground. As project manager, you may or may not have a say in reaching this compromise. The decision to open one branch office instead of two, for example, may have been made before you were ever asked to manage the project.

**ALERT!**

It is important to revisit your cost-benefit analysis at key time intervals once your project is completed. It is important to understand if the project really did create the promised benefits. Is it still providing benefits? How close were you in your estimation? Do you need to adjust your assumptions for the next time?

## Evaluate Your Strengths

Another reason a project may not be feasible for you as project manager is because it is not something you have time to complete or feel you have the background to accomplish. Everyone has strengths and weaknesses. Generally you will not select, or are not selected for, projects that would not be appropriate for you to handle. While research and a degree may be factored into the overall equation, the reality is that if you know absolutely nothing about golf, you may not be the person to set up and run the company golf tournament. Knowing about something, however, doesn't mean you need to be an expert. Many Major League Baseball managers and coaches were not always good ball players. The same holds true in other professions as well.

## Determine Your Availability

If you can only allot twenty hours a week to a project and your own business is currently requiring you to put in fifty hours a week, you may not be able to effectively take on the additional workload. Many people overextend themselves and end up not only jeopardizing the project, but wasting the time and energy of others. If the project can't fit into your schedule, don't agree to manage it. If the boss says it's your responsibility, like it or not, then you'll have to juggle or find a way to delegate your other responsibilities.

## *Has It Ever Been Done?*

So, you're studying the cost-analysis breakdown. The benefits outweigh the negatives, but only barely. You're staring at your screen thinking, maybe, just maybe, someone's had to do something like this before.

One of the most significant factors in determining whether or not to embark on a project is whether or not it's been done before. You may be hoping there is a template or at least some documentation of similar projects that have already been completed. While you won't become famous, you might stand a better chance of success if you can model your project after a previous endeavor and put your special signature or touch on it.

One of the most important reasons for keeping accurate documentation of a project as you proceed is so that the next project team can have something to look at to see how it was done previously—for better or for worse. Evaluating previous projects is very important at any level of project management. If you're planning a convention, a conference, or a seminar for your company or organization, surely you will want to look at the previous conferences and seminars. Historical information is useful, so find out where prior events were held, what resources were used, who was on the planning team, and whether or not the project stayed within budget.

**FACT**

Sometimes businesses start on a project hoping they will generate the funding later. This can be very risky, as many dot-com companies have found out. The first phase of the project should be to create a marketing plan to gain the funding necessary to proceed.

When analyzing previous projects, you need to analyze all the elements involved with an open mind. You also need to consider the time, place, budget, and resources of that project in comparison to your project. If, for example, the last team was clearly understaffed and everyone had to put in significant amounts of overtime to complete the project, then you will know from the start that you'll need a bigger team—which might require more money in your budget. On the other hand, if it took a team of five people a year to complete a project in 1991, a decade later you may find that it could take five people half that amount of time. Thanks to the Internet, more efficient computer systems, and a host of technological developments, teams and projects tend to progress more efficiently. Conversely, if someone planned a wedding for $25,000 in 1988, that same wedding today might cost $45,000. Account for a variety of factors when looking at previous projects. Obviously, the most recent project that is most similar to yours will be the most informative.

Here are some other considerations:

**Budget.** Of course, costs are higher today than they were several years ago. Make sure the budget accounts for the rising costs and higher rates charged by experts in the field. Also, look at whether the previous project came in under or over budget. See where the last team cut corners and determine whether or not you can cut those same corners if necessary.

**Personnel.** All factors being equal (comparable budget based on today's figures, a reasonable time frame, and so on), you may need to account for changes in personnel. Do you have the same level of expertise available to you that the previous team had, or will you need to look for someone with more experience?

**Leadership and management.** Just because the last chief executive said no problem to holding the annual new-client luncheon in his backyard, doesn't mean the new chief executive wants you anywhere near his property. A new regime means new rules to follow.

**External factors.** The previous project manager imported materials for the project from a foreign country. Because of internal political strife, the country has stopped all exportation of the materials you need. You can't control rules, laws, jurisdictions, and other factors. If you're planning an outdoor event, external factors can be as basic as the weather. No matter how similar all of the available resources may be, some things are going to be out of your hands. Try to be aware of as many of these factors as possible and see if you can work around them.

**Contingency plans.** Did the previous project managers have backup plans or strategies? Sometimes these are not included in the documentation if they were not implemented.

**Turnover problems and conflicts.** You may not be able to foresee who will leave halfway through a project or what problems or conflicts are likely to arise. However, if you see a trend that developed during the previous project you may be forewarned as to where the problem areas lie. If some of the same individuals are involved, you'll know ahead of time which people did not work well together. This can range from competitive sales reps to sibling rivalry among your kids. You'll be able to pay closer attention to issues where potential conflicts lie as identified by evaluating the documentation of previous projects.

When evaluating a previous project, you should also look at the subsequent results. Did retail sales increase after the company took its business onto the Internet? How long did it take for the benefits to appear? Will that same time frame work for your project, or do you need faster results to stay competitive? Treasurers usually have last year's budget handy when making up the current annual budget. Accountants have the previous tax return nearby when working on the current return. You too can benefit from having the documentation of previous projects handy, whether they are yours, your predecessor's, or ones you've researched that have similar key characteristics. Remember, no two projects will be exactly the same as long as human beings are involved. Try to use a close match to guide you.

## Going Where No One Has Gone Before

There will be many times, however, when you will encounter a project or an idea that has never been done before. This can be a stressful and nerve-wracking time, but it can also be some of the most rewarding experiences. Since the future is unknown, change is inevitable, and forward progress is a must in the business world; each project could be the next great thing.

Navigating the unknown is a scary proposition for many people. For project managers, it is a rite of passage and an everyday occurrence. Understanding and trusting the process of managing projects can ensure that you, as the project manager, bring vision, completeness, and unity to a project team. Who knows, that team may just be creating the technology needed to make the Starship Enterprise.

**FACT**

Xerox has a legendary research center in Palo Alto, CA where innovation happens. It was there that the Graphical User Interface (what allowed Windows to be Windows), the mouse, Ethernet, and several other ground-breaking items were created. Each project started here has the possibility of launching the next Microsoft.

## We Don't Have Time to Plan!

Depending on which study you read, as many as 80–90 percent of projects fail. Many of these projects fail before they ever really start. The greatest reason for failure is lack of planning. Later within the book, you will read about all of the types of plans that make up a project plan, but the key to all of them is that planning is an absolute must. There is no way around it. Imagine dumping a lot of wood, paint, and concrete in an area, then telling fifteen people to go build a house without talking to each other. How do you think the house will turn out? After some time, the team would eventually figure out that they have to talk in order to complete the house, but how much time passed before they realized this?

Proper planning is the crux of project management. It begins and ends the project and is everywhere in between. If you are faced with a situation in which a sponsor or stakeholder wants to proceed without a plan, the project is in trouble immediately. Running a project without a plan is like jumping out of a plane with no parachute.

As weird as it sounds, many projects will progress for months or years without a plan. If you don't have time to plan, then you are planning to fail.

## CHAPTER 2

# Setting the Wheels in Motion

Every project serves a purpose and has an aim or objective. If the project accomplishes its goal within set parameters, it is deemed successful. One of your first tasks as project manager is to determine how you will achieve that project's goal in accordance with the parameters set forth by the project sponsor. It is important that you carefully assess the project and have the terms, such as when the project is due to be completed and what the budget constraints are, in writing.

## Clear Vision

It's extremely important that everyone involved in the project has the same clear vision. Everyone should be able to clearly communicate the same goal or objective for the project. If the objective is vague or if anyone has a misconception of where the project is headed, encourage them to speak up before the wheels start rolling.

Contracts, project requests, charters, and statements of work are all written documents that include the details of a specific project in writing. Any such document serves as an important way of ensuring that everyone has the same understanding of the overall conditions of the project. Documents also serve as the primary resource if everyone has forgotten part of the original plan or if the team needs to verify anything.

Before you agree to proceed as project manager, consult with experts and team members to get a firm idea of how long each task will take. If you're planning a wedding, for example, you'll need to know how long the ceremony will run before you schedule the start of the wedding reception.

## Old Ways Versus New Ways

While you evaluate a project, prior to starting the wheels in motion, you will want to think about your methods of carrying out and managing activities. Do you have ironclad methods or are you open to change?

When planning a major conference, one person always says, "That's the way we've always done it, so we should do it that way again." Another person says, "Let's be open to new ideas. New people may provide us with better ways to accomplish some of our objectives." Who's right?

They are both right. Tried-and-true methods that work should not be discarded. They have proven to be effective, and there is a low level of risk involved—they are not likely to cause the project to go off track. But, new ideas open up the potential for positive growth. Examining new methods means matching them against tried-and-true methods of the past. Do they achieve the same and more, or do they achieve less? It's hard to measure quality, but sometimes you can improve upon a job well done.

**FACT**

Sticking with tried-and-true methods is less risky and offers a proven track record, but the methods may be somewhat outdated and limit your creativity. Trying new methods poses greater risk because these methods are often unproven, but they often allow for more creativity and can save you time and money.

Also, new ideas may invigorate the people involved and generate renewed enthusiasm. If a team is pulled together to work on a project, and they know that it will be the same routine as the last project, they are less enthusiastic than if there are some new elements to the project. Likewise, new team members can provide creative new ideas.

It's important to learn from the past while considering the potential advantages of new methods. Projects need to utilize the hard work and results of past successes as well as take advantage of advances in technology and education. Someone who is not open to change is limiting his or her potential for a highly successful project. Conversely, someone who refuses to acknowledge the previous methods may be so steeped in new methodology that he or she forfeits what can be learned from past history and experience for the sake of technology. To find the right balance, a project manager needs to be open to both sets of ideas, old and new.

## *Competition*

Among the many factors to consider as you size up and assess the project is whether or not your time frame or resources are impacted by competition. You may not be the first person with the innovative idea to sell baklava over the Internet; therefore, your project to get your new site, *www.ultimatebak lava.com,* launched by March 1st may require altering your time frame to beat your competitor, who is working on a project to launch *www.bestbak lava.com.*

If you learn that your competition is also working on a project to offer competitive products or services, you will have the added pressure of beating them to the punch. You may need to find ways to cut corners and create shortcuts to beat the competition, or at least have your product ready to go at the same time as your competitor.

**QUESTION?**

**What are deliverables?**
*Deliverables* is a common buzzword that refers to "the defined end products, results, or services produced during the project." A project goal can also be a deliverable.

Friendly competition to create a better product or develop the first of a particular item can be positive for a team that steps up to the challenge. Nonetheless, winning a competition at the risk of an inferior product or service is not really a victory, as you have not achieved the true goal of the project: produce a quality item or service that meets a specific need or solves a problem.

## Are You Ready to Roll?

Take a look at the following list of questions to see if you are ready to move forward into full-scale project planning:

- Have you established the goal of the project?
- Does everyone involved have a clear understanding of that goal?
- Have you identified all stakeholders (management, team members if any, customers, and anyone else the project stands to directly, or even indirectly, affect)?
- Will you be able to explain the objectives of the project to all the team members and stakeholders?
- Are you clear about what the stakeholders are expecting from this project?
- Have you identified opposition, if any, to this project?

- Have you defined the scope of the project (the size of the project in terms of budget, resources needed, potential impact on business or the community)?
- Are all the initial parameters in writing?
- Have you established a time frame for all deliverables?

Before you forge ahead, solidify your team, and put the plans on the drawing board (or on your software program), there's one more important step: Establish the rules of the game. Let's take a closer look.

# Do Your Homework

You'll hear constant talk about the project phases, starting with initiating the project and moving into the planning process. There are countless graphs, charts, diagrams, pyramids, flowcharts, and other manners of presenting the series of steps needed to effectively manage a project. Theories, methodology, and discussion of these steps are important only to the point at which you understand what the steps mean. Once that has occurred, it's time to stop talking, put down the graphs of the big picture, roll up your sleeves, and get to work!

Yes, there are a tremendous number of aspects and elements that can be discussed regarding projects, and plenty of buzzwords and project-friendly phrases, but the bottom line is that at some point it will be time to get busy. This separates those who talk about projects and those who actually do them. If you're a doer, then start the project by doing your homework.

## Research

Homework includes plenty of research. Gather information from as many applicable sources as possible. You will also need to verify that your sources are accurate, especially if you surf unfamiliar territory on the Web. In business, you will want to review the minutes of meetings leading up to the formation of the project. You may also want to look at the following:

- Company reports
- Previous project reports

- Pertinent documents
- External reports, such as neighborhood studies, demographic studies, and consumer studies
- Books, articles, and Web sites that pertain to the nature of your project

You may even review personnel files to find people with expertise in certain areas. You'll also want to use the Internet or your local library to gather facts and figures that support the projected outcome of the project. You'll need to scope out anything that exists in the media that may be helpful. Anything that can lead to resources will also be of value. As you build your team, you'll be able to delegate tasks accordingly, and the team members will be able to seek out information on their own.

Holding meetings with team members as you build the team will allow you to share and gain information. You will be able to describe the overall project and they may be able to demonstrate their knowledge of a specific area. Take good notes.

You cannot expect to lead a team effectively unless you know the project's scope, details, and place in the bigger picture. You need to be able to answer questions and show that you have a firm grasp of what is being done and how it will commence effectively. You also need to network—it's very important. Talk with other team leaders, especially those who have led similar projects, and potential team members, as well as others who you feel can provide information. Gather benchmark data against which you can measure vendor quotes, resource prices, your projected project time frame, etc.

Any project needs some degree of research before it gets off the ground. Besides making the initial determination of whether a project is or is not feasible (see Chapter 1), you'll need to investigate ways to proceed and research all possible pros and cons of the process you select.

Before you build a new bathroom in your house, you'll need to read up on the latest in bathroom fixtures and get an idea of how the plumbing operates in your home. You may have to look at blueprints of the house and assess the land before you start work.

Without doing solid research, how will you know if you have the best team members or whether you have someone who can't perform the job? You can't hire someone to create a new data entry system for your business if you don't know whether they've done such a project before. Likewise, you don't want a computer software program that is wrong for your project. Every step of the way, you will have to do research or have others do research for you and for the good of the project. If people are doing research on your behalf, make sure they know exactly what you are looking for so they don't waste your time searching for extraneous or unnecessary information.

Research and searching for information is also significant in helping you return to your stakeholders with valuable materials that may benefit them and even alter their projected results. You may have discovered a city ordinance that will force you to alter your plans slightly, or a new technology that will help you complete the project a week earlier than expected. Run your discoveries by your stakeholders; often, they will have information to share with you as well.

**ALERT!**

Avoid diminishing returns by using your resources effectively. Just because a computer software program has 800 functions, it doesn't mean you'll need all 800 for your project. Focus on the project, not the mechanics! Once you have everything up and running, move on.

## Action

One of the most common pitfalls of projects is failing to get them done on time without a mad rush to the finish line that often results in a less than satisfactory outcome. Many people who take on a project spend far too much time planning, plotting, and arranging and rearranging their schedule. After all that, they realize they've jumped into the take-action phase too late. A good project manager knows the value of the initial planning process, but also knows when the time is right to stop planning and start doing. Planning is important, but even a marvelous plan that never gets off the ground, or gets off the ground too late, is not worth the effort because the risk of failure increases.

# Three Common Mistakes

As is the case with any skill set, learning project management skills takes time and practice. During the course of a project, you will inevitably make errors and mistakes, but learning from them will help you hone your skills. Following are some common mistakes that occur while managing activities, setting up reward systems, and prioritizing tasks and activities.

## Too Many Pieces of the Pie!

One of the mistakes project managers frequently make is breaking down or subdividing activities into countless smaller tasks or chores. An endless list of step-by-step details through hundreds of tasks broken down by hours or even minutes can be problematic. First of all, at that level of detail, the project manager has left no room for changes in this tight and lengthy schedule. There is also no room for skilled professionals to take the ball and run with it. A Work Breakdown Structure that is too rigid and too detailed leads to micromanagement, which doesn't usually enhance the team spirit. The other problem with breaking down everything is that the process is not an effective use of your time. You don't want to hold up the project because you are up to detail number 1,376 in a list of 2,700.

By using a broader Work Breakdown Structure, you can list the tasks necessary for each person to perform, but look at end results rather than each nut and bolt. Naturally, if a safety inspector is going to review your project, you may have to detail many of the nuts and bolts, but for most projects it's advantageous to allow people to aim for results. You will read about the right level of detail in later chapters.

## Misdirected Rewards

Often projects are measured improperly. How often have you seen quantity rewarded over quality? How often has the loudest, most boisterous sales manager gotten his plan approved, while other sales managers with excellent ideas are overlooked because they aren't as loud or aggressive? Consider these other examples of misdirected rewards:

- The head of sales receives an all-expenses-paid vacation because sales are up, despite the fact that the company's reputation gets dragged though the mud by disreputable sales practices.
- The girl who sold 4,000 boxes of cookies for her school wins the award, even though she played hooky for a week to sell them during school hours.
- The player who scored the most baskets makes the All-Star team even though his lack of sportsmanship and teamwork cost his team a victory in nearly every game.
- The computer programmer gets a bonus for writing the most program code, nearly all of which had nothing to do with helping the project.

It's important to have a justified reward system if this is how you intend to motivate your team, but often, other conditions need to be considered as well. Reaching a goal while jeopardizing the reputation of a company or organization is not really an achievement. Suppose the goal is to provide an improved, user-friendly e-commerce component to your company. If you reward the programmer who wrote the most code, this reward is only justifiable if the code ultimately improved the system. If users find it easier to navigate the system and sales are up, then indeed this programmer deserved to be rewarded. If, however, you simply said whoever writes the most program code gets a reward, you may be rewarding someone who simply wrote plenty of code that effectively did nothing to improve e-commerce navigability or sales.

**FACT**

In Major League Baseball, the most valuable player is not just the player with the best statistics, but the one whose team most benefited from that player's presence. Likewise, your most valuable team member doesn't necessarily have to produce the most, but has to be significant in the success of the overall project.

Rewarding a job well done may not only mean quality over quantity, but staying within set boundaries. This means you, as project manager, need to set standards that are worthy of rewards (ones that help achieve a successful project without jeopardizing the business, other projects, or people). You can then reward measurable achievements, such as improved sales or better customer relations.

## No (or Unclear) Incentives

Let's face it, most people operate with a "What's in it for me?" approach to life. As a project manager, you may be in the position of establishing incentives and rewards. This can range from popcorn for a youngster to a bonus and promotion for a corporate team member. Not all projects require you to present a reward, but some incentive will generally provide a reason for team members to put forth that much more effort.

If there is a reward offered, it needs to be in proportion to the task at hand, and should be realistic in scope. Promising a child an expensive train set for passing a spelling test is a bit excessive. You are limited to the confines of your budget and an incentive plan that will encourage, not detract from, team spirit. You also want to set reasonable expectations—don't set a precedent that you cannot maintain in the future. With all of these variables to consider, it's no wonder project managers often do not offer any incentives or rewards for a job well done.

Volunteer groups are often the hardest to reward. A pat on the back, words of praise, or simply acknowledgement of a job well done is often the best appreciation you can offer a volunteer. An even better reward may come from the satisfaction of having a positive impact on something the volunteer personally supports, encourages, and believes in.

On the opposite side of rewards and incentives are consequences for a job done poorly. Yes, many people work hard not to get fired, not to fail a test, or not to be excluded from a group. While this is a form of incentive, it doesn't always produce the best results. A person working just hard enough not to fail isn't really working to exceed, but just to get by. There is always one student trying to get an "A" and another student happy to simply pass with a "D." Positive incentives and rewards give people more to strive for and produce better results.

## *Prioritize*

As you begin your project, make sure you have a list of priorities. The top-priority tasks are those that will lead most directly to the success or failure of the project. These are your core tasks. Some tasks may seem lower in importance, such as finding a rehearsal hall. However, you can't proceed with rehearsals for the original production of *Phantom of the Car Wash* without a place to rehearse. Therefore, larger tasks are sometimes contingent on smaller ones being completed first. This makes those little tasks high on the priority list.

A prioritized list of objectives will help you eliminate certain tasks if sticking to your budget or completing the project on time is becoming an issue. Priorities will also help you if you need to reorganize the project—you will know which tasks and objectives will need more attention. The same holds true with shifting team members. If two people are working on a low-priority task, such as printing the program for the theater production, and there's a need for more assistance on higher priority tasks, like costumes and lighting, you'll be able to make the proper adjustment.

FACT

Priority does not mean task order. Sometimes, the most important task is done last, after preparation. In other instances, the most significant task is that which begins the project and everything else depends on that task being accomplished.

Throughout the subsequent chapters, there will be further discussions about resources, objectives, working effectively with the project team, making decisions, and adhering to your priorities. A project manager must remember that these areas are not mutually exclusive. A project has a life, and like any living thing, there is growth and change throughout the process. There is overlap, which means determining what you will need and who you'll need go hand in hand. As you read further, you will see that project management means keeping tabs on the whole project by monitoring the numerous parts.

## Selecting the Right Project

In many cases, projects are chosen for the wrong reasons. It could be the flashiest or a pet project for one of the executives or it could be dealing with the coolest technology. Whatever the reason, many projects fail because they were the wrong project to pursue in the first place.

Each project manager needs to understand how this project fits into the overall strategy of the sponsor. If this is for a company, a project that is reducing the workforce may not fit into a company whose strategy is to double their employee base. If you are an individual, remodeling your home may not be a great project just before you sell.

As a project manager, you must understand which project to undertake. Many times this will not be your decision, but it is still crucial to know. Stopping a project before it starts because it is not the right fit can bring some of the same benefits as completing a successful project.

Develop a scoring criteria or a fit analysis to ensure that the project is the right fit. Work with your sponsors and stakeholders to make sure everyone is on the same page. If done properly, then your limited resources can be used much more efficiently to provide valuable projects.

## CHAPTER 3

# The Project Life Cycle

Each project lives its own life. The very definition of a project is a temporary endeavor that has a definitive start and finish. Many project managers use the phrase "from cradle to grave" to describe the project life cycle; this book won't take such a morbid approach. The project life cycle contains all of the steps necessary for a project, from beginning to end. Although many companies may have their own variation, a project life cycle usually means initiating, planning, executing, controlling, and closing.

## Understanding the Project Phases

Many life cycles follow a linear pattern. For software developers, it is usually design, code, test, user test, document, and go live. In project management, however, the cycle is not linear. Initiating and closing are phases that generally live on their own, but the planning, executing, and controlling processes are a cycle within themselves. During the execution of your plan, you must monitor how you are doing. Based on the results, you adjust your plan and begin executing against that one. This cycle will continue throughout the process until it is time to close the project.

It can be a bit overwhelming for many new project managers when they are assigned to a project. Following the standard life-cycle phases will allow a project manager to get started.

If you are unsure of how to start your project plan, then start with the standard five-phase life cycle. Then ask yourself what activities are required to complete each phase. This can jumpstart your thinking and get you going in the right direction. Many advanced project managers use this technique for their plans.

Many people will simply list tasks that are required to complete the actual work of the project. This can be a mistake and allow cost overruns. The reason is that up to 20–40 percent of the project cost could be outside of the actual tasks. For example: You have a project team of fifty people for a twelve-week project that entails a weekly, one-hour status meeting. If you did not list this as an item on your project plan, you may not have accounted for 600 hours. Understanding the project phases and what they contain will allow you to think of all of the items necessary to complete the project.

## Initiating

The most skipped portion of any project is the initiation phase. In fact, when most project managers get a project, it is well into the planning phase. However, this phase is one of the most crucial of the project. It establishes the target completion date and initial project team, and creates the actual scope statement. This phase is often overlooked because the overall project sponsors are the ones that select the project, fund it, pick the date, and then assign the project manager. However, you still have the opportunity to assist in the initiation process.

**FACT**

> The project sponsor is the person that is ultimately accountable for the project. However, this is not always an executive. Since anyone can initiate a project, anyone can be the sponsor. As a project manager, you may take direction from all levels in the organization.

The end result of the initiation phase is generally a project charter. This document formally recognizes the project and becomes the basis for planning the project.

## Planning

Planning is where the rubber will meet the road—another phase that is often overlooked. In Chapter 1, you read about the phrase, "We don't have time to plan!" This is an interesting phenomenon and one that is a cycle of emergencies. To illustrate this point, consider a real-life conversation between a consultant and the CEO of a company:

**CEO:** We are simply too busy to have a planning meeting.
**CONSULTANT:** What is going on?
**CEO:** We seem to be always in a state of emergency. Nobody has the time to stop and think about the next steps.
**CONSULTANT:** So things are dropped on you at the last minute, you don't have enough resources for the work, and every time you complete a task two more are waiting in the wings that you are unaware of?
**CEO:** Exactly!
**CONSULTANT:** And why would planning the tasks so that you could forecast the resources so that you could understand the workload not help you?
**CEO:** Huh . . . never really thought of it that way.

This conversation is not an anomaly—many project management consultants out there have had similar conversations. People get so involved in the details of the work they sometimes do not see the benefit of the planning process. However, with no plan, everything is the emergency. Where do you think the phrase, "A lack of planning on your part does not constitute an emergency on mine" started?

Planning is not a one-time activity; it is a constant, iterative activity occurring throughout the life of the project. As tasks complete early, late, or on time, the plan needs to be re-evaluated and adjusted, and these changes need to be communicated to all of those involved to continue the project.

Planning will consist of understanding the work involved, planning who should do the work, when it will occur, and how you will deal with issues, risks, changes, staffing, and communications.

## Executing

The execution of the project is really the implementation of your plan. While many organizations jump right in and start their project in this phase, it is only a small portion of the project-management effort. This becomes a confusing part for many project managers.

**If most of my expense is in the execution phase, why does it represent the least amount of project-management time?**
The reason is that most of the project manager's time is spent in the planning and controlling phase. However, most of the work done by your resources is in the execution phase.

Although the project can go awry quickly in the execution phase, it will be caught in the controlling phase.

# Controlling

The controlling phase is just as important as the planning phase. As discussed, there is a cycle between the planning, executing, and controlling phases. After you have planned the work and your resources are executing that plan, you must monitor to see how the project is progressing. Then, based on the results of monitoring, you will adjust the plan accordingly.

The controlling phase also consists of the greatest amount of communication. As the project manager, you are constantly seeking feedback on progress and results and communicating status to the team. This requires active follow up, status meetings, prodding of your team, and sometimes, constant pestering!

Once all of the information is gathered, it is back to the planning phase to understand the impact and adjust the execution phase to meet the goals.

# Closing

You will hear a magical number throughout this book: 2 percent. For the closing phase, it represents the hardest part of any project: The last 2 percent of a project is the hardest to close. This is generally the ancillary, nonimportant issues or features that were once deemed important, but somehow fell by the wayside. There are more projects out there that are sitting at 98 percent complete than you can imagine. In fact, most projects are close to completion, then float away into nothingness.

# Project Methodologies

Project management largely exists to bring order to chaos. It allows an individual or organization to plan and manage a significant change. A methodology exists to assist in creating a successful and repeatable process to provide consistency among project managers. A good methodology will:

- Change as the business does
- Be usable by all skill levels
- Be simple to follow

Project methodologies are often created by a Project Management Office (PMO), which is discussed later in Chapter 14. PMOs provide the standards and procedures to complete a project. It is important to remember that methodologies are guidelines, not absolute rules.

The weirdest thing about project management is that the moment you create a rule, the next project will break it! Be sure that rules are created around processes. For example, decide *what* should be communicated in a weekly report, not *how* it should be communicated. Project rules need to provide guidance while allowing flexibility to react to each project's needs.

A great methodology will help your organization standardize on procedures and terminologies. Although most methodologies evolve over time, an organization can jump-start theirs by purchasing one from another company or a consultant. If you or your organization decides to develop a methodology from scratch, be sure to involve many different people with different experiences to ensure your methodology accounts for all types of activities.

## Methodologies Versus Life Cycles

Did you think that methodologies and life cycles were the same thing? They aren't! A key difference is what they try to accomplish. A life cycle defines the stages or phases of a project, which can determine what activities are accomplished. Methodologies help set standards and procedures for how to perform each activity.

It is easy to get these terms confused, but remember that these two concepts work with each other when completing a project. For the purposes of this book, the next five chapters are broken out by life-cycle phase. The methodology will be the suggestions of activities and standards within the chapters.

## CHAPTER 4

# Project Initiation: You Have to Start Somewhere

Many projects start in the execution phase. This is also why many projects fail. The initiation phase of a project allows the sponsor (the person or group that is ultimately responsible for the project) to share his/her/their vision. This is the opportunity for the project to become officially recognized and funded, where vision turns into reality.

## Turn Vision into a Plan

All great plans, projects, and adventures generally start with a vision. A problem or opportunity has presented itself and something should be done about it. Whether it is to increase revenue for a company, paint a wall in your home, or purchase a new car, it begins with a vision.

Here's an interesting definition of a project manager: A project manager is an enabler that can create a cohesive whole of many parts and, focusing them, turn vision into reality.

This vision may be well defined and focused or may be very broad. It is the beginning of the project process. An advancement of project management is that the profession now understands that the vision can be broad. The vision of the project can be progressively elaborated as the project is better understood. One of the greatest examples of vision becoming reality through progressive elaboration was the statement made by John F. Kennedy in a speech to the nation on May 25, 1961. He said, "I believe that this nation should commit itself to achieving the goal, before this decade is out, of landing a man on the moon and returning him safely to the Earth." This was both a broad vision and a focused one. He outlined what the project would accomplish, but there were a lot of people that were charged with how to do it. Each project that was undertaken under this vision fed other projects, and the vision became progressively elaborated into a completed goal. On July 20, 1969, Neil Armstrong took the first steps on the moon. Shortly thereafter, the astronauts returned home safely. John F. Kennedy laid out the vision. The project managers brought the vision to a reality. The ability for a project manager to understand, articulate, and focus on the vision is the first step to running a great project.

## Creating the Playbook (Project Charter)

Every great team needs a playbook. In a football game, there are eleven people with different jobs and specialties all trying to achieve a common goal. The higher the level of play, the more precise the play needs to be. For example:

- **Pee Wee Football (thirteen and under):** There really isn't much of a playbook. In the younger children, you just hope they know which direction to run!
- **High School:** The playbooks become more sophisticated. Based on the school, it could get extremely sophisticated.
- **College:** In college, very few freshman get a chance to play. The playbooks are more sophisticated, and every person has a specific role. Timing becomes an important element in order to catch the other team by surprise.
- **Pro:** At the pro level, if you are one step off from where you are supposed to be, disaster could strike. If a wide receiver runs the wrong route, the other team will get an interception.

In the progression above, the teams have to be more and more sophisticated and their roles become more and more important. This is true of the project world as well. If you have a project that has a loose budget or time frame, the playbook doesn't have to be so sophisticated. However, if you have a large project team with a regulated due date, the playbook has to be tight.

## Why Is the Charter Important?

A project charter formally recognizes the existence of the project. It comes in many sizes with several elements.

**FACT**

To succeed as a project manager, it is important to establish a project charter. If you are given the project from the beginning or you are taking one over from someone else, create one. It will help establish the ground rules and start the communication between you and your sponsor in the right direction.

Charters can take many forms, but at a minimum it should contain a scope statement and target dates and cost, and establish the authority of the project manager. Without this document, it could be very difficult to get any decision made or run a successful project.

## Using the Charter

You may have heard of the term "scope creep." This term means that the scope of the project continues to grow or new items are introduced. Having a proper project charter will allow you to determine whether the requested item is in scope or if it requires a change request.

**QUESTION?**

**Why does it matter if a sponsor wants to add scope?**
Adding scope is perfectly acceptable in any project. However, this should also add time or cost. In many cases, without a scope change, scope creep increases the work but does not allow an increase in time or cost. Therefore, the sponsor will assume that they will get all functionality in the agreed-upon time and at the agreed cost.

It is important to understand the art of negotiation when it comes to additional scope. For the most part, you do not want to tell your sponsor no. It is much better to say, "Absolutely! It will add two weeks and $10,000 to the project." Then your sponsor can approve it or not. If you don't phrase it that way, the sponsor will believe that they can get the new requirements at the original cost.

## Everyone on the Same Page?

Once everything is set in your charter, make sure everyone reads it and signs it. An unsigned project charter is like an unsigned check: worthless. If you go through the trouble of establishing a project charter, then you have to follow through in getting it signed. Also, this will truly measure if everyone is on the same page.

Once presented, and before being signed, there will be some more questions raised. These questions are legitimate objections or questions that should be documented. Have you ever decided to make a big purchase? You research and research, make your selection, and get that buyer's tingle. Then, right before you actually make the purchase, you ask one more practical question. The answer to the question becomes the deal breaker. That is the same reaction you will receive when someone is about to sign the charter. Any objections or issues should be documented in the Decisions and Assumptions section of the charter and then redistributed for signatures.

A signature ensures accountability. If someone agrees to something but doesn't sign it, then they can always say they didn't understand, or what they agreed to wasn't clear. However, a signed document removes that ambiguity.

## Decisions and Assumptions

It is extremely important to record what you, your sponsor, and stakeholders were thinking at the time of the charter. Have you ever taken a note in a meeting and then read it two weeks later and not been able to remember what it meant? Imagine this problem on a large project. Also, many things are interpreted in many different ways. For example, if your boss says you have one day to complete a task, an immediate assumption is made. You may think that you have until the end of the business day, which is generally eight hours. However, a day is twenty-four hours long. So which definition is right? There is no right or wrong, but it is important to document the assumption. Even something as simple as saying, "That can be done in a day" carries an assumption. It is important to understand that assumption and document it.

The other key documentation to record is any decisions made. As you make decisions regarding what something means, what is part of the project and what isn't, and other items, document them within the charter. It is important to be able to come back to the charter later and understand what you were thinking at the time decisions were made.

## *Defining Specific Objectives*

Objectives lead to work—work designed to achieve the objectives. Therefore, the more clearly and succinctly you can define an objective, the better chance the work will be done with the correct objective in mind. When laying out your objectives or plan of action, keep the following in mind:

- **Don't talk tech, lingo, jargon, or slang.** Not everyone knows the terms, acronyms, code names, trendy nicknames, etc. Speak plain English (or the language of your team members).
- **Be clear and realistic about deadlines.** Nothing, as noted previously, can be done yesterday. Set realistic deadlines and make sure everyone is clear on what is due when.
- **Don't be so specific and regimented that your team ends up operating like robots.** Give them the leeway to be creative and innovative. Not only will they be more motivated, some marvelous new ideas come from allowing a degree of flexibility.
- **Don't be so loose that you have no parameters or direction to guide and focus your team.** You don't want people thinking that any old way they accomplish the job is fine. You'll need to be accountable for the methods employed by, and money spent by, your team. Finding out that your team saved money by buying the new computer system from some guy in the back of a van may not be a good thing!

The better you communicate the objectives, the more likely the project is to reach the desired conclusion. Miscommunication to, and misdirection of, team members are primary reasons for projects not reaching their goals.

Don't micromanage your team. It does nothing to boost morale, foster independence, or encourage growth. Regardless of your intent, micromanaging tells your team members that you don't have faith in their ability to do their work. The only times you may need to micromanage are when you are falling behind schedule or have a team member who is not doing his or her job properly.

The objectives of the project will become the measurement of whether or not the project is complete and one of the measures of whether the project was a success.

## Defining Key Resources

To complete almost any project, you will need resources, people power, and plenty of "stuff." Your stuff is whatever you need to complete the project, whether it's the goods to be sold or project-tracking software, heavy machinery, or pens and paper. The resources are key to making the project come to life.

List all of the significant resources in advance—those that you simply must have to make the project a success. Keep one eye on your budget and the other on your resources. Also keep in mind—and this is very important—you will very likely require additional resources along the way.

Committing to resources, both financially and contractually, means looking closely at your budget and the needs of the project. The tighter the budget, the more important it is that you run a streamlined project, and the more efficiently you'll have to utilize your resources. Your overall project resources will include:

- **How many people you need for the project.** This is not necessarily the number of people who will be involved at any level, but the number of people you will need to get the project accomplished. In addition to identifying whom you'll need, you'll need to determine for how long and at which stage each person will be involved.
- **Materials, tools, and supplies.** Determine what supplies are necessary to complete each aspect of the project. What will team members need every step of the way? Don't get caught without resources midway through a project on a tight deadline.

- **Tracking materials and technology.** If the project doesn't directly involve technology, as creating a Web site or installing a security system would, you'll need to determine what technology is and isn't needed to create, organize, and monitor the project. Depending on the complexity of the project, you may already have the computer capabilities to track the project. If you're putting together a golf outing for your fraternal association, you may simply fill in the names and information on an Excel or Word program. A camping trip for the neighborhood scout group may not require any technology, just a notebook to write down names and a list of supplies.

You should also discuss resources with your team members. Make sure everyone has what they need and knows how to use it. A new computer is wasted on a team member who is not computer literate. Also, listen to team members and look at similar projects to get an idea of what resources were required in the past.

# CHAPTER 5

# Project Planning

There is an old saying: If you fail to plan, you plan to fail. What seems to occur in many organizations is that they realize that they need better project management, but then will immediately tell the new project manager that they do not have time to plan. A project is supposed to be a unique endeavor that represents a change to an organization; a plan becomes the road map of how to get there. Without a good project plan, the project becomes lost.

## *Myths about Project Plans*

One myth about project plans is that they are overkill and a waste of effort. This could be true if the project manager is being forced to create a subplan in which he or she sees no value. It could also be true if a mandated template is used and the project manager does not understand all of the sections. In any case, it isn't the planning that is a waste of time, it is the manner in which it is being dictated.

One of the biggest myths about project planning is the schedule. So many project managers create a task list in Microsoft Excel or Microsoft Project and publish it as their project plan. There was little or no input from the team, the dates are rarely realistic, and it is a static list. This is not a project plan or even a project schedule; it is a task list.

## *It's Not Just a Task List*

A project schedule is so much more that a list of tasks and assignments. It becomes the heart of the project plan. A properly constructed project schedule can help you plan for risk, adjust to tasks finishing early and late, and communicate effectively with your team. Many project managers have yet to harness the power of a scheduling tool like Microsoft Project or Open Workbench (discussed in Chapter 15), and instead are using a spreadsheet tool like Microsoft Excel to manage their projects. This becomes such a large disadvantage because of the amount of manual work it takes to update the plan as well as the propensity for error.

You must take the time to learn and utilize a scheduling tool. The tool should update the entire plan for you based on entry criteria such as a finish date. By learning these tools, you can begin to manage the schedule instead of the schedule managing you.

A project schedule should ebb and flow as things finish early or late. In order to take full advantage of scheduling tools, you should understand the following.

## Task Dependencies

Tasks in project schedules should be linked to each other. There are four types of relationships. Each relationship is read as "Task 1 must _____ before Task 2 can _____." The relationships are:

- **Finish to Start (FS)**—Task 1 must finish before Task 2 can start. This is the most common relationship. The product can be ordered after the purchase order is signed. Ordering the product has a finish-to-start relationship with signing the purchase order.
- **Start to Start (SS)**—Task 1 must start before Task 2 can start. This dependency is most often used to link tasks that can start at the same time. A landscaping team can mow the lawn and edge the lawn at the same time. Therefore, "Mow Lawn" has a start-to-start relationship with "Edge Lawn."
- **Finish to Finish (FF)**—Task 1 must finish before task 2 can finish. This relationship is used to link tasks that can be worked in parallel, but one can't finish until the other does. A drywall hanger begins to create the walls inside a home. A painter can start painting the walls immediately after, but can't finish until the drywall hanger is complete. Therefore, "Paint Walls" has a finish-to-finish relationship with "Hang Walls."
- **Start to Finish**—The previous task must start before the next task can finish. This is the most uncommon of the predecessors, but is a defined dependency. There are rare cases to use this, but most likely the three prior dependencies will cover most scenarios.

Linking your tasks with dependencies will allow your schedule to expand or collapse as linked tasks are completed.

## Scheduling Rules

A properly constructed project schedule should follow these rules:

- Each task in the plan (except for the first task) should have a predecessor. This predecessor should have one of the dependencies associated.

- There should be no manually entered dates. The finish date for the project should "fall out" of the scheduling tool. The scheduling tool will use the durations, predecessors, and dependencies to set the end date of the project.
- Duration estimates should come from your team.

Following these simple rules will allow you to create a project schedule that can help with projection of completion dates, course correct when bad things occur, and communicate to the team when they should be ready to start their next tasks.

## *The Plans That Make the Plan*

One of the most common misconceptions about a project plan is that it is a schedule of tasks. There are several plans that make up a project plan. These include:

- Project Schedule
- Schedule Management Plan
- Scope Management Plan
- Quality Management Plan
- Risk Management Plan
- Issue Management Plan
- Communications Plan
- Budget

Don't let this list scare you though. It is not always necessary to include each one of these plans in every project; however, a project could include all of these plans and more.

Do not create one of the listed plans just so you can place a checkmark next to it and say that you have completed one; do it only where it makes sense. Project management is a set of guidelines, not rules!

All of the plans together make a project plan. They help you establish and understand what you will do, whom you will notify, and the effects of your actions when an event occurs on the project.

## *The Sum of the Parts*

A successful project is the result of various components interacting positively. If your project is to arrange and run a book sale to raise money for your school, you'll need to divide up the tasks. First, determine the scope or size of the project. Does the budget set forth by the sponsors (the PTA) allow you to buy 300 children's books to sell over two days, or 3,000 books to sell over two weeks?

Next, evaluate your budget. If $2,100 has been allocated for purchasing the books and you can purchase the average children's book for $3, then you are looking at about 700 books. If previous book sales indicate that books sell at an average of about 250 a day, you'll be looking at a three-day sale. Keep in mind that some of the parameters may have been decided beforehand. Make sure the numbers work. If, for example, the sponsor wants you to buy 700 books for a one-day sale, then you'll have to find a way to maximize sales by choosing a bigger location, using better promotion throughout the school, and having more volunteers on hand to sell books. You might, however, also propose a three-day sale to the sponsors, using your research to illustrate the possible benefits of an alternative plan.

**ALERT!**

Often, projects fail because key details were omitted from the project plan. It may help you to remember all the factors if you start listing everything you can think of. Once you have your team in place, they will be able to fill in the pieces you may not have considered.

Once you've determined the overall scope, you can start addressing the details. On smaller projects, you may be able to do several of the tasks yourself. Nonetheless, even for your own organization, it's important to have a list of all the details involved.

Using the PTA book-sale example, here's what your list might look like:

1. Set the date of the sale.
2. Set the timeline of interim deadlines.
3. Get volunteers.
   - Those who will help you plan and promote the sale
   - Those who will help you sell books
   - Those who will help clean up after the sale
4. Find the "in-school" location for sale.
5. Determine how books will be brought to the school and where they will be stored until the sale and after the sale. Are you buying books that can be returned to the publisher? Are you buying books on consignment? Are unsold books being donated to the school library? Always think about what happens to resources after the project.
6. Arrange for all necessary supplies, including cash register or cash box, receipts, etc.
7. Consider other items for sale, such as bookmarks, etc., but stay within your budget.
8. Set up day-of rules and guidelines; for example, "No refunds, but books can be exchanged on same day as sale," "Cash or personal checks only," etc. Also, determine who will be the cashier and handle the finances.
9. Coordinate all setup, including day-of and cleanup activities.
10. Day of sale: Set up and price the books (you may have already established a set formula for pricing, such as $x$ percent above cost to you).
11. Sell books.
12. Shut down and clean up. Break down at end of sale; return books to storage or wherever they are supposed to go. Don't forget to think about this part of the project.
13. Make sure money is accounted for and in a safe place.
14. Turn over funds to PTA treasurer.
15. Meet to debrief. While the event is still fresh in your (and your sponsors') mind, evaluate the success of this year's sale. Consider what you did differently that was better, what you did the same that always works, and figure out what didn't work (and why). Documenting this process will give next year's project manager a great foundation.

It's important that you cover all bases in your detailed plan of action. Your team will help you find gaps, if there are any, in your plan. They may also make additional or supplemental suggestions, such as, in the previous example, "How about having some refreshments on hand?" This was not a significant detail, as the project could proceed without refreshments, but it was evaluated nonetheless. Considering the limited space and manpower needed (or willing) to clean up, refreshments would not have been the best way to use the project's resources.

If, at the end of the book sale, everyone started walking out, and someone turned around and said, "What are we supposed to do with all of these extra books?" one of two things could have happened. It could be that no one planned the follow-through and closeout details, or the details weren't clearly communicated (or understood). In either case, it's clear that someone didn't accomplish his or her task regarding breaking down the sale.

Plan the delegation of tasks carefully to avoid any overlap. You don't want three people in charge of ordering bookmarks, or you'll have too many. Review all of the details with your team beforehand to make sure every task is covered and everyone knows what their responsibilities are.

Some projects will be broken down into numerous levels of details. You may have someone doing a task, someone else doing a subtask, someone doing a sub-subtask, and so on. Often, the more details you're working with, the more you may need to subdivide. Breaking down a project into smaller tasks is called a "Work Breakdown Structure." It is a systematic, prioritized account of all the work that needs to be completed, including the fine points necessary to plan, carry out, and track the project.

Some people are comfortable handling an entire task, but may feel more comfortable if the task is broken down into multiple parts. As a project manager, you can break down a task in any number of ways—whatever is most efficient in terms of time, money, and effort. For example, the person ordering the books can order storybooks on Monday, nonfiction books on Tuesday, and reference books on Wednesday. On the other hand, she may order all books from publishers ABC and DEF on Monday, from GHI and JKL publishing houses on Tuesday, and MNO and PQR publishers on Wednesday. She could also get all the books she can from a distributor one day and from Internet sources the next. It's important that you divide tasks realistically. Buying 600 books on Monday and 100 on Tuesday morning is probably not realistic unless your volunteer works for a publishing house.

Many factors must be taken into account when dividing a project into tasks and subtasks. Make estimates regarding the resources you have based on all logical and reasonable factors. For example, if someone works for a publishing house but would clearly lose his or her job by ordering 600 books at an employee discount without prior arrangements, you cannot make this a realistic task.

Detailing tasks is helpful because tasks can be easily understood and accomplished. The majority of people work better when they are working on smaller, more manageable tasks. However, it's important (and not always easy) to determine how much breaking down of a project you need to do. Yes, you may have a list of tasks and an order in which they should be done. You may have it broken down by days, perhaps by morning and afternoon. Should you then break each task down into how many hours or even minutes it should take? It depends on the overall time structure. If the project requires you to do a complete inventory of your business in one day before the potential new buyer shows up, then you might have to break down the project into an hourly schedule.

You can determine how many pieces of the puzzle there need to be by evaluating the following:

- The overall time frame of the project
- The complexity of the project
- The expertise of the person doing a particular task
- The complexity of the task

The last two items on the list are perhaps the most important. If a person is new to the job he has been assigned, you may have to detail the task more carefully. For instance, if someone ordering the books for the book sale has never ordered books before, you might detail who needs to be called, what needs to be filled out on the order forms, and how long each order should take. The complexity of the task will also be factored into the equation. More technical or detailed tasks such as those found in an engineering project may need to be further subdivided. This will tie in to the skill level of the team members.

**ALERT!**

When estimating how long a task will take, always allow extra time for external factors. Projects have been delayed by power failures, technical glitches, weather, illness, and various other factors. For every story about how a computer has facilitated the completion of a project much faster than it could have been done a decade ago, there's a story about how the computer crashed, lost a file, or otherwise caused a project delay.

The person planning the project needs to find team members who can work at the rate required. Sure, an author who works at a slower pace could easily handle the job with a six-month due date, but not within this particular time frame.

Sometimes the project sponsor will ask you how much of a given resource you need. If you are a contractor working with an assistant, you might have the opportunity to assess the project and give the sponsor an estimate of how much time it will take. You may not get the project if your estimate is not in line with standard rates and time estimates for the job you've been asked to do. If you're in the position of being able to set parameters for a project, get an idea of what other people would ask to do a similar project.

## Garnering Acceptance

Creating a plan is only a portion of the work in project planning. The team must believe in the plan. They must understand what it is, why it is there, and what the benefits are to them. As stated before, many people resist the planning process. The reason is that they really don't know what is in it for them. If people understood how the planning process benefits them, then they may be more prone to participate.

One of the key benefits to having a plan is not always being in emergency mode. A lack of planning will result in a lack of understanding of when your team is to perform their tasks. In the previous example, if your team member who was ordering the books for the book sale does not know when the book sale is, then a mishap is on the horizon. Imagine a plan with 1,000 tasks and forty resources. The when and where of a plan is very important.

Providing the resources (time, budget, materials) necessary to complete the project is another way that you, as a project manager, can help team members. With a good plan, you will know when each resource is needed, but you will also know how much is needed. This translates into operating efficiency and the overall improvement of team members' project experiences.

Understanding all of these factors can help you explain and garner acceptance of the plan. When your team first begins the planning process, they may be apathetic or skeptical. However, at the end of the process, they really start to see and understand why the process is so important. Following up with them one more time and garnering acceptance achieves two things: their commitment to accountability and their honest opinion of the plan. This helps you set the stage for selling the plan to the sponsors.

## Selling the Plan

So many project managers make the mistake of blindly accepting the end date given for a project. This is the key reason that many projects fail in the planning process. What many project managers don't know is that the date the sponsor gives is like the opening bid of an auction in which you are the seller. If the opening bid is more than what you were asking for, then you take the deal. If it is less, the negotiation is on. You begin to explain the value of the item, the future worth, the effort it took to create it, and discuss a new figure. In the end, you agree on a price and make the transaction.

The same is true with project end dates. There are some times that the end date is fixed due to a market date, regulatory issue, or mandated date. For example, planning the project that will produce *Dick Clark's New Year's Rocking Eve* has a pretty fixed date. There are other times when the date is selected out of thin air to create motivation for the project team.

Whatever the case may be, you have selected a team, created a plan, linked the tasks, received estimates, and documented all decisions. The output of all of this work is the time in which you and your team think the project can be done. Just like the auction, if the date you planned is before the date expected, you are ready to get to work. If the date you had in mind is later, then you need to start selling your plan to the sponsor.

- Are there requirements that should be removed from the project?
- Will we need more money to get additional resources or materials to speed up the project?
- What will it take to complete the project earlier?

> You will be surprised how many mandated dates are changed when the plans are presented and reasoning is given. Many of these dates just sounded good or were a goal in mind when the project was started. When you come back and validate your reason for changing the date, it then becomes reality.

Whatever the case, sell, sell, sell. Remember the team member who is wondering how all this planning is going to benefit him? Right here is where it matters. A sponsor said, "I want this in this time frame." Your team said, "We can do it in this time frame." It is up to you to close the gap. If the gap is closed properly, the team will get the time needed for the project. Late hours and weekend work will not be necessary.

## Project Baselines

After all of the work and planning, it is time to draw your line in the sand. This is called creating a baseline. A baseline is the simple recording of your current plan so that when the project begins, you can measure your progress against what you planned your progress to be. A project is measured in time and cost, so actual performance compared against planned performance (baseline) is the determining factor.

When tasks complete early or late or are completed for more or less money, the actual figures get recorded. Then you compare those against your baseline to see if you are ahead of schedule or behind, over budget or under budget, and how efficient your team is.

Creating a baseline is like drawing a line in the sand because a baseline can be changed based on a change request or significant event, but it must be agreed upon by the team. Remember the old Bugs Bunny cartoons where one character draws a line in the sand and says, "Cross this line, and you are in trouble." The other character crosses the line, and the first character quickly draws a new line and says, "Now, cross this line, and you are in trouble." This scenario goes on and on. Creating your baseline may feel like this, but you have to measure against something!

# CHAPTER 6

# Project Execution

Project execution is where the work actually gets done. This phase of a project generally requires the most investment of time and cost; however, it is the smallest investment from a project management standpoint. Project cost and effort generally follow a standard bell curve through the project life cycle. However, the project management effort follows a reverse curve. Confused? The project manager is doing a large amount of work during the execution phase; however, most of it is categorized in the controlling phase.

## *Track, Report, Change, Plan, Track*

As discussed in Chapter 3, the planning, executing, and controlling phases are a cycle within themselves. It is important to consistently update the project plans based on the actual occurrences. During the execution of a project, the actual work is being done. It is also the time that most issues will arise.

**ALERT!**

No matter how much you plan, or manage the plan, issues will arise. It is part of the project management process. If you expect that they will happen, then they are much easier to deal with than when you expect everything will go smoothly and it doesn't.

You should communicate with your team at regular intervals to get results from them. However, do not wait to do this in the project status meeting. Talk to the individuals prior to the status meeting so that you are prepared to deliver the right message. Also, if you wait until a status meeting to get updates, you are conditioning your team to only communicate once per week. Team members will forget to work on an issue or task, see the meeting on the calendar, and then try to scramble at the last minute to show progress. If you ask on a constant basis, but are not consistent in the elapsed time between progress checks, it conditions the team to move forward.

## *Getting the Right Answers*

The two worst questions to ask during the execution phase are:

- Will you be done by the date provided?
- What percentage of the task is complete?

Many project managers ask these questions, get generic responses, update the plans, and miss the targets. As PMI states, 90 percent of a project manager's time is spent communicating. However, it needs to be proper communication. Asking what percentage of the project is complete and whether it will be done on time are subjective. Also, these questions allow someone to give an automatic response. It is allowable to ask these questions, but only if you intend to follow up with more pertinent questions. These questions should be more direct and qualifying. For example:

- You say that you are 50 percent complete, but three days have passed on a five-day task. Are we behind schedule?
- Do you anticipate any issues or outside influences preventing you from meeting the committed date?
- Can you tell me how you have determined that you are 80 percent complete?
- What do you have to do to get the remaining 20 percent done?

These questions help you dive into the responses to uncover what is really going on.

As much as possible, have these conversations one on one prior to a status meeting. You do not want to embarrass or put a team member in a bad position by interrogating them in front of the entire team.

You will get automated answers if you ask automated questions. A status check is not intended to allow a project manager to move through a task list and place check marks to show that things are moving along; they are designed to ensure that the project is progressing at the correct pace and to identify potential issues that could derail the project.

## *Sending the Right Message*

To communicate, you must be truthful. As an individual, business person, mother, father, or project manager, you are only as good as your word. The moment people start to mistrust what you say or report, you lose all power as a project manager.

Being a project manager is a unique position. You generally do not have the normal motivational packages that are available to standard managers. You can rarely give a raise or bonus to an individual, grant time off, or promote a team member. Therefore, your standing in the eyes of your team members and project participants is everything. You must be honest and truthful with where the project stands. It is what it is.

If the project is over budget or late, it is just as important to report this as it is if it is under budget or early. The earlier you present this information to your project sponsor, the better. You must give them ample time to react to a situation. Holding on to bad information with the hopes that it will get better will end in disaster for all.

Sending the right message also means controlling your demeanor throughout the presentation of the status. Frankly, if you are freaking out, so is your entire team. If you lambaste a team member because they are late, then the next team member is unlikely to be truthful with you.

Show compassion, honesty, and integrity. Your team will pick up on this and will begin to open up in several ways. Mostly, they will be honest with you in return, and this will improve the chances of a successful project.

## Progress, Progress, Progress

During the gathering of information on progress, there is a key opportunity to firm the bond between you and your team. As you check in, do not forget to reward the team for their accomplishments. In the beginning, you asked them to estimate the unknown and create a plan for something that they have never done before. Now, the project is moving forward and you are requesting progress. If everything is going according to plan, don't forget to congratulate the team. Thank them for their efforts. Make sure that they understand the small wins that can lead to the overall success of the project.

Consistently search for progress information from your team. Do not expect that everything is progressing as planned. If a task is supposed to start, call the team member to see if it did. If a task is finishing five days from now, see how the progress is going. So many project managers wait until the project status meeting to check how things are progressing. What many will find is that nothing occurred since the previous status meeting, and now an entire week has been lost.

## Let Your Plans Ebb and Flow

Most project managers will fail to update the plan once it is written and approved for the first time. Whether they are lazy, do not understand the tool they are using, or some other reason, the project plan is not progressed. Without a plan that shows progress or lack thereof, how do you communicate the needs to the team? When a task finished early, how do you notify the next team member that the next task needs to start?

Assuming that your plan was set appropriately, then the dates will expand and contract based on early and late dates. The project plan is then ebbing and flowing. If tasks are finishing early, then you can continue the momentum by notifying the team members to start the next task early. If it is finishing late, you can talk with the team members to make sure they are ready to go as soon as it finishes so that no more time is lost.

Communication will always be the key. Letting your team members know what is coming can help move the project through to fruition.

## Showing the Real Date

Showing the real date is the one item that can really save a project manager from the firing line. There are times that the real date is adjusted because the project manager doesn't want to tell the team or the sponsor that they are behind. The funny thing is that the sponsor will find out eventually.

There is one tricky instance of this to keep in mind. In managing project communications, what you are really managing is expectations. A project is only early or late based on the expectation of when the project would be completed. So if a project is running late, show it immediately. However, if it is running early, do you show that, too? This is your call, but general practice is to keep the original date posted and to use the early time as contingency time. This will set the proper expectations and keep the project coming in early. It also accounts for Murphy's Law or an overexuberant team member reporting better progress than actually occurred.

**QUESTION?**

**Why is showing the real date so important?**
If you adjust the date or don't progress the plan because it moves the date later than the original due date, then are you telling the truth? If you are not telling the truth, then what are you telling?

In any case, show the real date. If a project runs off course early and you are reporting that on a weekly basis, is it any surprise to anyone if it comes in late? Managing expectations is what will determine project success.

# CHAPTER 7

# Project Controlling

The controlling phase goes hand in hand with the planning and execution. However, it is just as important and active as the planning phase. In the controlling phase, the project manager is making adjustments to all of the plans based on the actions and information received in the execution phase. This is the stage where you react to the information, help understand the new direction, and continue to monitor to make sure the project is progressing as planned.

## *Making the Right Adjustments*

A great trait for project managers is having the ability to keep a calm exterior in times of duress. It is important not to panic. The most important part to understand about the "It is what it is" approach is that there's nothing you can do about the past. It is all about the future and how to recover from bad news and keep the momentum when the news is good.

As discussed earlier, create an atmosphere where it is acceptable for your team to give you an honest status. If you freak out every time a task is late, chances are tasks will continue to be late and you will not be told about them. In making the right adjustments, take a look at that all-important project plan. Where should you try to add resources? Where should you try to remove requirements?

If you are running a project that is a fundraiser, and one task is to create the announcement and the other task is to stuff the envelopes and mail them, what is the right adjustment if the announcement task is completed late? Would you reduce the amount of envelopes to stuff? Probably not, because that would reduce the likelihood that you would reach your donation goal. How about adding another resource to stuffing envelopes so that you can compress the time it takes?

This is a rather simplistic example, but there are three main adjustments that you can make in a project plan to shorten a task.

- **Fast Track:** To increase the schedule, you work parallel tasks to shorten the time frame.
- **Crash:** Crashing the schedule means that you add resources to shorten the time frame.
- **Remove Requirements:** Remove a requirement or task from the project.

These are your general options in trying to adjust the time frame. Be careful when selecting a strategy to shorten your project time frame, especially when choosing the "Crash the Schedule" option. There is a law of diminishing returns that means adding resources will not always mean a shorter time frame. Once you have decided which option you will choose, it is back to the planning phase for you.

## *The Cycle Within the Cycle*

You have received your project update information, made a selection in how to adjust, and now you take the outputs from this process and start the planning cycle over. Have you caught on to the cycle within the cycle yet? When you are updating a project plan, you are actually performing functions in all three of the phases—planning, executing, and controlling. It is important to remember that the movement between phases is fluid. It is not as simple as start planning phase, stop planning phase; start executing phase, stop executing phase; etc. A discussion of all of the phases could occur in one conversation. For example:

**PROJECT MANAGER:** How is the work coming on the painting of the house?

**CONTRACTOR:** The walls came up late, and we did not get started on time.

**PROJECT MANAGER:** Is there any way that we can make up the time?

**CONTRACTOR:** I could bring on another one of my workers and we can split the work to complete it faster.

**PROJECT MANAGER:** Will that add to my cost?

**CONTRACTOR:** It shouldn't, since we will do the work in half the time with twice the resources, the cost should be the same.

**PROJECT MANAGER:** Sounds good, but if we start to see that we will not make up the time or that cost will be impacted, let me know.

In this example, the project manager moved throughout the phases:

- **Executing:** Requesting the status of start and completion times.
- **Controlling:** Assessing the impact of the status and making proper adjustments. Also, requesting feedback if things do not go as planned.
- **Planning:** Placing the new resource into the plan, adjusting the time to half of the original duration, and assessing the cost impact.

You may not always know that you are progressing through the phases, and that is all right. With practice and an understanding of how the technical components of project management work, you will begin to see the results of the cycle within the cycle.

## Ask All of the Questions

You will find as a project manager, there are loopholes in any system. If you don't believe it, ask any parent whether or not this is true. A parent can tell a six-year-old to only interrupt an adult conversation if it is extremely important, but then the child interrupts to state that she watched Barney today on television. The parent gets mad at the child, but in fairness, telling that to the parent was important to the child. The parent then has to define what an extremely important conversation is to the child. Before long, the child will find another loophole and the cycle will continue.

The same is true for your project team. In the example of the house painting, there was a very key question asked. That was, "Will that add to my cost?" when the contractor stated that they could bring another worker to the project. If you don't ask all of the questions, you are generally in for a big surprise.

**ALERT!**

Projects will have a tendency to go out of control exponentially based on the number of assumptions that are made. Be sure that you are handling the obvious ones, such as time, cost, and quality.

For the sake of this story, let's say the project manager did not ask about the cost of bringing another resource on. Two weeks later, after all of the work is complete, the project manager receives the bill for the house painting, and it is twice the cost. When the irate project manager calls the contractor, they will say that they were asked to get another resource and the one that they had available was more expensive than the one already on the project. Therefore, the project manager created one issue by solving another. Let's explore the proper conversation for this matter:

**PROJECT MANAGER:** Will adding the additional resource affect my cost?

**CONTRACTOR:** Yes, the resource that we have available is $50 per hour instead of the $25 per hour quoted.

**PROJECT MANAGER:** So, my choices are to finish the painting of the house five days late or have it cost more?

**CONTRACTOR:** Yes.

**PROJECT MANAGER:** Let me talk to my sponsor and I will get back to you. Please proceed as originally planned, and I will let you know.

By asking all of the questions, you have uncovered another potential issue. Again, this is a learned skill, but if you always keep time, cost, and quality in mind as you are searching for options, you should be able to avoid huge errors.

## *How to Communicate Change*

So, you have made the right adjustments, asked all of the questions, and now find yourself with a significant change. In this case, it is a tradeoff between time and cost.

As a project manager, it is important that you present your sponsor with issues and proposed solutions, not just issues alone. When communicating a change, make sure that you have thought through several options so that your sponsor can get you your decision in a timely manner.

To complete the story, the project manager has the following conversation with the sponsor:

**PROJECT MANAGER:** The walls for the house were not completed on time. We now have a decision to make. I have talked with the painting contractor and they can get another resource, but it is more expensive. We can either finish the project five days late, or spend the additional money needed to complete the project on time. Which would you prefer?

**SPONSOR:** I am on a really tight budget, so let's finish five days late.

Some of you are chuckling as you are reading this, thinking that your project sponsor would say, "Finish it on time and for the cost provided!" Although there are many sponsors like that, we deal with facts and reality. It is what it is. In this story, if the project manager didn't uncover the additional cost by asking all of the right questions, then they would have saved time but spent more money. This is exactly what the sponsor did not want.

Change is an interesting phenomenon. Many consultants love change because it generally means more dollars and more revenue. But there is a responsibility involved in change. Change for the sake of change can mean that the intended result of the project is diminished. For example, if you are painting your house and you hire a company to perform the job, there is a fee associated. When they have finished the first coat, you realize that you do not like the overall color, so you ask them to paint a different color. There is a fee associated with that. Ten coats of paint later, you are satisfied with the color. The outside person looking at your house sees one color. A real estate broker sees one color. You see one color, but the cost is ten times the amount intended, so the value of repainting your house diminished greatly.

It is important that when you communicate a change, you are giving an unbiased approach. A more responsible action by the painting contractor would have been to paint several small, inconspicuous squares of different colors to inspect the overall color, paint one side of the house and check to see if it is acceptable, then complete the painting of the house. The cost would be significantly less and the customer would not have diminished the value of the work. Instead, the contractor just went out and painted the whole house each time, driving up the overall cost.

**FACT**

Change is inevitable. Ensure that you are exploring all options before blindly accepting a change. Make sure your changes are responsible, ethical, and keep as much of the original intent of the project as possible.

When you communicate a change, make sure you are providing the whole story so that everyone understands why the change was made, the positives and negatives of the change, and what other alternatives were suggested.

## Measuring Against the Baseline

Remember the line in the sand? This is where it is time to compare against it. In the controlling phase, every piece of information received in the executing phase is compared against the baseline to determine what to do next. This includes inputting the project statistics, seeing the variances, and determining which areas need to go back to planning. The only way to truly determine if a project is early, late, or on time is to measure against a baseline.

**QUESTION?**

**Can a project have multiple baselines?**
Absolutely! Many of the project software programs support multiple baselines, and it is a good practice to have baseline intervals. If a change is executed, rebaseline the plan, but keep the original for reference.

Reporting where the plan is versus the baseline is the biggest part of the project controlling phase. All corrective actions should bring the plan back to, or as close as possible to, the baseline. Also, if the plan is updated properly, then bringing a plan back to the baseline ensures that you will complete the project as originally planned.

## Determining When to Panic

As the great Kenny Rogers sang, "You've got to know when to hold them, know when to fold them, know when to walk away, and know when to run." The same is true about project management. There are several types of project managers (as covered in Chapter 23) and they all communicate differently. One thing that must be communicated consistently is when you are unable to determine a way to bring the plan back to the baseline.

Remember that this book teaches you to anticipate issues and to know that at least 2 percent of the project is going to go wrong, no matter how good of a project manager you are. If you run every little issue up the flagpole or discuss them in great length at team meetings, your message will be lost when it is really time to panic. When should you panic? The answer, really, is never. It is not good to panic; it leads to rash and unjustified decisions. I am not saying be a robot, but there's that recurring theme again: It is what it is.

> There is no reason to panic if a task or two is late, because they may not have been critical to the time frame of the project. Only when the plan is unable to be recovered to the baseline is it a dire issue.

By now, the phases should have taught you how not to panic. You have already followed these steps:

- Received the feedback from the team
- Explored strategies to recover the plan (i.e., crash, fast track, etc.)
- Assessed the impact of the available strategies
- Gathered the facts and options

Now it is time to give all of the information to the sponsor for the decisions to be made. Even if the sponsor is mad, it doesn't change the status of the project or the options available. A great sponsor can come up with ways to solve the problem utilizing options you were unaware of. In any case, you don't determine when to panic—you determine when to escalate.

## CHAPTER 8

# Project Closing

Believe it or not, the closing of a project is the most difficult phase to accomplish. There are more projects that are sitting at 98 percent complete than there are completed projects. As the project winds down, there are a few trailing issues and small tasks that should be done, but don't feel so important. These will drag on and on until they're eventually forgotten, and new projects are underway.

## What Is the Definition of Done?

To get great estimates from your team, it starts with a simple definition. What does *done* mean? When you ask someone, "How long will it take you to build the house?" there is ambiguity. One contractor may say one year, one may say three months. How do you know which one is right? If the definition was set in the beginning that done means ready to move in, then the contractor would not have said that they were done in the first place.

Make sure everyone understands what they are being asked to estimate and you will arrive at better estimates. This also allows you to set what done looks like when the project is complete. When each person has finished her task, what will it look like when it is done? In the house-building example, if the scope wasn't set properly, the house that is built may not be what was envisioned. A great result for a project means beginning with the end in mind.

## The Last 2 Percent

As mentioned earlier, there are many projects sitting at 98 percent complete. This is because the last 2 percent of a project is the hardest to close. A great way to determine a company's project-management maturity is to look at their last fifteen completed projects. In looking at the documents, take the following quiz:

1. **Is the project plan updated?**
   *Yes = 5 points, No = 0 points*
   **Bonus:** Are all tasks marked complete?
   *Yes = 10 points, No = 0 points*
2. **Do you have an issue and/or risk log?**
   *Yes = 5 points for each, No = 0 points*
   **Bonus:** Were issues and risks added throughout the project?
   *Yes = 5 points, No = 0 points*
   **Bonus:** Are all issues and risks marked complete?
   *Yes = 5 points, No = 0 points*
   **Bonus:** Are all issues and risks updated with the proper resolutions?
   *Yes = 10 points, No = 0 points*

3. **Was there a project close-out meeting?**
   *Yes = 5 points, No = 0 points*
   **Bonus:** Did you create meeting notes for this and send them out?
   *Yes = 10 points, No = 0 points*

If you scored less than 20, don't worry, many people will. If you scored between 21 and 30, you are well on your way. If you scored 30+, congratulations!

**QUESTION?**

**Why is it so hard to close out the project?**
Generally, there is more work to be done than resources available. Many people get too busy and start the next project without completing the mundane things it takes to close the current project.

If you are a vendor or contractor, the last 2 percent means a whole different ballgame. Many clients are afraid to sign a project-completion document for fear that they missed something and want the vendor and or contractor to remain available. The last 2 percent for them is waiting for a test to be run, a document to be approved, etc. In most cases, it is stalling, but they do not want to end the contract unless they are absolutely sure that it is complete.

The difficulty of closing the project is in direct correlation to the definition of the project. This scenario again lends itself to the definition of done. How well the project was defined will determine how easy it is to show that it is complete.

# Lessons Learned

The infamous lessons learned: Do they really exist? For many people learning about project management, they have heard this term quite a bit. In theory, a lessons-learned session is supposed to identify issues, risks, and pitfalls of a previous project and document them so that they can be avoided in future projects. However, this step rarely gets done.

Many team members feel that a lessons-learned session is for complaining or placing blame about project mishaps. Others are just too busy to attend. Either case is an excuse for the real reason, which is that many people see little or no value to a lessons-learned session. This is because most companies mandate some sort of session, but do not have a way to store or retrieve them. They become busywork and therefore are pushed aside or completed with little effort.

The real reason to perform a lessons-learned session is to truly learn. First, many issues on a project are communication issues. A session to discuss them, in an open and honest atmosphere, allows team members to solve the communication issues and build a stronger bond for the next project. Many times, larger issues are a result of some small misunderstandings along the way. These can be avoided by an adjustment to a form or an earlier notification of a need. If these issues are not explored, they will most likely occur again and again. The greatest way to show value in lessons-learned sessions is to publish them. Create a repository of them for others to find. An even better way is to bring a list of previous lessons learned to the planning meeting for your next project.

## Closure Documentation

The closure documentation should be as important as the beginning. The old you (prior to reading this book) may have just let the last 2 percent go. However, the new you (after reading this book) will understand how important closure documentation is to your future project success.

Many project experts say that the key to a successful project is looking at historical documentation prior to planning a new project. This is your chance to create your historical documentation to plan your next successful project.

A closing packet signed by the sponsor is ideal for the project closing documentation. This packet should be the last item for each project. This should include:

- Complete and updated project schedule
- An issue and risk log that has all items closed or transferred with resolutions detailed
- A team assessment including evaluations of each team member's performance
- Lessons learned
- Completed budget report detailing all project costs
- A project statistics report that shows actual performance compared to baselines
- A project completion report for the sponsor to sign

**ALERT!**

Having a project methodology that requires a detailed closing package is a great way to assist in closing the last 2 percent of the project.

The detailed closing packet can be used as a communication tool as well. If you are having difficulty closing the last 2 percent of your project, then detailing the outstanding items and presenting them to the sponsor for signature will determine the importance of the remaining items. If they are necessary, the sponsor can mandate completion and you can use referent power to pass this along to the team for action. If the sponsor signs off, then the last 2 percent can be transferred to ongoing issues and closed out of your project. Either way, the closing package can help facilitate the closure of the project.

## *The Handoff*

While projects by definition are finite, their impact should continue after they have been completed. If not, one may question what the point of the project was in the first place. Many projects roll themselves into operations. The company should now be using the information or system that resulted from the project. A transitional period will often take team members directly from the project into their roles in the daily operations of the company.

Now that the project is deemed complete, it's important to determine:

- Who will maintain it once it becomes operational?
- When will upgrades be made?
- Who will handle troubleshooting?

Setting up the system was the project; using the system is the operational process that follows. Often, people from the core project team are the perfect fit for these positions. In fact, some may have been borrowed from similar positions to work on the project. If you used the services of an expert or outside consultant during the project, you may need to continue using that person on an ongoing basis after the project ends, at least until someone else has been trained to take over.

Regular corporate operations may also change because of the project. You have to look at how the project affects the manner in which business is run, including corporate communications, cultural implications, and so on. A successful project should have an impact, and when the project is drawing to a close, that potential impact needs to be addressed. For example, what will the flow of company information be now that lower-level managers have access to the same information as the top executives? The technical staff can often train upper management and senior VPs on processes and procedures for the system. As the knowledge base shifts, what new procedures will have to be addressed?

The transition that takes the project from completion to real-world activities will require reviewing reports and other data generated throughout the project to answer questions that arise. Therefore, it's important that you organize and store all key documentation.

It's worth noting that almost every project has a carryover effect. Rarely does a project end without any discernable trace. Even a small-scale school fundraising project will result in that money being spent on something—and that purchase will hopefully be educational or helpful for the children who attend the school.

The effects of a single project can also be widespread. Projects in small businesses or large corporations frequently result in new and efficient methods of assimilating and storing data or enhancing production, communication, or marketing efforts. Projects from a wide range of places, including laboratories, may result in the discoveries of new medications or create new and useful products.

From personal growth to expanding global technologies, projects differ in numerous respects and can impact one person or millions. Whether it is keeping the weight off after your two-week project to lose ten pounds or maintaining communication with the space station after your project was to supervise its building and launch, the steps necessary for making the transition from project into actual operations are vital. It is this transition that can ultimately make all of your hard work worthwhile. After all, if the project was to build the space station, it's worth your effort to make sure it is operational and that the team is trained how to use it efficiently.

## The Sign Off

While the sponsor, stakeholders, or management will officially sign off on the completed project, you will also have to finish your tenure as project manager. Along with the need to see that all loose ends are neatly wrapped up, you will want to take time to review the decisions you made and the strategies that you implemented along the way. Which ones worked? Which ones did not work as you hoped they would? Was your style of leadership effective? You may not be able to determine all of the answers yourself. If you have a thick skin, you may want team members to tell you what they liked and disliked about how you ran the project. Ask for honesty and be prepared to receive it.

As the project winds down, you will be faced with moving on to the next situation. In the corporate environment, there may be another project waiting for you. Or, you may be resuming business as usual. Having put so much effort into one specific project, you may feel let down when it comes to an end. Your daily routine may seem boring by comparison. On the other hand, working nine to five might feel like a vacation! Whatever you are feeling as the project winds down, don't allow yourself to give less than your usual commitment to the project. Just as you don't want team members to slack off as they see the finish line approaching, you must tell yourself that although the end is near, you will need to muster up one last burst of energy.

During the course of the project, try to find a few moments to line up your next project. Don't wait until this one is in the final stages. However, you also don't want to divert your attention from the current project, so stay focused.

If the project is yours to sign off on, then you need to determine if everything has been completed to your liking, as you are management, sponsor, and champion. Carefully monitoring the project along the way should have eliminated any major surprises at this point. Carefully evaluate what you were looking to achieve and compare it to the finished project that is now before you. Don't sign off on it if you feel that more work is needed. On the other hand, don't pursue perfection at the risk of never having a marketable product, or falling behind the competition. Maintain high, but realistic, expectations.

## Disassembling the Team

How one disassembles a team depends on the nature of the project and the team. If the project was a one-time operation such as helping your buddy move, it's over. There's time for a parting beer, some handshakes, and "I'll see you soon." However, if the project is one that will require more work in the future, you need to determine who can do each job. Perhaps someone who set up the computer system wants to stick around and move into the operational side as systems manager. Others will learn new skills on the project with the express purpose of continuing to use them on a regular basis once the project moves to an operational phase.

Projects can promote learning, which can lead to greater talent on your workforce. Integrating people from the project into the regular flow of production is generally very effective, particularly with new companies or businesses that may need people to fill open positions. People who make the transition from the project team to the daily routine created by the project often have a more intimate knowledge of the inner workings of the new system or product since they were involved from the start.

## How Do You Feel?

Now that the project is completed, do you feel a sense of relief? Do you feel a sense of accomplishment? Do you feel that you have achieved your project goals? Do you feel that, as the project manager, you have supported your team and fulfilled the stakeholders' expectations?

All the evaluations won't tell you how you feel about the project. People have worked on very successful projects and come away feeling empty. Sure, they made money, but they felt they did not learn or grow in any way. Some projects succeed despite unpleasant working conditions or unscrupulous methods that take a toll on team members. Other individuals will feel a strong sense of learning and growing from a project that went nowhere. Filmmakers will often recount early flops that taught them about how to do it right in the future. You might even recount a personal project that went no place, but from which you made a personal discovery, like a hidden talent or a new friend.

After the project phase is completed, sit down and assess what you personally got from the experience. Ask yourself:

- Did I learn from any or all aspects of the project?
- Did I grow?
- How will I continue my affiliation with the product, service, system, or function that resulted from the project?

At the end of the official project phase, you can do a personal overview of your project management skills. Be honest. These are some of the questions you may ask in your self-evaluation of the project and your role in it:

- Did I deal well with other team members?
- How well did I communicate my ideas?
- Did I keep management, stakeholders, and any other key parties informed of the project's progress?

- Was I able to maintain the schedule I planned?
- Was I flexible enough to make alterations in plans when needed?
- Did I deal with conflict situations well?
- Did I catch risks in time?
- Did I take any unnecessary risks?
- Did I monitor properly so that I felt I had a firm grasp of where the project was at any given time?
- Did I reach the planned objectives of the project? If not, why not?
- If not, could I have prevented the project from failing or was it out of my control?
- Did I have proper contingency plans?
- Did I make the right call to use—or not to use—contingency plans?
- Did I learn new skills regarding project management? Specifically?
- Would I do it again? What would I change and what would I keep the same?

Take a few moments to assess what type of leadership qualities you displayed. While working in a leadership capacity, it is often hard to step back and take a look at exactly how you are doing. Assess your leadership skills by asking yourself these questions:

- Do I usually take time to go back and review information before making decisions, or do I just make the decision and move forward?
- If a team member asks me a question and I don't know the answer, do I seek outside help in finding the answer or try to research and solve it myself?
- Do I allow for a learning curve, or learning while doing (trial and error), as I go?
- Do team members consider my approach methodical or direct?
- Do I include gut feeling and intuition in making decisions, or rely strictly on data and specific information?
- Am I closer to believing that conflict situations can sometimes work themselves out, or am I closer to the idea that immediate intervention is necessary?
- Am I flexible in my methods, or do I try hard to keep the same methods in place as much as possible?

Obviously, there are no right or wrong answers to these questions. The situation, environment, and time frame will often dictate which answers are more suitable for a particular project.

**FACT**

You can make a positive argument for either approach, and certain leaders will vary from one method to another depending on the team and the project. The ability to adapt is one characteristic of an effective project manager.

The first choice generally indicates a less aggressive approach, such as stepping back to reevaluate or letting the conflict work itself out. In nonpressure projects, such as those over long periods of time or those for which the outcomes are not highly consequential, you may use intuitive feelings, review rather than move forward, and so on. In projects where time is critical, you may not have the luxury to visit and revisit an issue; it may be necessary to act quickly and rely on data alone.

Along with the situational understanding of these questions, there is the style of leadership you display and how that affects your team. A high-energy team in a hard-working, fast-paced environment may expect someone who is more direct, stays with proven methods, and uses facts and figures for decision making. A smaller organization, a casual setting, or an artistic or creative project, however, may need a leader to be particularly flexible and adaptable to new ideas. The team may look to you as someone who will follow a gut feeling now and then, and not always go by the book.

While you cannot completely play the chameleon role and change your leadership style for each project, you can consider the following:

- What type of leader will get the best response and results from this particular team of individuals?
- What does this particular project call for in terms of flexibility or rigidity?
- Before I take on this project, can I be the right leader for these people and this job?

There's nothing wrong with determining that a particular project needs a specific type of leader, and you are simply not the person for the job. Not every leader fits every role. Perhaps if more leaders evaluated the situation carefully and truthfully, they would know when they were not the right fit.

## Down the Road

A project may be evaluated further down the road to determine whether sales indeed increased, customer service improved, the movie was a hit at the box office, or the patio you built held up all summer long or started leaning to the left by late July.

For a fair assessment of the impact of your efforts, look at the project results after three, six, or twelve months. You can learn a lot about your initial plans and all of your hard work when you examine the results from a distance.

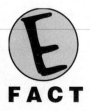

**FACT**

A card, note, or simple thank you to each team member means a lot. Let everyone who was involved in the project know that you appreciate the team's hard work. Hold a party or go out for dinner and make a toast, hand out small awards or give gifts to say thanks. Even if the project didn't meet final expectations, you should let everyone know you appreciate their efforts.

Ongoing evaluations will provide details for future projects. Teams can look at the fruits of their labor and see how the project results stood up over time. In the case of a new product, the data may tell you when a newer, updated version needs to be created. With technology, that may be ten minutes after you've signed off on the project.

Some projects are meant for short-term purposes and others are meant to have long-lasting implications. Know the limitations and evaluate accordingly. If something was created to last for six months, you should have realistic expectations if you evaluate it after one year.

Now that you have learned about the phases of project management, you'll take a closer look at many of the activities in project management.

## CHAPTER 9

# Assembling the
# Best Project Team

When a team wins a major sports championship, it's generally due to the efforts of the team as a whole, not a single player. As bright and shining as a star may be, other players need to step up and fulfill their roles for a team to win. Likewise, for your own project, it is unlikely that there is no need for interactivity and coordination among various aspects of the project. The bottom line: A good, well-organized team gets the job done right.

## *Your Team's Core Members*

At the center of your team are core members, those who were involved in initiating the project and laying out the parameters. Some of these are stakeholders, who will move into active roles in the project. The degree to which initial stakeholders and sponsors get involved in the actual project may vary greatly. Team members will become stakeholders as this becomes their project. Sponsors are very often not involved unless it's their own project—they're paying everyone involved, and they want to do a lot of the work themselves.

There are various levels of involvement by the sponsor. Someone may begin a project by handing you instructions and a budget and saying, "I'll be back in six months, good luck." You may sit down with upper management and find that although you are project leader, many of the other managers who worked with you in getting this project off the ground are planning to stay involved in various capacities.

**FACT**

With more and more people working off-site via technology and the Internet, there are projects in which the team members never meet. Even in these circumstances, communication is vital, and team members usually establish an e-mail relationship with one another.

Sometimes core project team members are found and sometimes they are already attached to the project. The team that works to plan the project is generally a core team, a starting team designed to get things lined up and set goals, objectives, and parameters. Some will continue on to the actual project team, while others won't.

## *Selecting Your Project Team*

Your project team will do the tasks necessary to bring the project to fruition. You will have to act as your own scout, seeking out the people who best fit the positions you need to fill. Although you may begin by assessing contractors to help you build that new family room on your house, you will also need to decide who will paint the room, furnish it, and so on.

Team members come in all shapes and sizes. They may be top professionals or your eight-year-old who is helping you plan that big summer trip to Europe. As long as each one brings something to the project, he is a valuable team member. What can your eight-year-old bring to the project that you don't already know? He can give you the expectations of Europe through the eyes of a child. Children look at the world differently and present ideas that they would enjoy. Rest assured that successful project managers at toy companies have consulted with children at some point.

**The right team members:**
- Are reliable
- Are trustworthy
- Are available
- Are flexible
- Have something to contribute
- Make an effort to get along with other team members
- Abide by the rules and parameters of the project
- Ask for help when they need it

**The wrong team members:**
- Show up only when they feel like it
- Are not honest about their skill level
- Must do everything their own way
- Make no effort to work as a team
- Complain frequently
- Think they know everything

It's up to you to carefully pick the right team members for the actual work on the project. You will need to look at your work breakdown structure and determine which positions you want to fill first. For example, if you're planning a wedding, do you hire the caterer or the wedding coordinator first? On some projects, you can have several people come on board at the same time, while on others, team members will join at various intervals as their responsibilities dictate.

A task breakdown sheet will help you assign the right people to the right project tasks. This can work in conjunction with your master plan on your work breakdown structure, which is your overall project blueprint including all tasks organized in a hierarchical chart. To start building your team, you'll have to assess the skills of each potential team member. Do you need a professional publisher with ten years of publishing experience to put out a newsletter for a small business? Probably not.

**ALERT!**

Project managers seeking team members often have a laundry list of qualifications they're looking for in a person. In reality, only a handful of those qualifications may be necessary to perform the task. Don't make the mistake of searching for Superman when Clark Kent will do.

Besides having a task breakdown sheet of all the tasks that need to be done by each team member, you need to determine how proficient a team member needs to be and how much experience he or she should have to fill a role. It's very important that you don't sell your needs short, but equally important that you don't mistakenly believe that only an expert will do.

If your business depends on building a Web page that will be easy to navigate and can handle a high volume of e-commerce, then your nineteen-year-old nephew may not be your best choice, no matter how skilled he is. On the other hand, to build a small Web site, you need not hire a team known for designing sites for multinational corporations.

Two common mistakes that subvert effective teams are:

1. **Hiring someone who's underqualified because they are:**
   a. Charging less money for their services
   b. A friend, family member, friend of a family member, or someone else for whom you are doing a favor
   c. Available now, and you need someone right away

2. **Hiring someone who is overqualified because:**
   a. You feel their credentials will impress your stakeholders
   b. You believe that a higher level of expertise is needed when it really isn't

You need to have a fairly good estimate of your actual needs to find the right person. Fill real jobs, not ideal ones.

Assessing talent often relies on an intuitive feeling that the candidate has a keen understanding of what the short-term task and long-term project are all about. Often, a resume or background information will tell you only what the person has done; it won't indicate what else he or she could do using past experience and overall knowledge. Try to get a feel for the quality of someone's work. Just because a person has done a certain job over the past ten years doesn't mean he or she has done it well. Again, some people excel and some people just get by.

Following are ten things to keep in mind when choosing your team members:

1. If your expectations are unrealistic, you will waste a great amount of time seeking the perfect person.
2. If you find someone overqualified, he or she may very likely become bored with the project and lose interest along the way.
3. Individuals with general experience in an area are often more valuable to the team than someone who specializes in only one specific task. Generalists can also provide help in other areas. Naturally, if the task requires a specialist, it's worth your efforts to find one.
4. The hot, trendy, young technological genius fresh out of school may know a lot, but does not always have the actual hands-on experience necessary to do the job in the real world. Don't be sold only on the basis of a graduate degree—experience in the workplace is very valuable.
5. Are team members willing participants or are you hoodwinking them into participating by withholding bonuses or threatening to ground them for a week? Willing team members are more valuable than those who have been coerced, threatened, or cajoled.
6. Someone with a high profile may also have a big ego. You don't need a prima donna on your team.
7. Technical or sales skills are great, but can the person get along with others? You need team members with people skills.
8. Seek out people who have worked on similar projects before, even if it was on a lower level or smaller scale.

9. Think in broad terms. A person might not be good for one task, but might fit another task perfectly.
10. Find people who are trustworthy and loyal, which isn't always easy. You'll find that it's important that people have some sense of dedication to the project. You don't want them running off mid-project and leaving you high and dry. Look for some sense of commitment.

## R-E-S-P-E-C-T

In any project, whether you're working with top-level executives or top-level family members, you need to have respect for your team and you should expect the same in return. If you treat people in a polite, easygoing manner, you will most often get better results than if you are the stern taskmaster. Following are some tips on how to win respect and influence team members:

- **Listen to everyone's ideas.** If someone offers an idea that will work, thank the person and give credit for his or her input. If an idea isn't suitable for the project, explain why it may not work this time, but how it may be worthwhile in the future. Never be demeaning or condescending.
- **Do not embarrass team members.** If you need to discuss a problem or something that was done incorrectly, do it in a private meeting (see Chapter 10). Remember that no one is perfect; mistakes and accidents will happen. Your time is better spent learning from the mistake and correcting what you can than delegating blame.
- **Reward team members for a job well done.** Often just saying the words "good job" is a boost for the team's morale—and it costs you nothing.
- **Treat all team members equally.** Showing favoritism will cause dissention within the group.
- **Lead by example, and treat yourself as you would a team member.** If showing up late for the family patio-planning session warrants an extra chore, give yourself an extra chore.
- **Talk to people, not at them.** This is basic common courtesy and makes people feel like your equals, not your subordinates.

- **Be accessible.** When you are not, have an adequate system for getting all messages. If the kids are working on a family project while you are at the office, let them know how they can reach you, and make sure your secretary, assistant, or answering machine is taking all messages.
- **Return all phone calls and e-mails promptly.** This shows respect for those you're working with.
- **Don't gossip!** It can be tempting to talk about other people, but while gossiping is not appropriate at any level, it is certainly not something that should be done by the project leader.

Mutual respect includes understanding that each team member, including you, the leader, has multiple responsibilities. Each team member needs to remember that there are other aspects of the project, and that you may not be able to respond to each request immediately. Team members also need to understand that there is a priority system and that you may have more pressing issues that need your attention.

## *Where to Find Team Members*

On smaller projects, team members are probably all around you. Friends, family, and neighbors may be available to pack boxes when you move. Club members are usually willing to help plan the year-end holiday party or summer blowout. Your sales staff is ready, somewhat willing, and hopefully able to help you complete your store inventory. And with competent direction, your department is going to help you bring your corporate project to fruition.

You may have to move people in and out of a couple of possible jobs until you find the best fit for their talents. If you have three people who are all good at one task and nobody to fill another, you may have to reevaluate the assignments. Depending on the scope, complexity, or detail of one task, perhaps two people could share one responsibility. When putting together the new company softball team, or the neighborhood little league team, you might have three people who want to play first base and no one who wants to play third. While all of them can handle a groundball or catch a popup without too much trouble, you'll need to determine which, if any, can actually throw the ball accurately. Strong throwing is necessary for a third baseman, so you may need to assess that skill in these three infielders. If none of them can throw accurately, you'll need to find someone else.

Try to determine what other skills a person can handle. Someone with multiple skills may be very valuable to your team. When the pianist took ill and couldn't make it to the cocktail reception one project manager had planned, his backup turned out to be the senior vice president in charge of sales. The project manager had no idea the executive loved to play the piano and was, in fact, more than happy to take over the role. You'll find plenty of surprises in your initial talent pool. Aside from the qualities and attributes you know about, make an effort to ascertain secondary skills so that you have versatile team members. This will come in handy when you suddenly realize that you need more people on one end of the project, or you need to replace another team member.

If you need a specialized resource, such as a consultant or contractor, you'll probably need to look outside of your immediate circle of friends, family, or coworkers. You, and others on the team, may have to bend a little to accommodate a specialist who may be tightly booked, or has a personality that doesn't lend itself to winning friends and influencing people. One organization often referred people to an attorney who specialized in a very specific aspect of law by saying, "You don't need to like him, but he'll do a good job for you."

The team–project manager relationship is a give-and-take situation in which both sides need to treat each other as they would like to be treated. The same holds true for the relationships among team members. A team that respects its members will function much more efficiently.

Be creative—think about how you would either promote yourself or find opportunities to be a team member, and do your searching with that in mind. Potential participants for your project can come from a variety of sources, including the following:

- Other departments in the company, or other groups or committees in an association or club
- Networking or word of mouth (often the best and most widely used source for smaller projects)
- Newspaper, newsletter, or trade journal articles and advertisements
- Personnel agencies

When borrowing people from other committees or departments, or if neighbors help on an otherwise family-based project, keep in mind that these people may have other projects they are working on. Make sure they can afford the time to help you. Despite the best intentions, if he or she is overloaded, the quality of work (and therefore your project) may suffer.

Finding team members through networking is always desirable. You'll avoid advertising and agencies, which will save time and money, and you'll get a recommendation that (hopefully) comes from someone you trust. Sometimes, the best way to find additional team members is to ask those who are already on board. If they've worked on similar projects, they may know of other good resources for your project. Keep in mind, however, that even if another team member recommends someone, you should still check that person's qualifications. Sometimes friends and family members have exaggerated opinions of people they recommend.

Someone you know and trust may be ready and willing to become a member of your project team, but that's no indication of whether he or she is able to do the job. Be fair to yourself (and to others) and get qualified people for the job.

When finding team members through outside sources, such as advertisements or an agency, you may have to pay top dollar. Make sure you know exactly when to run the ad or call the agency, and when you need to have this person start. Don't hire someone at a high rate for two weeks when they only have three solid days of work to do. You don't want to pay people to sit around, especially someone getting high hourly or daily rates.

## Getting It Down on Paper

Not unlike when you post a job in a newspaper or on the Internet, you'll need to provide a job description to team members, particularly for complex tasks. In this case, you'll have to be more specific about the actual tasks and responsibilities of the particular job. It always helps to put it down on paper, whether formally or informally. List what you want the team member to do. The degree of detail will depend on the job and the person expected to perform it, but it's always advantageous to lean toward the side of caution by being more specific. You can always lead in with, "I'm sure you already know most of this, but . . ."

Writing down important details sets clear expectations. On an important or large-scale project, whether it's personal or professional, make sure you have the work agreement in writing. An informal project or a family project can have an informal contract, which simply brings everyone together on the project.

The formality of the agreement should match the significance (not the scope) of the project. A small project (in scope) that may take only a few hours could be critical to your business or your personal investment, and your expectations need to be clearly communicated. The agreement:

- Helps you find the precise abilities you're looking for
- Ensures that you will remember all the tasks to explain to each team member
- Provides stakeholders with a document detailing what is expected of each team member
- Assists in settling disputes about what work did or did not need to be done

Job descriptions may be part of your work breakdown. For example, if the work breakdown requires computer use, you might note that you need someone proficient in a particular program.

There are various ways to structure your list of team members and tasks. Often, it's best to start by listing the tasks, then fill in the team members along with their skills. Keep in mind that as you start working with your team, you may need to reassign tasks and responsibilities, so either use a pencil as you change your records or create new computer files as your plans are modified.

Following is an example of what your list might look like if your project involved developing a Web site for a home-based business:

| TASKS | |
|---|---|
| Applications Development | Phil E.—System integration background |
| Web Architect | Mike J.—Graphic design background |
| Layout and Design | Steven F.—Web design & IT consulting experience |
| Content Editing/Writing | John M.—Journalism experience/Web content |
| Advertising and Sales | Abigail M.—Former advertising account manager |
| Marketing | Lauren H.—Former corporate marketing manager |

After filling in your first list, you might discover that Steven F. has a better technical background and has worked more closely with Web architecture than Mike J., so you might move Steven F. to Web Architect, and Mike J. to Layout and Design.

Before filling in the personnel for the specific tasks, you might fill out a skills chart like the one that follows. In this chart, the candidates are rated by their proficiency in the assigned area based on their backgrounds. Next to each person's name is a number. In some cases, the number is in parentheses, which indicates that the person does not have experience, but has trained in that area by taking classes or a special training program. Sometimes, you'll find someone fresh out of school who has taken top-level courses and displays the necessary knowledge to perform the task. You will have to assess the training program as well as talk to the individual to help determine his or her ability to apply the skills to your project. Often, it will be necessary to check with other people and outside sources to evaluate someone's background and knowledge. You may, for example, look on the Internet to find out whether a degree from the John Doe Computer Design Institute is worthwhile or if it is a fly-by-night operation.

## SKILLS CHART

*The ratings are based on a 1–5 scale, with 5 being excellent and 1 being poor. A dash (—)*
*indicates that the person does not work in that area.*

| Skill | Mark | Karen | Gladys | Fred |
| --- | --- | --- | --- | --- |
| Technical | 5 | — | 2 | — |
| Layout and design | 3 | 3 | — | — |
| Writing | — | 2 | 4 | — |
| Sales | — | — | — | 5 |

What can you tell from this chart? Mark's experience shows that he clearly excels in the technical areas necessary, but Gladys has enough courses or training under her belt to be of some assistance. Karen or Mark could handle layout and design equally well, but since Mark is needed for the technical end (his top strength), Karen will take on the role of layout and site design. She has a good background in the area, but is not an expert. Gladys clearly has the most proficient writing background, but Karen has done some content writing and editing, and can fill in if necessary. Fred is a crackerjack salesperson, but lacks the other qualifications necessary for this particular project.

ESSENTIAL

If you expect to manage future projects that will need team members, put together a skills directory. In a skills directory, you can build a list of potential individuals, cross-referencing names and skills. The directory will be a great resource for you, or for networking purposes.

A skills chart should tell you who does what, how proficient they are at particular tasks, and, in some cases, how much background they have. For example, you might list college or postgraduate degrees next to the names. You can also learn who might be a good candidate for training in a particular area. Consider adding a column for noting what type of supervisory experience someone has in the event that you need to have supervisors.

# Determining Availability

Just because you want someone to work on a project doesn't mean they can do it. You might not be able to get your kids to pitch in on the yard cleanup project when they have final exams. Likewise, your brother-in-law might not be able to help you run the camping trip for your lodge because he's an accountant and it's tax season. In business, people have other work to do and may be part of other projects. While you can't delay your project or work around everyone's schedule, you may need to be somewhat flexible if you want certain individuals involved. You'll need to weigh the level of help a person can provide and determine whether it is in your best interest to try to be accommodating or get someone else whose schedule is not as tight.

## Coordinating Staff

Once you've drawn up your work breakdown structure and listed your personnel on a task breakdown sheet, you'll have an idea of who will be needed at each stage of the project. This may also be flexible. If the flowers for the wedding are ordered a week later than planned, as long as they still arrive on time for the big day, it doesn't matter. On the other hand, if the computer systems are not set up for a week it will throw your entire inventory schedule off. Some things can wait and others cannot. The project comes first, so if you need to replace the person because the task cannot wait, then do so. The more advance planning you can afford yourself, the easier it is to book prospective people onto your project.

## Picking Up the Slack

Keep in mind that there are instances when you, as team leader, will have to assume some of the work yourself. On smaller projects with fewer resources and fewer people involved, this should go without saying, particularly if you are the initiator or major stakeholder. After all, if it is your small business, you need to be in there doing some of the work. On larger projects, you may take on a role in the project, but you may also have a full-time job managing the project. If you have more than one project to manage at a time, you most likely won't have time to roll up your sleeves and get involved. Don't overextend yourself; you still have the job of project manager.

## Ancillary Roles

Besides doing a particular task on a project, you'll need individuals to take on secondary roles, often involving the overall team. For example, someone handling the money at the school bake sale, by watching the flow of traffic, might be able to give you an assessment of how it might flow more smoothly. Perhaps you need a monitor stationed near the checkout area directing traffic. Other people may serve as critics, giving you their opinion of how a project is running and how it might be improved. While doing their own job, people may see or have ideas about other areas that can be improved. Someone writing Web content may be able to assess how the overall layout looks or how easy the site is to navigate, since they are also working on it in a different capacity.

**FACT**

Full-time, professional project managers working on corporate projects have little time to do anything else besides manage a major project. They generally aren't expected to do much beyond that, since project management is their area of expertise.

Besides having their roles in the project, members may have a team role as well. The first baseman of the ball club may also be cocaptain of the team. The same holds true on a project. The person in charge of creating your marketing plan may also be in charge of setting up an after-work get-together to help boost morale. Team jobs may coexist with project jobs. You will have team members critiquing the project, inspecting the work to make sure it meets the high necessary standards, coming up with new ideas, and helping maintain team spirit. Various team members will do the team jobs in addition to their assigned project tasks.

## Who Has the Authority?

Everyone asked Marjorie how many books to order for the school book sale. She gave them the go ahead to order 500. Janet, the head of the PTA and project leader, was a bit taken aback, explaining that the PTA's budget would never afford them more than 250 books. The problem was that everyone involved was under the mistaken assumption that Marjorie had the authority to okay the number of books to be purchased. She didn't.

It is very important that everyone involved in a project understands who has authority to make decisions and who doesn't. It's also important that those with authority document their decisions for discussion and future reference. People who are put in positions of authority need to know how far that authority extends. Being the person in charge of ordering the books does not automatically mean you have the authority to order the computer software as well.

## Set the Parameters

Carefully clarify each person's authority—both for the individual and the group. For example, you may allow your brother to order all the wood for the tool shed you're about to build, but only up to $400. Any spending beyond that, he'll need to discuss with you. If everyone knows who has authority from the start, then people will know whom to turn to when they need something done—they will also know who is making (or approving) decisions that are not within their responsibilities. If everyone knows (or can find out) the parameters, there are fewer opportunities for misinterpreted authority.

Sometimes there are layers of authority. For example, only two people in an association may be authorized to sign checks, the president and the treasurer. However, they may not be the people to authorize the purchase of a new basketball hoop. The sports coordinator may need to give the okay and then talk to the treasurer for funding. Everyone needs to know the chain of command in an organization, group, or company so that they go to the right person to get approval for their needs.

## Delegate Responsibly

As project manager, you need to know when to delegate authority. You delegate authority to relieve yourself of some of the workload and responsibilities. However, you only want to delegate responsibilities and authority to people who won't abuse it, who are responsible and can handle the decision-making process, and who have a clear idea of where the project is going and how to get there.

A checks-and-balances system will often let you know how well people in a position of authority are doing. You might distribute a random, anonymous questionnaire to team members asking them to assess how working with various people has been: good, fair, or poor. If someone in a position of authority is receiving a number of complaints, then you need to address the issues with this person. Likewise, if someone in authority is receiving great praise, you need to compliment him or her. Let the person in any leadership or authority position know that he or she may be monitored. Sales representatives working on phone sales calls often inform you that the conversation may be taped for review purposes. This ensures that even though they have been given a position of authority to make sales, they cannot abuse that position by offering you something beyond that which they are selling, making a subsequent deal, or abusing their position in any other manner.

**ALERT!**

Anyone who is in a position of authority must maintain that authority only for the good of the project and not for personal gain. Potential abuse of authority and power calls for parameters to be put in place for everyone in authority roles. Set up those parameters and let your team know that abuse of power will result in some manner of "big trouble."

Keep in mind that as project leader, although you can delegate authority, you are still responsible for the work getting done and for the people to whom you have given authority. This means you may have to intercede or get involved in some manner to make sure something gets done. While you don't want to embarrass anyone, there may be situations in which you have to overrule someone else's decisions. Explain why, and that it is not personal, but a matter of doing what is best for the project.

## Building Commitment

Getting people to work on a project out of the goodness of their hearts is wonderful in volunteer organizations. The problem that such organizations often run into is that someone doesn't do what she said she would, and because it's a volunteer organization you really have no recourse—you can't fire a volunteer. In such organizations, you need to build a good rapport with other volunteers and provide extra pats on the back and praise for a job well done. After all, appreciation is a form of reward.

To ensure that those around you will participate in a personal, family, or neighborhood project, you may need to trade favors or remind people of what's in it for them. In business, participants can move up the ladder, receive raises, or other such perks. Team members have a much better attitude if they know what they can gain, rather than working not to get fired. Sales projects, such as those in the Boy Scouts, Girl Scouts, or schools, have rewards for those who have sold the most boxes of cookies or rolls of wrapping paper. Similarly, a shining star on a project team may be selected for a vacated management position. Let team members know that their work can be rewarded.

**FACT**

If you put someone in charge of a particular aspect of a project, no matter how big or small, that person is responsible to you. Likewise, you are responsible to whoever put you in charge of the project. Because you are in charge, you cannot blame your team members for things that go wrong. The sponsor is depending on you to complete the job, which includes being responsible for your team.

Once someone has agreed to work on a project, they have a moral, ethical, or contractual obligation. This is not to say that a crisis may not interfere with their ability to complete their job; you need to afford a level of understanding.

## Finding the Right Mix

Putting together a project team is like putting together a complicated recipe: You often have to try a few variations before it tastes right. At every level, as project manager, you will need to ensure that you have both skilled individuals and the right blend of personalities. Mixing and matching both skills and personalities takes time and patience. You'll be rewriting or deleting and adding to your plan many times. It's a good idea to run your selections by others who know the individuals you are selecting. Others can tell you which team combinations are like oil and water.

When you sit down with all of the project's key players individually, you may not get an accurate assessment of how well they will interact in a team environment. It's easy for someone to tell you he or she is a team player, but you won't find out for sure until the project gets under way. No ballplayer is going to say, "I hog the ball every opportunity I can," although that may turn out to be the case. In the sample team, Fred may not be the ultimate team player, but if his role is more independent on a daily basis, it may not matter. Also, he's the only crackerjack salesperson you've got, so everyone may have to deal with a little more attitude when he's in the office. While you hope everyone is gracious, people who are harder to replace are sometimes aware of that and can be more demanding. If you don't have other, more suitable, resources, accommodate difficult personalities, unless they threaten to bring down the whole project. (There is more on dealing with difficult personalities in Chapter 18.)

Learn which members of your team need to be praised often, who can work contentedly on their own, who needs handholding, and who will be a constant challenge. Keep these assessments to yourself—they should not be shared with other members of the team.

Finding the right mix is also made more complicated by the constraints of a budget. You may have to accept someone who is not as talented in one position because you are forced to pay top dollar for someone else. Be careful not to spend too much money paying people who are less vital to the project. Often, it's best to work your way down, starting with the most significant positions first, but be careful—you might spend two weeks looking for a technical manager and lose other great potential team members because they took on other jobs rather than waiting for you.

Keep in mind while selecting a team that more team members mean a wider variety of personalities. As project leader, you will need to look for the strengths and weaknesses from a personality standpoint. Someone may be a marvelously talented designer, but is quite shy and says very little at the meetings. You may have to gently draw this person into the group dynamic. A salesman might be very outspoken at the meetings and intimidate or even turn off other team members with his or her approach. You'll have to try to channel this individual's enthusiasm into his or her work and limit their participation at the meetings.

Take a look at the following skill/personality assessment matrix. In the same way you build a team with complementary technical skills, you should build a team that will complement each other interactively.

| SKILLS / PERSONALITY ASSESSMENT MATRIX | |
|---|---|
| **Skills** | **Personality** |
| 5  Expert | 5  Gets along well with almost everyone |
| 4  High | 4  Strong in a positive sense |
| 3  Average | 3  Average, generally agreeable, perhaps mild mannered |
| 2  Below average | 2  Strong in a negative sense (grating or condescending) |
| 1  Poor | 1  Difficult to get along with |

A 5/5 in the two categories might seem perfect, but be realistic. Not only is that combination unlikely, keep in mind that there can be too much of a good thing. You'll have many 3/4 or 3/3s on your roster as well. A solid cross section is fine, as long as you have a blend of thinkers, talkers, listeners, and doers.

And what about the extremes? Poor skills but great personality (1/5) is not desirable unless you need someone to boost morale or bring in new recruits. Some organizations (usually not in business) have a key role for someone who does basically nothing, but gets along well with everyone and puts a smile on people's faces. In reality, then, he or she is actually doing something—although it may not be a defined task—by helping to keep team enthusiasm and motivation up. The other side of the coin is the

5/1, an expert whom you cannot replace even though his conduct is not always beneficial to the team.

Following is a summary of the process by which the project team comes together:

1. Define the goals of the project clearly.
2. Divide the project into tasks that need to be done.
3. Define what roles need to be filled to complete each task.
4. Define the attributes the person filling each role needs to bring with him. List the attributes that would make up the ideal candidate, then be realistic.
5. Determine who, if anyone, from the process-initiating team will move onto the team that does the actual work.
6. Make sure all key stakeholders are kept abreast of the team-building process, unless otherwise directed.
7. Scout for team members. Make a list of possibilities. Look both inside and outside the group, office, family, or immediate circle.
8. Set up team rules, regulations, and parameters to which the team will adhere.
9. Review the qualifications of all potential team members.
10. Review the availability of all team members.
11. Discuss compensation and additional resources needed for team members.
12. Review your decisions with anyone who is involved in the decision-making process.
13. Meet team members individually to discuss what is expected of them and when.
14. Select team members and fill in your work breakdown chart.
15. Determine who will have authority.
16. Meet with team members together. Establish team rapport and build team spirit.

This is just the beginning!

## CHAPTER 10

# Effective Project Leadership

To be effective as a leader means communicating what it is you want, need, and expect people to do in such a manner that they respectfully do the tasks or activities involved. Leading people can mean directing them to perform specific new activities or tasks they've done before. Whatever the case, an effective leader makes people feel good about themselves and in the work they do. Effective leadership also combines technical or subject knowledge with listening and people skills, and takes some time to master. Organized, qualified, and successful managers will always do well.

## Team Huddle

Okay, the team is ready to take the field. Do you have any final words? Knute Rockne became legendary for his pep talks before sending his team onto the football field. As project manager, you will need to provide more than pep talks; you'll need to fuel the fire behind the team and then manage the team throughout the ensuing project. This will mean constantly monitoring and keeping track of what everyone is doing without micromanaging. It will mean sticking to a schedule that may need to be altered as you go. It will mean taking time out from your original plans for conflict resolution.

You may find yourself immersed up to your eyeballs in a project, or you may simply manage to squeeze it into your schedule without much difficulty. It all depends on the scope of the project, the team you are working with, and your level of expertise.

Your first responsibilities as project leader are to do as follows:

1. Introduce the project team to one another, or if they are meeting via videoconference or conference call, let others know who is on board.
2. Make sure everyone understands the goals and objectives of the project.
3. Make sure everyone is clear about his or her tasks and responsibilities to the overall project.
4. Establish clear lines of communication.
5. Set basic ground rules.
6. Establish and explain your method of tracking the project, such as status reports and meetings to discuss your progress.

## What Kind of Leader Are You?

"Uh-oh, here he comes . . . let's go!" If this is the response you overhear from team members when you approach, there's something wrong with your leadership style. While you don't need to be everyone's pal, you do want the team to feel comfortable around you and seek you out with problems or questions. If you are a leader who is also part of the team, you need to have a sense of camaraderie. If you are busy managing the team and they are doing the actual hands-on work, let them know that you are counting on them and have confidence and faith that they can do the job. Refer to it as "our project," not "my project."

To determine what kind of leader you are, consider which of the following leadership styles best describes you:

- Are you a taskmaster? Are you focused solely on production?
- Are you a people person? Do you focus on communication between team members and take a consensus to get decisions made?
- Are you Pavlovian? Do you believe in behavior modification? If they do the work, will they be rewarded as they go?
- Are you a micromanager? Do you look over everyone's shoulder?
- Are you missing in action? Do you start and end the project, but basically disappear for the duration of the process?

Most likely, you will combine aspects of the first three leadership styles on the list, while trying not to fall into the last two categories. Managing tasks, working well with people, and providing rewards for a job well done are all part of being a good leader. The project and the circumstances surrounding it, however, will dictate your primary style. Don't be surprised if you need to use a little of each approach for different situations. Often, project managers, while focusing on the task in hand, will have to deal with difficult personalities and even stroke some egos to encourage particular individuals.

**FACT**

To be both a manager and a leader, you need to combine the skills of planning, implementing a schedule, and monitoring progress along with effectively delegating, communicating, and listening to other people. Just as being knowledgeable does not make someone a good teacher, management skills and MBA credits don't automatically make you a good leader.

Be flexible enough to switch gears when necessary. Let the nature of the project, the scope, the time frame, the progress of the project, and the people determine which style of leadership you'll use on which day.

Consider the following scenarios. Each situation requires the project leader to tap into different styles in order to keep the project focused and moving forward. While all leaders will have a preferred style (one that seems most natural to them), the best leaders are able to adapt and use each style when necessary.

- **A crisis arises**—things are blown way off course! Take control, make unilateral decisions, and get the ship back on course; be task oriented.
- **Morale is declining**—the campers are not happy! Use your people skills, get everyone involved, take a consensus before making a move, ask for people's opinions, and make nice until the team is happy again.
- **Many questions are left unanswered**—the team just doesn't know what to do next! If the problems are in the system or revolve around aspects of the project itself, then you may need to take a more analytical approach and hunt and gather information and materials. Have your team work together to seek and find what needs to be learned. Turn all attention inward, and get the structure of the project back on track, then return to project business as usual.

## *The Importance of Consistency*

A good leader is consistent. From child rearing to dealing with a group of consultants, it's important that you be consistent. If you want something done a certain way on Monday, you want it done the same way on Tuesday, unless new technology or some unexpected events dictate otherwise. The manager who constantly changes how things are done confuses team members.

Likewise, the manager who favors one team member over others causes dissention in the ranks. The way in which you conduct yourself, your decision making, and your level of respect for your team should remain consistent. This way, people come to know what to expect of you and what you expect of them. A Jekyll and Hyde personality can hurt team morale if they don't know who they'll find sitting in your chair when you swivel around to talk with them.

Consistency does not mean inflexibility, however. Changing your style of leadership to fit a particular situation is part of the project management process. If you are used to making unilateral decisions but this aspect of the project requires a consensus, then you will have to change your approach. The same is true for becoming more task oriented when necessary. Consistency means reacting in the same manner each time a situation arises. For example, every time the project is close to falling behind, you will switch to a more task-oriented approach. You will still remain the lovable leader, but you'll have to be more focused on everyone just buckling down and focusing on their work.

Parents may reprimand their children one minute and hug them the next, but they still consistently love them. You will consistently be there for your team, whether you have to get tough with them or have the time to talk casually and be a people person.

## First-Rate Teams

Some people manage projects and some project managers manage people. The work needs to be done, but unless your project is comprised completely of automated technology or robots, you will have to deal effectively with people. The modern employee is empowered. He or she is no longer subservient or unaware of his or her rights. But it goes beyond empowerment. The workplace is full of knowledgeable individuals who are well versed in their fields and in the companies that employ them.

Outside of the workplace, you can find people who excel in any one of numerous areas. From party planners to highly skilled contractors, there are top people available to meet any project need. And, when there are not, the training materials available on the Internet, in adult learning environments, and in books will make team members experts by the time a project is completed.

Besides knowledge, you need to lead by example, which means displaying confidence. The team will follow your lead. If you are tense about getting the project finished and complain about the project, your team will pick up on your uneasiness and uncertainty, and morale will be affected. If you have serious doubts about a project, your team will also have doubts. If you exude confidence, they too will exude confidence. You shouldn't tell them everything is going well when it's not. However, it does not help to worry team members with situations that are out of their control. If other means are necessary to solve problems in one area of the project, then you will address that specific area with those involved, not have everyone needlessly concerned.

**ALERT!**

As the leader, you need to stay on top of the project. You should know the project inside and out—after all, you don't want your educated team members showing you up. This isn't to say you must have the skills to handle every task, just that the big picture is very clear in your mind.

Your demeanor throughout the project is very important. You cannot wear your problems on your sleeve. Keep outside issues and project issues in their perspective places. For example, when a project meeting is called, it is to talk about the status of the project, not to whine because you weren't made VP of sales.

Following are ten tips, besides having a confident attitude, for becoming a successful project manager:

1. Listen when others talk
2. Do your homework and be well versed on the project
3. Manage people, not just projects
4. Be ready to manage in various situations (be flexible)
5. Delegate work to others
6. Give people latitude to do their work (don't micromanage)
7. Get the opinions of others
8. Monitor work closely (take good notes)
9. Keep all stakeholders apprised of your progress
10. Know when you need to ask for help—don't try to be a know-it-all

# Senior Management Reporting

A key aspect of effective project leadership is how you choose to communicate with senior management. As Rob Thomsett, author of *Radical Project Management* states, "Projects fail because of context, not content." Therefore, it is how you are reporting the progress of the project to your senior managers that can make or break a project. Consider this: Your project is behind schedule and over budget.

This is a common occurrence throughout projects. However, it is how you deal with this common occurrence that will determine how your project is perceived. Are you going to do what most project managers do and pray that it will get better? Most people are so afraid of the repercussions of the situation that they will actually ignore it and hope that it will get better on its own.

**FACT**

Any project has both internal and external concerns. The external concerns may include how the project is shaping up and whether there are problems relating to the project's place in the real world. Internal problems can be late status reports or incompatible software. Often, the internal problems will affect the external results.

This issue tends to go hand in hand with project management maturity. Most young or new project managers do wish that some miracle will occur and bring the project back in line. This leads to misinformation, and most of the time, an even larger disaster. Truth be told, the sooner that you reveal the situation, the better it will be in the long run. Many experienced project managers understand this. Often, a requirement can be removed, extra staff added, or any combination of things to bring a project back on track. The difference between a new and experienced project manager is that the experienced ones get their sponsors and/or senior management involved as soon as possible.

It takes a tremendous amount of leadership to reveal that things are not going as planned, but this goes beyond you as the project manager. Do you think your team wants to work this hard only to be considered a project failure? Absolutely not! Be in tune with your team, continue to present solutions instead of issues, and keep senior management informed. These are all signs of good project leadership, and will ensure that you are managing the context properly so that the delivered content is a success.

**CHAPTER 11**

# Creating the Schedule

Whether you call it a roadmap, outline, or blueprint, you'll need a plan of action to get your project from the drawing board to completion. Your schedule is critical for the success of the project. Most often, on medium to larger projects, you will have a combination of graphs, charts, and diagrams laying out the tasks to be performed and their time frames. You will want to be able to view tasks relative to each other, to the allotted project time, and to the budget. Maintain graphs and charts to measure progress, and as tools to report back to your team and other stakeholders.

## In the Beginning

The schedule should provide a variety of ways of measuring success as you monitor your project. You will start off with your baseline, which will be your initial project schedule for a specific time. This baseline schedule remains fixed and is used for comparison against your current project schedule. Baseline dates are, therefore, the initial dates for starting and finishing a task. These will be used with your current schedule for comparison purposes to see if tasks are being performed on schedule. This can also be used to calculate where your project costs are in conjunction with the budget.

As you plan your schedule, there will be several key dates, including your project start date, the start dates of individual tasks, and the completion dates of the tasks and the project. You will see as you build your schedule that there will be some variance regarding when you can start and finish specific activities. You will have designated start and finish dates as well as earliest feasible start dates, which mark the earliest date on which the activity could be scheduled to start based on the scheduled dates of all its predecessors (other activities that need be completed first). This date is also calculated by resource scheduling, meaning that the date cannot be set if resources have not been purchased or set up for this activity. You'll also find an earliest finish date lurking on the other end of the activity. This date is based on the calculated start date.

## The Network Diagram

A network diagram is essentially a flow chart that includes all of the project elements and how they relate to one another. It is widely used because it is easy to read and not only depicts the sequence of activities in the project, but also shows parallel activities and the links between each activity. Network logic is the collection of activity dependencies that make up a network diagram for a particular project. In other words, certain tasks are dependent on one another to complete the project. This creates a logical stream of events that will lead to completion of the project.

You'll need to analyze, organize, and put into sequence the activities that need to be completed. You'll also need to carefully determine how long it should take to complete each task and in what order they will be performed. Setting up dependencies, or tasks that depend on the previous one being performed, will be vital to a smooth-flowing schedule. Setting deliverable dates—when tasks need to be completed or products delivered—will also be part of the equation.

## Lining Up the Pieces

Even when doing a smaller personal project, it's important to have a schedule. You may be able to get by with a to-do list when planning a vacation or a party, but there is still a need to organize and prioritize. For example, you can't plan a trip to France without a passport for each family member. Because of the length of time it takes to receive a passport, this will need to be a high-priority item, scheduled early on in the sequence of events leading up to your trip. No matter what the project, the sequence of events is significant to completing the project.

**FACT**

A good project manager wears many hats. Identifying stakeholders and defining their roles, clarifying project objectives and goals, doing plenty of research, assessing skills, putting the team together, promoting effective communication between team members (and everyone else), monitoring the project, and about ninety-nine other tasks fall under your jurisdiction.

Determining dual tasks is also important. If a project has fifty tasks that would each take a week to complete, your initial estimate might be that the project would take one year to complete. However, if five tasks could be completed simultaneously every week, you'd have the project finished in ten weeks. Therefore, you need to carefully determine which tasks can be done simultaneously.

Refer to this diagram as you read through the chapter. As a visual and organizational aid, the diagram will help you plan and track dependencies and concurrent tasks.

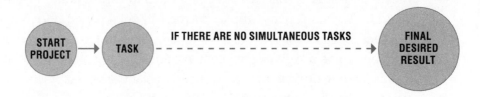

### The network diagram lets you do the following:
- Define the project's path
- Determine the sequence of tasks to be completed
- Look at the relationship between activities
- Determine the dependencies
- Set up simultaneous tasks
- Monitor your project by establishing benchmarks, milestones, or deliverables—these are markers to determine whether your project is on, ahead of, or behind schedule
- Make adjustments as tasks are completed
- Take a broad look at the project path and clearly see the relationships and dependencies between tasks

There are complicated network diagrams and simple ones that you can figure out at a glance. The ease with which you can follow the network diagram depends on how complex the project is and how well you have defined everything that appears on it. You can use one color to indicate the tasks that can be completed simultaneously and another color to highlight tasks that are dependencies, or dependent on the completion of a prior task.

Your network diagram will have a critical path, which is the route from start to end that must be completed to finish the project. This is the spine, or what drives the network diagram. The activities that need to be completed along the critical path and all other paths (which ultimately connect to the critical path) are typically connected with lines and arrows. Then you will label the activity. As activities are completed, you should clearly mark them completed or highlight them in another color or manner. Each activity should include the number of days it will take to complete the task.

**FACT**

Elapsed time or duration is how much real time is needed to complete an activity. A consultant may estimate he'll need twelve hours to do a task, but he probably won't work twelve hours straight. If he works four hours a day for three days, the duration or elapsed time is three days, so you'll need to factor three days into your schedule for the task to be completed.

The benefits of the network diagram are that you can see not only the tasks that need to be done, but how long they should take to complete and where they are in relationship to one another. Each task is defined in a box, and the boxes are laid out horizontally to show the sequence of tasks. Two rows (or more) of parallel boxes indicate that these tasks are taking place simultaneously.

A good network diagram, like a treatment for a screenplay, blueprints for an engineer, or a game plan for a football team, includes all the details that need to be taking place. This allows you to get a good estimate of how long the activities should take and helps you monitor the flow of the project on a task-by-task basis. You can easily see where you might have to add more time or manpower, or where the flow of activity in one area is ahead of another. When putting together a museum guidebook, you might have writers creating copy while photographers are taking photos. You'll be able to see that the photographers have completed taking the pictures, while the writers have not yet completed their first drafts. Therefore, you may need to call in another writer.

## Building Your Network Diagram

No matter what the scope of the project is, unless it's a one- or two-person operation with few individual tasks involved, it's helpful to have something on paper. Build yourself a little network diagram and use it as your guide. If nothing else, it will give you a sense of accomplishment as you color in each task en route to your conclusion. Anyone who has ever tried a serious diet (one approved by a doctor and not a fad diet) knows the benefit of celebrating milestones along the way to achieving their project goal. If your goal is losing twenty pounds in a month, then every five pounds lost may serve as a milestone along the way.

**FACT**

The network diagram doesn't place tasks in order of what is more important or more costly to complete. Sometimes the most important task (which might be judged by difficulty to accomplish, significance to other tasks being completed, or simply by time or cost) comes at the beginning of the project and everything else is the icing on the cake. In other projects, all the preliminaries, such as planning the wedding, lead to the main event.

While a diet is a uniquely individual project, you can set it up for yourself horizontally on a network diagram just as you would for any business, community, or home-based project. To set up the diagram, you take the list of all the tasks involved and see which ones must be accomplished before moving on to other tasks and which ones can be done independently of each other. A museum guidebook, however, is more team oriented, and its diagram would first include the tasks that the writers needed to do along with the tasks the photographers needed to do, plus perhaps a third column of tasks ad sales representatives needed to do. At first, the ad sales reps are dependent on some initial copy and graphics being completed so they have something to show sponsors. Then all three—the writers, photographers, and sales staff—can work simultaneously until the material needs to come together and be presented to the printer. Along the way, you might want to select specific milestones, such as an outline from the writers, a list of photos from the photographers, or a list of local retailers to contact for advertisements.

**QUESTION?**

**What is a milestone?**
A milestone in a network diagram is a box that defines a task or series of tasks that have been completed. These are checkpoints that you can look at to see whether you are or aren't on schedule. Milestones may, and often do, include deliverables.

If you're working on paper, use a pencil and eraser. Be prepared to rewrite your diagram a few times until you've included everything in sequential order with milestones and all. Look at the sample network diagram to guide you. On a computer program, you'll be entering and reentering your information a lot.

## Reviewing Your Network Diagram

Once you've completed your network diagram, review it carefully before hanging it on the wall like a Picasso (believe me, when you're done, it will feel like you've created a masterpiece). Check to make sure all the activities on your detailed task list are included and be sure the sequence makes sense. Remember, you can't edit the museum-guide copy if you haven't written it yet. If several tasks taking place simultaneously need to be finished before a next step can be started, make sure all arrows from the first tasks lead to the second. In other words, the tasks of writing, photography, and ad sales all have to be completed before the box that says "take to the printer," so all of these activities lead to the same final box.

It's really pretty simple once you start putting it on paper. In fact, why not fill in a blank network diagram with a task you'd like to accomplish? First, however, you need to make a simple work breakdown sheet for yourself on a piece of paper listing the tasks needed to complete your project. Then, start filling in the network diagram. Feel free to add more boxes if necessary, and don't forget to pencil in your milestones in some of the boxes. (Remember, milestones are simply signposts that let you mark your progress.)

## Verify Your Estimates

In most cases, unless you are very familiar with the task at hand, you should check with whoever is going to do the work to find out how long it will take them to complete it. If the time frame sounds unreasonable, research how long it takes someone else to do the same task. For example, if a printer says he can have the job in five weeks but you feel, based on your experience, that it should not take that long, check with a couple of other printers to determine their turnaround time. If two other places can have it done in three weeks, clarify why your printer cannot do it in that same time period. Often, team members or outside vendors like to pad their own schedule in case they have to push the work back a few hours or a few days. This is fine if you have some flexibility in your schedule. However, that isn't always the case, especially in business.

Once you've set up the time frames in your network diagrams, go back and reconfirm that they are okay. Suppose you accepted the printer's estimate that he could do the job in four weeks because you like his work and have that much time available in the schedule. You still need to confirm that he indeed understands that you have it on your schedule to be completed in four weeks, and have that due date clear on both of your calendars.

### Estimating the Unknown

Many times, you will be asked to estimate a task and will have no idea of what it will take. In this case, follow these steps:

- Break down the task into individual steps
- Come up with Best Case, Most Likely, and Worst Case time estimates for each step
- Add up each column and apply the following formula:
  *1 Best Case + 4 × Most Likely + 1 Worst Case) / 6*

The formula (BC + 4×ML + WC) / 6 is called a PERT formula (Program Evaluation and Review Technique). This formula was started in the engineering world and has been widely applied to project management to estimate the unknown. There are many more formulas within PERT, but most project managers stop here. Even with this formula it is difficult to get the right answer, but it has helped many a project manager create a better estimate when the work effort is truly unknown.

## Absolute Completion Date

When you tell your children you want their homework done by six o'clock, knowing you really want them finished by seven, you're setting one time for their benefit and a second one for yours. Likewise, you know the last possible date something can be completed on the project, but that is not the date you put down on the network diagram or tell the person doing the task. If you're printing a special end-of-year holiday brochure to come out in November, you may tell your copywriter that you need all copy in by September 15th, knowing that it won't be sent to the printer until September 30th.

**ALERT!**

Make sure team members know when their work needs to be completed. This is especially important when the start of one task depends on the completion of another.

You should have a completion date for each task and an absolute drop-dead completion date, which is when the work absolutely, positively must be finished. Promote your deadlines and keep your absolute deadline in a separate place. Just as budgets get padded, so do schedules. Often the manager or boss who must have it tomorrow really doesn't need it until the day after—she's just not providing you with that information. By determining the latest a task or activity can be completed without interfering with the overall project, you have some room to maneuver when you need to make adjustments to the schedule.

The same holds true for a start date. What is the date you plan to start an activity? If there are delays, what is the absolute latest date you could start the activity and still get it completed in time to keep the project running on schedule? You may have to look at other tasks to determine this because other tasks may be dependent on this work getting started and completed at a certain time.

If you're not sure how long something should take to accomplish, get the best and worst time frames and use the average number plus 10 percent. If, for example, one source indicates that you can get all the necessary supplies to Boston in seven hours, but another source says that with heavy traffic it has taken as long as nine hours, you might take the average of the time estimates and come up with eight hours. Add 10 percent to play it safe and you have 8.8 hours, which rounds off to nine hours for your time estimate.

## Cut Yourself Some Slack

Slack, or float time, is essentially the extra time between how long you've allotted for the task and how long it will take to complete it. If you've allotted ten days for a task but you actually need only six days, you'll have four days of slack or float time, which you can use to your advantage.

While you want to have some time to play with, if your project is running late, you can use the slack in the schedule to pick up the pace of your project. You may find places where you can double up your resources. For example, if you can't start rehearsals of the community production of *Death of a Salesman* until Friday when the rehearsal space opens, you might have some of your cast double up on other activities, such as putting together the program, selling tickets, or building the set.

Don't use precious slack time for a round of golf early on in the project—it will come back to bite you. Perhaps, if you're six days ahead of schedule in the final week of the project, you can hit the links. Even then, it's a risk!

Unfortunately, slack time is often used to solve problems, resolve conflicts, and make changes brought about by external factors. From cleaning up the mess in your new office to spending a day calming two feuding relatives who can't plan a wedding together, you'll find your slack time disappearing quickly.

# Various Projects, Various Methods

The network diagram is in vogue in the business world. Other popular tools are the Performance Evaluation and Review Technique (PERT) and the Critical Path Method (CPM), both of which are more technical in nature, but are basically used for the same purpose: to schedule, chart, and monitor a project. The PERT method uses differing degrees of likelihood, while CPM includes activities and circles for milestones. You'll find other tools, too, but many are more complicated than necessary for the vast majority of simple and smaller projects.

No matter what method you use, you need a way to follow the progress of your project.

- Have each task clearly displayed.
- Be able to see multiple parallel tasks and see their relationship to one another.
- Have a clear understanding of the order of the tasks.
- Know when you've reached key goals (milestones, signposts) along the way.

If your method gives you a clear overview of the project and all the various components within it, then whatever you're doing is just fine.

# The Famous Gantt Chart

The Gantt chart is a well-known standard in program management that dates back to 1917, when Henry Gantt, a pioneer in the field of scientific management, invented it. The chart plots a number of tasks across a horizontal time scale. It is easy to understand and allows team members to maintain the status of their tasks against planned progress. In its most basic usage, the Gantt chart puts tasks on a series of horizontal timelines. The timeline can measure the progress in hours for a short-term project, months for a long-term project, or weeks, as shown in the example on page 120.

| PROJECT: PRODUCING NEW SALES BROCHURE | | | | | | | | | | | |
|---|---|---|---|---|---|---|---|---|---|---|---|
| | | | | | Number Of Weeks | | | | | | |
| **Task** | 1 | 2 | 3 | 4 | 5 | 6 | 7 | 8 | 9 | 10 | 11 |
| Gathering resources (team, materials, etc.) | ▓ | ▓ | | | | | | | | | |
| Sales research | | ▓ | ▓ | ▓ | ▓ | ▓ | ▓ | ▓ | | | |
| Writing | | | ▓ | ▓ | ▓ | ▓ | ▓ | | | | |
| Graphics | | | ▓ | ▓ | ▓ | ▓ | ▓ | | | | |
| Editing | | | | | | ▓ | ▓ | ▓ | | | |
| Printing/Production | | | | | | | | | ▓ | ▓ | ▓ |

The Gantt chart shows timelines for each task and the overlap between tasks. You can clearly get an idea of what tasks are being performed in any given week. You can also use the chart to gauge where you are. For example, if, in week eight, graphics are not complete, then you are behind schedule. Gantt Charts are easy to read at a glance, particularly if you use different colors for each task. You can show progress on the Gantt chart by using light colors or no colors on the initial timelines for each task, and then coloring in the boxes as the work gets done.

What the Gantt chart doesn't tell you, is who is performing each task or if tasks depend on one another. For this information, you will need a task member schedule or task list. Therefore, while the Gantt Chart is very helpful in terms of a timeline, you'll need to use it in conjunction with other scheduling tools.

## *Task Schedule or Matrix*

You will need to refer to your skills chart (discussed in Chapter 9), in which you will see the various skills of each team member, to establish a schedule for your personnel or team members. This task schedule, also known as a resource assignment matrix, will indicate who should be doing what and where they should be in the process. When setting up this matrix, defining the relationship between individuals is as important as the relationship of individuals to their tasks.

Review the task matrix with team members to make sure they know when they are expected to do their assigned tasks. Make sure everyone is available during the times they are needed. If there are limits to their availability (part-time employees, your children helping you after school, volunteers giving their time one day a week), make sure you schedule accordingly. Obviously, a task that takes six hours a day cannot be performed efficiently by one person who is only available for three hours a day. However, if you've budgeted for six hours daily on that task and it needs to be done in $x$ amount of time, you can solve the problem easily by hiring two people to do the task.

Do you have a communications plan? If you don't, you should. The plan indicates how you will communicate important information to your team and others, including milestones, changes in the plan, and the overall progress of the project.

In business, community, and other projects, you will run up against team members' vacation schedules. Make sure you ask before the project if anyone will be away during any part of the project. Schedule their task(s) accordingly. If they need be around for the entire project, then they either have to reschedule their vacation or you need to find someone else as either a replacement or a fill-in while they are away. It's often difficult to fill in for a short time when someone is away from a project. It's best to have someone available for the duration. Remember, the project comes first.

One word of caution: It's tough enough managing a project; the last thing you need to do is create a task list or a schedule that is so complex it will occupy your day just checking off what is being done. If you're spending all of your time walking around checking off a lengthy list of tasks, you'll have no time to look at the overall progress being made on the project or address problems or conflicts that arise. Don't overload yourself with data-entry duties.

## *Anticipating Pitfalls*

It's important to try to anticipate any potential pitfalls that could ultimately spell disaster for the project. There will certainly be surprising, unforeseen developments along the way, which you will try to deal with accordingly. After all, you do need to expect the unexpected. But there are ways to reduce the probability of problems that might occur.

Look at factors surrounding your project that could directly or indirectly impact your goal. Is there an upcoming labor strike? A change in leadership (in your company or in one that you do business with)? A change in politics? New zoning laws? Policy changes? Is the economy heading into a recession, thus affecting your sponsor's ability to adequately bankroll the project? Is there a for-sale sign on the catering hall you just booked for your manager's retirement party?

Contingency planning needs to be part of your overall initial planning stage. Such backup plans also need to be mentioned at meetings so that other team members can suggest alternatives should problems arise. The more people you have thinking of alternative plans, the more likely you'll be prepared to handle problems and avert potentially disastrous situations. While you do not want to take time away from the project, you do need to have some backup plans in place from the start of the project. For example, if a shipment is going to be delayed, are you ready with the FedEx number handy? You may have to pay more, but your project may benefit by staying on schedule.

Not only do you need to have contingency plans ready in the back of your mind and in the minds of your team members, you need to know how (and when) to switch to plan B if necessary. For example, at what point does the outdoor wedding become an indoor wedding because of the weather? When it looks like rain, when it starts to rain, or does it depend on the forecast? You also need to know who will make the changes and move the seating indoors. Who will tell the guests? Planning contingency tasks is as important as planning the project.

Sometimes projects grow. For example, the ninety-person wedding now has 110 attendees. It's not important how it happened, it's just important that the project scope changed. Can you adjust? Likewise, your promotional video, which was going to twenty-seven offices across the country, is now being slated to appear in Japan as well. Subtitles! Who will translate? Who will add these subtitles?

**ALERT!**

If you have project files in your computer, always back them up regularly on floppy disks. It's a good idea to make hard copies, too. A project can be lost or set back several days or even months because a power failure or computer crash erases the work.

Naturally, you can't anticipate what new developments will arise, but you can have some basic plans in place. Be resourceful when projects change or grow. There's more on planning in Chapter 5.

## And the Calendar Says . . .

If you're not quite ready for elaborate charts and diagrams, you might opt for scheduling a project on a simple calendar. Using a different color for each task or assigning a color for each of the three or four people on the project, you can make up an easy-to-follow schedule such as the one that follows. You might also use initials for team members.

| JUNE | | | | | | | |
|---|---|---|---|---|---|---|---|
| **TEAM MEMBER** | **SU** 4 | **MO** 5 | **TU** 6 | **WE** 7 | **TH** 8 | **FR** 9 | **SA** 10 |
| AJ | | TASK A | | | TASK B | | |
| DJ | | TASK A | | | | TASK B | |
| ST | | TASK A | | | | | |

In this example, each "Task A" is a different activity for the project. "Task B," however, might be the same color, indicating that AJ and DJ worked on the same task at the end of the week. Task B was only one day of work for DJ, but AJ had enough to complete to take her into Friday.

A calendar can be posted in a central location so everyone can check their status and note how many days are remaining in the project. We've all seen children (and adults for that matter) mark off a calendar with how many days are left until vacation. In this case, you're marking off how many days until the project is complete. Just make sure each day's task is complete before you mark it finished.

Add milestones to your calendar or create a milestone schedule. You can highlight important events by circling the date on the calendar or pasting a gold star next to key tasks that you have completed. These will indicate that you have reached an important point or a milestone en route to completing your project.

In some cases, you might not list tasks on a daily basis, particularly if they are repetitive by nature. You can simply include the milestones that need to be reached on certain days. For example, someone might be painting six similarly sized offices over the course of two consecutive weeks. You can make a line for a continuing task as in the previous example, rather than writing "paint office" in each box. At the end of the first Friday, you might mark down "Finish painting three offices" as a milestone or marker.

A milestone version of a more detailed schedule can give stakeholders who are not actively involved with the project on a daily basis, or the sponsors, an idea of when key goals within the project have been reached. For example, the backer of the film will know when shooting wrapped and the postproduction phase begins.

## CHAPTER 12

# The All-Important Budget

Money. It may be the root of all evil, but it's also the backbone of nearly all projects. In an ideal world, you'd start a project with a series of blank checks, and whatever you spent would be just fine. But unless you've got a billionaire funding your project, you've got to keep tabs on where your project is in relation to your budget at all times. The majority of projects begin on a tight budget, yet your soda pop allowance will often have to accommodate some- one's champagne tastes. You might be able to handle that if you keep one eye on the budget throughout your project.

# *Ready, Set, Budget*

In many corporate projects, you are told what your budget will be without participating in the process. However, when starting a personal project or a project in your own business, you have to put together your own budget. You can use software and other technology as a guide, but you'll still be responsible for the actual money behind the numbers. It will still be your call as to exactly how much you can set aside for this project.

Budget building requires certain skills, including being very well organized and meticulous in your planning. Putting together a budget for a month-long family trip to Aruba or a budget for building a new warehouse for your business means breaking down the project into each component and determining the cost. It is a demanding process in which you need to visualize the way each task is to be completed. If, for example, your project is to plan a fiftieth anniversary party for your aunt and uncle, you'll need to start out at the beginning and think your way through all the details. Ask yourself questions as you proceed:

- How many people will attend?
- How much will you spend on invitations and postage?
- How much will the facility cost?
- Is catering included? If not, how much more will it cost?
- How much will decorations cost?
- How much will you need to spend on entertainment?
- Will you need to pay hotel costs for out-of-town guests?
- How much will you spend in transportation?

The list will continue through all of the details with an approximate amount based on research and acquiring cost estimates. Often, the budget builds as you answer these questions. Once you determine how many guests will attend, you can determine how many invitations you will need. Of course, a party for twenty will cost less in each area (invitations, food, etc.) than a party for 200. You'll find that the different elements of your project, scope, and budget will drive each other.

The need to combine resources with manpower is essential in putting together a budget. If you're leasing or renting equipment, you'll need someone to operate it—you don't want equipment sitting around unused. Likewise, you don't want people on the clock for an eight-hour day if the equipment is only available for three hours. Coordinating resources and manpower takes careful planning. Make sure they go hand in hand.

It's also important that you have enough work to keep full-timers working full time. If you're hiring someone for a thirty-five-hour workweek (and paying them a weekly rate), you'll be spending extra money if you only have twenty-two hours of work for them to do. You might hire someone on an hourly basis instead. However, if you are paying this individual $2,000 for the week and the rate of $100 per hour would put you at $2,200, you would actually be saving money with the weekly rate, even if the person isn't busy all the time. If you have this person on your payroll, he or she could be doing another task during those extra hours.

**QUESTION?**

**What are the elements of a budget?**
Similar to resources, budget elements are the people, materials, and tools (along with anything else) necessary to complete a project. They are the individual aspects of the budget to which money will be allocated. The anticipated project cost at the start of a project is known as the budget cost.

Use either/or scenarios to determine which is the most cost efficient way to run your project. Often, someone will rent equipment thinking that they will only need it for a short time, so they will be saving money. In the end, they need the equipment for a longer time frame and end up spending more money than they would have if they had purchased the equipment. Therefore, it's important to judge your needs in terms of equipment and time frame. No, you need not buy a forklift (which you'll probably never use again) for a two-week job, but if you buy a computer for a two-week job, you'll probably use it on your next project and the one after that. Keep in mind the practicality of buying versus renting for long-term usage.

It's also very important that you know the going rate for consultants, experts, or any specialists you may require. If the going rate is $75 per hour and you have found an expert looking for $175 per hour, guess who you shouldn't be hiring? But while you want to keep costs down, keep in mind that if this expert is the only one available, you may need to pay the higher rate, and factor it into your budget.

Let's say you're building a patio. For this project, you might estimate spending $2,500 on wood for the patio plus $75 an hour for the contractor for ten hours, assuming this is the estimated time he assumes he needs to do his part of the job. This would give you $3,250 in the budget for the patio ($2,500 + $750). Add to that $500 for paint, assuming you'll do the painting yourself (which saves you money), and $300 for additional supplies, including screws and tools. This gives you a budget of $4,050. Tack on an additional two hours for the contractor, in case he underestimated his time, and you'll be at $4,200. If you know you have $4,500 in available funds, you could put aside the remaining $300 for miscellaneous expenses—all those extra items that come to mind after you've put your budget on paper. Try to think of everything up front so you don't need to dip into those miscellaneous funds too often. In business, the extra funds, or a small portion of the budget, becomes petty cash, which usually disappears quickly.

**ALERT!**

Don't sell your project short by hiring inexperienced personnel for low pay. More often than not, you will be left with substandard work.

When determining the cost of anything from renting office space to planning a catered meal, have an estimate of the size or quantity you'll need. Don't rent an office space for twenty if you only have five and aren't expanding. Similarly, don't plan a buffet for fifty when you've only invited twenty-five. The size of the party, office, room, or any other space you will be renting or buying is a factor in estimating the cost. The more accurate your estimate, the less money you'll waste on too much space. Track RSVPs or confirmations as they come in to be sure your estimates stay realistic.

Another important aspect of putting together a budget is research. After all, how are you expected to know the costs of all materials and rates for services rendered unless you do your homework? You'll need to check with associations, network with professionals in the field, review similar project budgets, use the Internet or the library, and ask whomever you know what the going rates are for resources, especially when it comes to hourly, daily, or weekly pay rates.

**FACT**

When starting a project, you might decide to buy a copier to use for the project. The copier, purchased for your project, is considered a *direct cost.* If, however, you lease a copier for general office use, your budget would include a percentage of the overall cost based upon your use of the copier for the project. A cost not directly applied to a project (or function) is an *indirect cost.* It's to your advantage to utilize resources for multiple purposes and multiple projects.

You may get significantly different quotes from vendors. There must be a reason. Before you jump at what seems to be a bargain, make sure you aren't missing some important information. Are you getting an authentic reproduction of what you believe to be an original? Is the material substandard? Poor quality? Illegal? Remember, a deal that sounds too good to be true probably is.

## Affecting the Bottom Line

As much as budgets are one aspect of the project you're managing, they are also a project in their own right. You must have time to plan and research, you need documentation, and you have to identify your resources—which may include either a financial planner or a small loan.

### Time

Time plays a key role in your budget in two ways. First, you need adequate time to cover all your bases when preparing the budget. This can be very difficult if someone wants it done yesterday. If you're under great pressure, overestimate the major areas so you'll have some money in reserve when details in those key areas rear their ugly heads. For example, if you're installing a new computer system, you may budget for overtime and incentives under staffing costs. If you're not familiar with the new system, or who you will assemble as your team, it would be a good idea to factor in the cost of a specialist as well. If you don't need a specialist, then the worst thing is that you've come in under budget. The more time you have to prepare your budget, the more carefully you can examine all of the details.

Time is also a factor when planning your budget. How much time do you have to complete the project? A project on a short schedule may not afford you the luxury of lower costs. A printer, for example, might be able to have your programs for opening night ready in six weeks for $600. However, you only planned to do this show three weeks ago; hence, you'll need the programs in two weeks. This will be a rush job and will cost you $900. A shorter project time frame usually means higher costs. Whenever possible, try to plan far enough in advance to avoid paying higher rates or rush charges when something is needed in a hurry.

## Expertise

The need for experts will also affect your budget. No, you probably won't need a professional wedding planner to plan a wedding unless you don't have enough time or are anticipating an unusually lavish affair. Most often, family members plan the wedding and either the bride and groom or their parents become the project managers by default. On the other hand, you may need to hire an aeronautical engineer before you can proceed with your project to reroute a runway at the international airport. There are many levels in between these two scenarios that will require you to bring in someone familiar with the task at hand. Factor in more money for experts, knowing that in the end the job will be done right. Make sure you get a firm estimate of how much the expert charges and how long he or she will be needed on the project. Also, make sure experts communicate in language that everyone else on the team can understand.

## Supplies (Resources)

Supplies are another key factor in your budget. Make sure you know exactly what you need to buy or rent before you start. Make a mental picture of whatever it is that you are building, moving, planning, or creating, and determine what you'll need as you proceed through the project. Often, when doing projects at home or with friends, family, neighbors, or in the community, team members bring in or donate the majority of your supplies. If your neighbor already has a ratchet set, and he's helping you build the tool shed, borrow his if you can. Always make sure you know what you're getting.

Try to pad the budget by 5, 10, or even 15 percent to allow for extra cash for supplies. When things break (and they will) or you're running short on an item (and you will), you'll still have some money left to cover unplanned expenditures.

While you probably won't count every paperclip (unless the sponsor has you on a very tight leash budget wise), you'll need to maintain a firm grasp on where supplies are going and what they are being used for. Look for places where you can double up. For example, if someone needs to work on a computer for only one hour a day, let them use someone else's computer while that individual is at lunch. It's not cost effective for this person to have his or her own computer.

Also, be aware of availability in an office situation. Just because no one has used those three offices on the third floor in six months, it doesn't mean they will be available next week. You may need to rent office space. Make sure you cover all bases and double check all availability when renting, borrowing, or using existing materials. Here are some other budget tips:

- Include everything you can think of that might cost you or your sponsor money—from nuts and bolts to a city permit to importing the fake snow for the Christmas pageant.
- Research rates and prices carefully. Get quotes. Find out what the quote does and does not include.
- Look for places where you can beg or borrow (but not steal) supplies or materials.
- Determine how much more contingency plans will cost you. Will moving the wedding indoors cost $2,000 more than having the outdoor affair you are planning? Are you prepared for that expense?

## *Let the Budget Work for You*

Your first draft of the budget isn't your final project budget. You'll need several revisions before you complete your detailed budget. The budget can then help you in several important ways.

First of all, you can use the budget to determine if the cost of completing the project will outweigh the benefits. If it costs more to complete the project than you stand to gain from it, perhaps it's time to stop before you start. In whichever way you are measuring the benefits, whether it's short-term increased sales, improved morale, stress reduction, or long-term increased property value, the budget gives you one side (in black and white) of your pros-and-cons sheet for doing the project.

**ALERT!**

If you are not financing the project yourself, make sure you get the budget approved by whoever is putting up the funding. Get the first completed budget approved as well as any revisions that need to be made as you proceed.

The budget also lets the sponsor determine from a financial perspective whether outside assistance is necessary to finance the project. The budget keeps the flow of funds going into what is most necessary for the project's success. And finally, you can look at the budget as one way of monitoring the progress of the project.

Once the project gets started, the budget will be a key factor in determining how well the project is going. Too many projects go over budget and are axed for that reason. Get a good grasp of the budgetary needs before you begin.

Let's look at a sample project of creating a guidebook for tourists visiting the local museum. The curator has hired you to manage this project, which entails putting together a small printed book with photos to sell at the museum gift shop. He wants the guidebook to capture the key exhibits of the museum, and would like it to be ready in three months, before the spring tourist season begins. You ask him how many he wants to print, but he is not yet sure. You ask him if he wants you to work on site or off.

He doesn't have any office space available, so you'll have to use your own office, which you already have.

You look through the museum and estimate how much needs to be written to get about forty pages. You take note of approximately thirty ideas for photographs.

You contact printers and get estimates of how much it would cost to do a forty-page book with color photos, and one with black-and-white photos. You get estimates of how much it would cost to print 5,000 and 2,000 and 500 copies. You discuss possible turnaround times. You also get price quotes for an illustrator (in case you use one for the cover), a writer, an editor, a graphic designer, and a photographer. You get an estimate of how long it would take each of them to perform their tasks.

You return to the curator with what you have found. He decides that 2,000 copies would be sufficient, judging by the last tourist-season attendance figures, and that a forty-page book would be fine.

Next, you draw up a rough budget based on your findings:

| SAMPLE PROJECT BUDGET | |
|---|---|
| **Expense** | **Cost** |
| Writer ($40 per hour × 60 hours) | $2,400 |
| Photographer ($50 per hour × 8 hours) | $400 |
| Photographer expenses (travel, film, etc.) | $100 |
| Editor ($25 per hour × 10 hours) | $250 |
| Layout and graphics | $400 |
| Cover design and illustration | $250 |
| Printing (2,000 at .90 each) | $1,800 |
| Indirect cost to use your office/computer | $1,000 (% of rent + computer usage) |
| Travel (to and from museum/printer, etc.) | $50 |
| Miscellaneous | $350 |
| **TOTAL PROJECT COSTS** | **$7,000** |

The museum could have 2,000 guidebooks available for the tourist season for $7,000, or $3.50 each. If the museum sells them at $7.00 each, they will make a 100 percent profit, or $7,000. If the curator sees this as a cost-effective project that will have a benefit to the museum, then he or she will give you the go ahead.

**What is the difference between budgeting from the bottom up or from the top down?**
If you start with an overall estimate for the project and then allocate funding to various areas of the project or to lower-level managers, you are budgeting from the top down. However, if you start with team members and the tasks they do and work your way up to the total budget by adding the sum of the parts as you go, you are budgeting from the bottom up.

## And the Project Goes On

As the project continues, the budget will change. You'll find yourself needing $500 less for flowers and $500 more for centerpieces, or the contractor will need $1,000 more to finish the job. You'll need to move the numbers around accordingly. Of course, the problem arises when there are no numbers to move! (More on juggling in the next section.)

The other situation that you will need to pay close attention to is the schedule with regard to the budget. Allocating $10,000 to a project that needs to be completed in two months doesn't necessarily mean you need to spend $5,000 each month. You may have greater start-up costs and find you'll spend $7,000 the first month and only $3,000 in the second month. However, if you've spent $9,000 in the first month, you'll be in trouble in month two.

A budget need not be evenly distributed across your schedule. You do, however, need to know if you're falling behind whatever pace you have set for yourself. Set up a system by which you will monitor your budget as the project proceeds. It's important to subtract money as it's spent, but it's also important to keep track of expenses that have been agreed upon but not yet paid. If, for example, you've ordered the supplies for the new office but have not paid the bill for the supplies, you would have to make a note that your $10,000 budget to move the office is now down by $3,000 for new supplies, or at $7,000 remaining in actual funds. Chances are, a lot of that $7,000 is earmarked as well. It's similar to balancing your checkbook. There are checks that have cleared your account and outstanding checks that you have just written.

Making sure that everyone involved in the project fills you in on all financial commitments is just as important as tracking actual expenses. Have team members keep written records of their expenses and any vendors or outside sources who are still to be paid. Get photocopies of signed agreements or contracts. Make sure each person on the team is aware of his or her budgetary limitations. When a team member is buying materials, you need to set a maximum amount that he or she can spend. Likewise, you can set maximums for what can be spent on consultants' fees or other hiring costs. Make sure it is clear that this is all that is in the budget before the individual begins the work. Make it clear that you, or whoever is paying the bills, will not pay more than the maximum. This may also mean having people record their time.

It's easy to maintain control over the budget if you limit the number of people who can spend money or make financial promises or agreements. Make sure anyone operating under a budget understands the ramifications of spending more than their budget allows.

Depending on your relationship with the team members and the nature of the project, you may have a system worked out that allows each team member $x$ dollars with which to handle their tasks. They are expected to stay at or below that total. On the other hand, you may have a centralized budget, and each person may need to get an okay from you, the treasurer, or whoever is keeping track of the budget before making any financial commitments.

When working on a conference, the chairperson of the speakers' committee promised several out-of-town guest speakers that the organization would pay their travel expenses. His budget was only $3,000. After making this promise to several people, he was asked to provide an estimate for those travel expenses. He researched the airfares and it came to $8,000. He had therefore made promises that would cost $5,000 over his budget. He had two choices: either call back some speakers and rescind his promise (at great embarrassment to the organization), or help locate $5,000 in another part of the budget. Ultimately, the $5,000 was found elsewhere. What this committee chair should have done was add up the costs as he went along and stopped at $3,000, or asked if there was additional money in the budget before making the promises.

## A Juggling Act

Juggling the budget is essentially taking from line A to pay for items on line B. The problem with this is that while you may still have the money sitting there on line A, it is most likely earmarked for another significant part of the project. Otherwise, why would you have budgeted money on line A in the first place?

**ALERT!**

Monitor your project closely. Try to foresee any and all reasons to change your budget ahead of time so that you are ahead of the budget and it's not ahead of you!

Essentially, the only way to avoid getting into budget trouble is to plan your budget very carefully and stick to it throughout the project. If you need to juggle, you'll need to take money away from the lowest priority area of the project and place it into a higher priority area. That may mean you'll have fewer new lounge chairs on the new pool deck, but at least you'll be able to pay the contractor to finish building the deck.

Inevitably, there will be decisions that need to be addressed throughout the life of the project. Unforeseen circumstances may mean spending extra money. For this reason, it's wise to look for one area of the project where you can cut costs early on. This may give you a place to turn when such emergency funds are needed. Look at the lowest priority items first and consider them your luxury items, those that will be there if the budget allows and nothing unforeseen takes the money. Perhaps you want a hotel suite on your trip to Paris. You may have to settle for a more standard room if you're stuck paying a speeding ticket because you were late leaving for the airport. Expect the unexpected and be glad if you can afford any luxuries in your budget.

## Budget Busters

Budgets go off course for various reasons. Don't tuck away the budget and say, "We'll look at it when we're done and see how well we did." To avoid blowing your budget, you need to pay careful attention to all the details. Among the leading causes of such monetary mishaps are the following:

- Inadequate budget estimations (underestimating costs)
- Lack of properly researching pay rates and resource costs
- Basing costs on old price structures
- Failure to include all significant details
- Poor communications with team members about their responsibility to stay within the budget
- Failure to properly document expenditures
- Not properly addressing emergencies and other changes as they occur throughout the project and impact your budget
- Falling behind on your schedule and needing to spend more to meet last-minute deadlines

These budget busters can be avoided, but others cannot. For example, technical glitches can turn into nightmares that can wreak havoc with your budget, or materials you ordered may be delayed. Consultants and experts may also need to put in more hours on the project to overcome potential pitfalls. Whatever the reason, many well-intentioned projects have been scrapped or run into the ground because of budgeting disasters. Look at New York City's long-anticipated Second Avenue subway. Every city has its share of projects that simply didn't have the budget to either get started or get completed. Many companies and new businesses run into similar problems trying to introduce new products or ideas. Sometimes the project is delayed, and sometimes it comes to an abrupt halt.

**FACT**

There's nothing wrong with letting the budget do what it's intended to do—set boundaries. If funds were unlimited, you'd love new uniforms or a fancy restaurant reception, but they're not. Let the budget say no for you: "I'd love to have custom-made uniforms, but it's just not in the budget." "I think the cocktail reception would be great at a restaurant, but the budget limits us to the hospitality suite here at the hotel . . . my hands are tied."

Even personal projects may be scrapped because the money is no longer there. For example, you may have planned and budgeted to make home repairs as your fall project, only to find you needed to spend the money to repair the car after an accident.

Remember, the budget needs to be carefully planned, reviewed, and monitored throughout any project. Expect that there will be changes. Make sure you work with a system that you are comfortable using. Don't work on a software program that you don't know, and if you prefer to use a notebook or any other manner of maintaining the budget, that's fine, too. You want to avoid making errors on your budget simply because you couldn't figure out the calculations on the program or on the page. Spreadsheets, software or actual, are just that—places where you can spread numbers out. Do it.

Also, keep a separate budget for the project. If you incorporate it into another budget or use the budget for other things, you will only confuse yourself and jeopardize the project. You can always set up a separate project account for your personal or small business projects.

## CHAPTER 13

# Monitoring Progress

As the project moves forward, you will need to establish how you monitor your progress based on a number of criteria, including time, cost, and performance. Your system must highlight potential problems so that you can steer the project back on track. You may come upon a detour and need to find another route in order to arrive at your destination on time. Naturally, the sooner you find out about upcoming roadwork, the sooner you can plan an alternate route. Likewise, the sooner you discover potential problems, the sooner you can make plans to circumvent them.

## Why Monitor?

Monitoring a project is vital because it lets you communicate to stakeholders, sponsors, and team members exactly where the project stands and determine how closely your initial plan of action resembles reality. It allows you to validate any decisions you will make in regards to implementing changes. Your data will benefit anyone who has an interest in the potential outcome of the project. Monitoring your project also allows you to make the necessary adjustments regarding resources or your budget. If you learn, for example, that you have more people than you need on one task but need someone in another area that is lagging behind, you can make the adjustment.

**FACT**

Regular monitoring helps you avoid disasters. Just as checking the gas gauge in your car as you drive helps you see how much gas is left in the tank, monitoring your project helps you avoid running out of gas before you reach your goal.

As your project comes to life, keep these questions in mind:

- Are you on schedule?
- If not, how far behind are you, and how can you catch up?
- Are you over budget?
- Are you still working toward the same project goal?
- Are you running low on resources?
- Are there warning signs of impending problems?
- Is there pressure from management to complete the project sooner?
- Is there public opposition or any other opposition to the project being completed?

These are just a few of the questions you should ask yourself as you monitor the progress of your project. Monitoring will allow you to make comparisons between your original plan and your progress so far. You will be able to implement changes, where necessary, to complete the project successfully.

If you need to monitor for the sake of providing reports to outside sources, including stakeholders and sponsors, let the team know that the information is needed for other sources. Make sure you are addressing the concerns of the customers, partners, stockholders, upper management, and others involved in the project. Get a clear idea of who needs to know what so that you don't have to burden your team or waste your own time gathering extraneous information. Sources seeking information on the project may include:

- Stakeholders
- Government offices
- Sponsors
- The media
- Politicians
- The community

Other reports (internal and external) may also need to include your project data, including:

- Quarterly or annual reports
- Operating budgets
- Cost-variance reports
- Marketing materials
- Supply inventories
- Compliance reports

## *How Often to Monitor*

Do you keep progress reports on a daily basis? On a weekly basis? Do you need frequent review meetings? How often you monitor a project depends on several factors:

- The scope of the project
- The number of people working on the project
- The skill level of the individuals working on the project

- The schedule/time frame of the project
- The familiarity of the project (are team members taking on tasks that they have not done before?)
- Communication needs (are stakeholders, upper-level managers, or others waiting for, or expecting, regular updates?)
- The complexity of the project (are there numerous technical details?)
- The level of risk associated with the project
- The resources associated with the project

Let's look more closely at each of these factors to help determine how often to monitor a project.

## Scope

Larger projects will generally require closer and more frequent monitoring, since numerous activities are taking place and there is a greater likelihood that some areas of the project will fall behind or that a problem will arise. A larger project will need a more formal system of monitoring while a small, or family, project can be monitored informally.

## Number of People on the Project

When more people are involved, the chance of human error is greater, no matter what the overall scope of the project. Unless everyone is doing the same task, it takes closer monitoring to make sure each person stays on track. (Don't overdo it, however. More on this later.) Usually, more people will mean more monitoring. However, fifty people performing the same activity may be easier to monitor than ten people doing ten different tasks, because you will be able to use the same baseline criteria for the fifty people.

Get to know more than one person at the company (unless it is an individual subcontractor). If you can't reach one person, or if your contact leaves the company, you can still get in touch with someone who can find out what part of the work is completed and what needs to be done.

If outside contractors, suppliers, consultants, and others are necessary to help complete your project, it may be hard to keep track of their progress, especially if they are working off site. It's to your advantage to include them in aspects of the project. Keep them updated on the project's progress, include them in team get-togethers, etc. The more involved they become, the more accessible they will be, and the easier it will be for you to get the updates you need. You can set up the how and when of supplying you with a progress report, but you'll often get better results by establishing a good rapport with outside vendors and resources.

## Skill Level

You may have experts who have done the same activities many times before. These individuals may not need to be monitored as often or as closely as people who are doing a task for the first time. So as not to micromanage, you may simply set up more frequent checkpoints in the process or have more meetings to closely monitor individuals who are less familiar with specific tasks. You can also make it clear that people should be able to approach you with questions or problems, especially if they are being trained or are new to a specific task.

## Schedule

If the project requires presenting deliverables every couple of weeks, you will want to monitor on a weekly basis (at the least). A longer project with more time committed to each task and no deliverables until the end result may allow you greater intervals before you'll need to monitor the progress. You can judge your progress based on when the team reaches specific milestones on your original schedule, which is a very common way to monitor projects.

Remember, each person needs to stay on schedule. The farther behind the project falls, the more closely you'll have to monitor progress. Generally, there's a little slack built into the schedule, but the further behind you fall, the less slack there is to play with. If, for example, you know that the project can run three days behind schedule, and you're already two days behind and not even halfway finished, you'll need to monitor more closely to see where you can pick up the pace.

### Familiarity of the Project

If you've never done this project before, you'll need to monitor more closely to make sure you haven't veered off course. It will be important to have a prototype or some form of blueprint or document on which to base your project. If, for example, you're setting up a backyard swing set for the kids, you'll have to check the diagram more closely as you go and double check for safety each step of the way. When a team has done a similar project in the past, you can monitor more loosely.

## Communication Needs

If stakeholders or others expect monthly, weekly, or daily updates or reports, you have to furnish them with the latest project news. That news will come from monitoring your project to respond to their needs. Make sure you address the needs of the individuals waiting to hear the latest developments. High-profile projects, such as the building of a new bridge or a new convention center, will often require you to provide frequent updates to numerous media sources as well as politicians and other government offices.

## Complexity

The more nuts and bolts there are in the project, the more closely you'll need to oversee what is going on. Complex projects are more likely to have potential for error, so they need to be tracked more closely. These may include numerous tests for quality assessment.

## Risk

"Risk" is a relative term. Building a power plant takes much closer monitoring than planning a convention. A project that can be potentially detrimental to the world at large obviously requires much closer monitoring than building the backyard pool. The risk that your new corporate offices will not be ready on time does not affect the world at large; however, it does affect the success of your company and the jobs of many people.

Projects involve two levels of risk. One is the risk of the project failing in the larger picture and the other is internal risk, meaning that the project won't get completed. While your first risk is that of the project failing, the greater risk lies in the consequences of the project failing, which will affect the stakeholders. But how? Will the company fall behind in the market place, causing lower sales figures and costing people their jobs? Will people simply have to wait fifteen minutes longer for the bus because the new subway-line project bombed? Basically, if a project fails and no one is affected by it, then there wasn't much risk involved. But if the project fails and shuts down the city of Pittsburgh for two weeks, there was significant real-world risk involved. Monitor accordingly.

Don't assume that because a team worked on a similar project a month ago they won't need any monitoring this time around. You'll still need to monitor for accuracy, safety, and other issues. Remember, every project is different, with unique concerns and issues.

## Resources

What do you need to complete the project? Resources may seem plentiful when you start out, but they can run out fast. From labor to paperclips, it's important that you keep an eye on what is running low. Do you need toner for the printer? Are you out of cement for construction? Has your art director just left for another project? Monitor what you have and what you need.

Once you monitor the project (as often as necessary to keep you abreast of what is going on), you will need to do something with the data you have gathered. The point of monitoring a project is that someone will gain insight from the information. After all, if you monitor a project and no one ever reads or evaluates the data, what is the point? Gather the information, then compare and analyze what you have gathered and make an assessment of where you stand in each area.

## Performance Periods

Call them performance periods, segments, or anything you choose . . . as long as you determine a time frame in which activities will get done.

Companies have quarterly reports every three months to assess how well they are doing financially. Projects need the same type of breakdown. This allows you to analyze and review the project through each period. It also gives you time to review the intended goals of the overall project and discuss the upcoming phases with team members.

Performance periods will help you subdivide the overall task into more manageable segments. Select appropriate amounts of time. If your time periods are too short, there may not be enough progress to monitor. On the other hand, if monitoring occurs too infrequently, some aspect of the project can go wrong and be undetected before turning into a major problem.

## Gathering Information

Once you've assessed what you'll be looking for and how often you'll be monitoring the project, you'll need to determine exactly what information needs to be gathered:

- When each activity began and ended
- The resources used for each activity
- The expenses incurred for each activity
- The number of man hours put into each activity
- Whether the goal of the activity was accomplished or not (this may determine whether you can move on to the next activity or task)

To make all of this information worthwhile, you need a measure of comparison. This is where you turn to your original plans. Did the start and end dates of the activity coincide with your projected start and end dates? Did you use the anticipated resources or did you run short or have materials left over? Where are you in conjunction with your projected budget at this point in the project? Did you anticipate more or fewer man hours to this point in the project?

All of the comparisons with your initial plan are vital to determining where you stand at any given time in the process. Compare the performance of your team with the original plan and look for reasons why there are differences. To better your understanding of the comparisons, you may want to meet with team members and get further details. In these meetings, you can discuss progress, assess any setbacks, resolve issues, and evaluate performance. Team members can often provide valuable suggestions on ways to perform more efficiently. Perhaps the resources are at fault for the delays.

Prior to meetings, you should study the details of your tracking or monitoring system to find the most glaring differences between scheduled and actual performance. If everything is running smoothly, you may simply want to tell everyone how well they are doing and keep up the team spirit by using the review meeting as an opportunity to reward everyone in a small way.

While you may not need as lengthy a discussion as you would if the project were off schedule, it's a good idea to get some notion of why things are going well. You will want to document what you are doing so that you can repeat your success on the next project. Just as people learn from their mistakes, they also learn from their successes. (And don't get too overconfident if the project is on course; things can always take a turn for the worse.)

**ALERT!**

If a team member is at the root of a problem, work on constructive ways to resolve the problem and let the team member maintain dignity and respect. If, however, someone is not performing his task or cannot do an adequate job, he may need to be replaced.

More often than not, one area is lagging behind or one task is falling behind schedule. You need to assess why. Did you underestimate the time it would take to perform the task? Are you using improper resources? Is the right person doing the right task? Whatever the reason, you need to find the source of the problem, then you need to try to prevent that task from falling further behind schedule.

## Monitoring at the Individual Level

For you to monitor a project, it will require that individuals provide updates of where they are and how long it has taken to get there. Monitoring needs to start with team members. However, be careful not to stifle positive attitudes, productivity, and creativity by imposing too much clerical work.

Make sure team members know how you want their reports to read. Don't make the process overly complicated or team members will shrug it off or not hand in the reports on time. Remember that less is more. The less you ask of your team members, the more likely it is that they will provide you with timely updates. Get basic, but specific, information as opposed to nitpicking for details. The setting will dictate the level of formality necessary and the amount of information to be reported. Keep it simple. Let's look at a few examples:

1. Someone volunteering to make costumes for the community center theater production may simply tell you she has completed five costumes in three days and has three more to complete in the next couple of days. Since this is a volunteer position and there is no pay, you don't need an hourly assessment. You may, however, want to ask if she has all the resources she needs to complete the task.

2. Someone writing a brochure may write down that she has completed the first draft of three (out of four) pages of copy in seventeen hours. She estimates that it will take her one more day to complete the first draft of page four. This example would include hours, since the copywriter is being paid by the hour.

3. Someone on a project to assemble 200 new vacuum cleaners for demonstration purposes will have a report that tells you that between January 4 and January 8, twenty-nine shipments arrived and the first hundred of the vacuum cleaners had completed phase one of assembly. It took 300 man hours at a cost of $12,395. This example may require more detail since the project has a greater scope and a larger budget. Ask team members:

   - To provide the information that you need
   - To hand in written reports on time
   - To report potential problems
   - To include milestones reached
   - To let you know if they need more resources to complete the task

You will need to evaluate reports or updates from team members, whether it's a verbal update, as in the first example, or a more detailed report. Can you find solutions to the problems that are presented early on, before they become large-scale problems? It's important that you address these concerns.

It's also important to ask the team members for comments on the project. Comments will run the gamut from rantings to significant predicaments. You will need to determine the severity of problems and make a hierarchical list starting with significant actual problems and continuing with potential problems. If you are out of a particular resource, that is a problem. If you will run out of a resource if you keep using it at this rate, that is a potential problem. Both need to be addressed. Make sure, however, that a potential problem is real and based on the current project assessments and not on a hunch or a guesstimate.

Getting written or verbal comments from team members can help you avert potential problems. Be sure to take notes. It's likely that people working directly on individual tasks will be able to point out key areas of concern.

Rank all current problems 1–10, with 10 being the most serious. Then number all potential problems as 1–10, with 10 being the most serious. Look at your lists. Those problems ranked 5–10 on your current list of concerns should take precedence, with potential problems ranked 5–10 addressed next. Then you can take care of the smaller problems ranked 1–4, and finally, address the potential problems ranked 1–4.

Comments will also need your attention. Let team members know that time is limited and that you would appreciate concise comments that pertain only to the project. Separate those that pertain to the project and those that pertain to the project team, such as conflicts between members. Rate them and prioritize them as well. Discard those that are not project related. Also, look for consistencies. If one person says that the work area is too warm, you can suggest opening a window near where that person is working. However, if twenty-two people say they are too hot, you'll need to seriously consider a better air conditioner. A consensus of opinions can point you to key concerns of team members.

Your lists of immediate and potential problems will provide significant points for discussion in project review meetings and will also give you key points to summarize with stakeholders. Depending on the problem and the stakeholder, you can determine which information to pass along and which can be solved without alerting others. For example, customers don't need to know that three of your team members have left and need to be replaced, as long as deliverables are ready on time. Stockholders, on the other hand, may want to know if one of the three people who left is also the CEO.

If you see a problem on your list that you can solve with a quick phone call or flick of a switch, make the change or have someone else do it. It's always nice to knock out a few problems quickly.

Determine which problems need to be communicated to others and which ones you are expected to handle. The level of authority you have and the nature of the project will dictate your best course of action. It's very important to know what is for public consumption, what is for key personnel to know, and what is and isn't for the media to sink their teeth into. Some projects will require detailed accounts or public posting of every written document. Others will require that you make the changes and move on. Judge carefully who you apprise of current and potential problems. Remember: Problems can become magnified when they are communicated to the wrong people, or are not communicated to the right people. Either way, your position as project manager could hang in the balance.

Some activities in a project seem to follow Murphy's Law: Whatever can go wrong will go wrong. If you're lucky, these nightmare aspects of the project will be minimal. Any activities that have proven to be troublesome in previous projects are worth monitoring more closely. You may also have to monitor people who've been tardy or lazy in the past more closely, but first give them the benefit of the doubt—a new project might mean a new attitude.

# *Three Steps Forward, Two Steps Back*

Once there was a beautiful, natural waterfall that flowed magnificently, taking crystal clear water from high up in the mountains down to a river below. The stream of the waterfall was continuous, flowing steadily in the same direction.

Once there was a project that emerged from a mountain of paperwork. It was designed to put the paperwork into a series of computer databanks so that work could flow more smoothly. Unlike the waterfall, these databanks would need to be set up by programmers through an elaborate technological system. The project flowed smoothly for some time, like the waterfall, until someone realized that there was trouble way back in the early stages of the flow—technological pollution, so to speak—which meant that the water would no longer flow crystal clear to the bottom.

**ALERT!**

Don't try to play hero and do everything yourself—ask for and get help when necessary. If someone higher up in the pecking order (whether it's your boss, PTA president, or your dad) has told you to report any problems to him, do so!

The waterfall method of completing projects, which has one activity flowing into another and into another, has not proven very effective for technological projects. It has become increasingly obvious that one needs to move forward with caution, and after proceeding through one, two, or three phases, there is a need to go back and make sure phase one still works as intended. Often, changes in a project will occur at many of the early stages, affecting all the information processing that will follow. Therefore, it is often a three-step process—one step forward and two steps back—to make sure everything is still working properly.

Technology presents many complex issues:

- The technological team needs to satisfy the needs of the potential users. Both the needs and the users can change often as the project progresses.

- There is a need for interfacing, both within the company or business and externally.
- The technology itself changes very rapidly, particularly in the course of a yearlong project. What was cutting edge on day one is old news on day 365 of your project.
- An intended goal can be achieved in many ways. Try to get a consensus on which course of action would be best to follow.
- Testing is crucial and needs to be factored into the schedule. Results need to be clearly defined. Programs need to be tested individually and the system needs to be tested as a whole.
- Good communication is critical.

The last point derails many projects. How often has one learned that the technical team and management did not clearly understand one another? How often has the technical team had to go back to phase one, two, or three and make changes that would affect the phases that followed? How often has someone wanted to do it his or her own way only to find out the method did not work? More often than not, a lack of clear communication is at the root of the technical problems that slow a project down.

For example, many of the dot-coms that failed in late 2000 and early 2001 were victims of poor communication between management, sales, content developers, and the technical team. Frequently, someone had a great idea, or thought it was a great idea, but the technical team was not informed of all the details. In other instances, the technical teams clearly did not share the same vision with the creative team. Then there were cases where something simply could not be done, or would cost much more to achieve than was feasible. Poor management and the inability of the management, creative, sales and marketing, and technical teams to get on the same page was at the root of many dot-com disasters.

## *Monitoring Expenditures*

Few projects can succeed without money. Your purchase orders, vendor bills, checks, credit card bills, and other documents will be used to verify what is actually being spent on the project. As you learned in Chapter 12, your budget should clearly illustrate the sum total of what needs to be spent.

You, or someone handling the disbursements and expenditures, should have a system in which every payment is approved, using the original invoice only, to make sure that no bills are paid in duplicate. Make sure purchases are accounted for and subtracted from your budget. Just because the new computer isn't sitting on your desk doesn't mean that $2,000 from your budget hasn't already been spent. Remember that the $150 for shipping the computer needs to be accounted for in the budget as well. Make sure any additional expenditures that were not in the original budget are addressed and noted immediately—don't wait for the end of the next monitoring period, such as the weekly status report. It's important that a $500 change in the budget on a small project be incorporated on Monday when the purchase is made and not on Friday when the status report is handed in. Someone, very likely you, needs to review and approve any and all additional expenses.

In your budget, always plan for at least 10–15 percent more for large-item purchases because of shipping, handling, taxes, and other expenses. Also, allow for unforeseen expenses, but set a limit in this area—say, $500 under "Miscellaneous"—unless there's a major emergency.

If your accounting department is handling the payments, they may not be keeping separate records for your particular project. That means you must take on the responsibility yourself and keep track of the project budget. If they are handling the budget for the project, you must make sure to have steady communication and know exactly what they have and have not yet included as expenditures. The best way to monitor expenditures is to set up a system at the beginning of the project that accounts for all expenses. Use software if you choose, but remember, it's up to you and your team to make sure the correct data is entered.

To judge your project's success in relation to your original projected budget, you'll need to compare how much you have spent in conjunction with how much you have in the overall budget. Using a system known as Earned Value Analysis, you can determine whether you are ahead of or behind your budget at a specific point in the project.

For example, suppose your total budget to move the office to the new location is $40,000 and you have a time frame of two months. After one month, you've spent $20,000. Are you on budget? If all work to be done, including all expenses (such as resources and manpower) is equal in both months, you're fine. However, this is not always the case. You will have different needs and costs at different points in your projects. You need to look specifically at the project's schedule and resource expenditures to that point, both actual and projected. If you had planned to spend only $15,000 through the first month and you have spent $20,000, you have overspent by $5,000 at this point, based on your projection. This is known as your cost variance.

Your proposed budget has an additional $25,000 to be spent in the second month of the project. You have only $20,000 left in your actual budget. Therefore, you will either need to ask management or whoever is sponsoring the move for an additional $5,000 or find a way of saving $5,000 in the next month.

**QUESTION?**

**What is Earned Value Analysis?**
Earned Value Analysis is how you analyze the progress of the project. You compare the money budgeted with the money spent and the work achieved. You can determine whether you are ahead of or behind your projected budget.

If you take the actual cost of work performed and divide it by the budgeted cost of work performed, then multiply your answer by the total cost of the project, you can get a rough estimate of how much you would spend at the current rate. This is important if you are over budget and see upcoming spending continuing at a similar rate. It's a rough estimate because there are variables that will come into play that will impinge on your budget. You may also find ways to save money.

Your Earned Value Analysis tells you it's time to do one of the following:

- Find ways to save money
- Ask your sponsor for more money
- Eliminate a portion of the project that may be extraneous and will not impinge on meeting the goals of the overall project
- Hop a plane and leave town

## *Project Evolution*

As you monitor your project, you will discover changes or alterations that need to be made to your schedule or budget. Insignificant alterations are usually easy to make, while large-scale changes take more time to plan and often need approval from various sources including sponsors, stakeholders, and upper management or supervisors.

Just as a living organism grows, your project will grow and evolve into something more than just plans or blueprints. And just as your children come home and surprise you with new words they've learned from their friends at school, there are outside factors that will pop up during the growth of your project that you will have to address. No matter how much you monitor, you will never be completely prepared for every unforeseen event, such as new shipping charges, a new ordinance, or a labor strike. But the more carefully you monitor progress, the more you will be able to handle those issues that are within your control.

### *Be Prepared*

As you make changes and alterations to the schedule or budget, make sure you keep everyone apprised. If the people working on a project don't know that the due date is now Tuesday instead of Thursday, they'll be late in finishing their activity. Keep all necessary people informed of any changes that affect their work. Also:

- Be ready to explain and justify any changes you have made
- Make sure you get all necessary approvals before making changes
- Work within the system and ask team members to do the same

### Be Clear

It is important to be very clear when you give instructions. If you ask someone to make sure everything remaining in the office is packed up for a move, the individual may pack everything up in any number of ways. Asking someone to pack everything up is vague. However, asking someone to pack up everything in cartons that are labeled and taped, so you can easily identify and load each item onto the hand trucks in the morning, is much more specific. You need to spell out details and let the team members know what achievement or end result you expect of each task.

More specific directions will result in less frequent monitoring because you've clarified the process and the desired (and expected) results of the task. Never assume people can read your mind—let individuals know the details you are seeking and the end result (achievement). Achievement-based assignments keep things clear for all concerned.

## Monitoring Yourself

Are you becoming a pain in the neck? Are people spending more time filling out progress reports than doing actual tasks? Do team members duck into restrooms to avoid you for fear of being given the third degree? If you are overmonitoring, you can become the project's worst enemy.

While you do need to monitor a project's progress, you also need to know when to stop monitoring the project itself. You can keep a log of project activities that does not require constant input from other team members. However, when others are involved in monitoring the project, they are using valuable time. Keep monitoring to a minimum unless you are working with complex projects or highly sensitive materials that need to be double checked or tested often.

Resources such as equipment and materials have a way of disappearing. You need to monitor that, so they don't grow legs and walk off the project. Short of locking up every pen, you'll have to keep a rough inventory of the tools, materials, and equipment involved in your project.

If you do need frequent updates on a more complex project, keep the updates simple. It's easier to fill out a concise form, even on a daily basis, than to have to write out pages of details. Too much paperwork will lower the morale of your team members, and that will show up in their work. You'll also find that if you require too much reporting, team members may start ignoring the reports or handing them in incomplete or late.

You don't want people to feel micromanaged. On a smaller or less technical project, you might begin by informal monitoring, such as walking around to see how everything is going and asking people informally if there's any problem. For many projects, such informal discussions or weekly team meetings and summary reports will do the trick. For larger projects, you may hold team meetings on a monthly basis but still want weekly status reports.

If the people working on the project are not highly experienced, or you are not familiar with their work, you might monitor more closely at first and then once things are on track, loosen the reins a bit. It all depends on your approach and the people on your team.

The basic rules of thumb are:

- Make sure you are clear about what you expect from team members regarding their assigned activities.
- Make sure people know what you want on your reports.
- Monitor just enough to feel comfortable with and remain in control of the project.
- Monitor to track and gain insight into the flow of information, but don't waste people's time.
- Make sure monitoring is not a burden to your team.

To establish the most effective monitoring process, keep status reports short and to the point. If you are working on a community, family, or small business project, you might have weekly meetings to get status updates. Ask which tasks have been completed in the past week, which ones are still in progress, when they will be completed, and how much money has been spent so far. Ask if there are any questions or if your team members anticipate any problems. Also, ask for suggestions to make things run more smoothly. Remember, there are no bad suggestions, just ones that may or may not work well on your particular project.

For more formal tracking methods in business or on larger projects, you can write each of these questions down and present a stack of status forms to be filled out at the end of the week. A simple form e-mailed to team members each week is often the simplest method. Make sure there is room to fill in suggestions or comments. Whether or not you use many (or any) suggestions, it helps make everyone feel involved in the project if you ask them for feedback.

Suggestions are also helpful because:

- You never know when someone will have a brilliant idea
- It keeps people thinking about the project
- It makes team members feel involved

## Tools for Monitoring Your Project

For small projects and personal projects, you can use notebooks, graphs, diagrams, day planners, personal organizers, or other tools to post your schedule and project updates. Don't make things more complicated than necessary by using high-tech tracking devices for simple projects. You don't need an elaborate software system to run a bake sale, plan a wedding, set up a small business, or build a jungle gym for the kids. The tracking system should match the scope of the project. Many software products, such as those offered by Microsoft, are designed primarily for corporate or large-scope projects. (Several are listed in Chapter 15.) You can always use a spreadsheet program, such as Excel, on your PC if you want to track a simple, small-scope project on your desktop.

The easier the monitoring tools are to understand, the quicker you'll be able to explain them to others and read (and analyze) them yourself. A tool is only useful if it serves a productive purpose. If monitoring means being able to easily gather, read, and utilize information for comparisons, you need a tool that does this without distractions.

# *Monitoring Intangibles*

Okay, it's easy to have everyone list how many hours they've worked on the project. It's also easy to write down what work has been completed and what work still needs to be done. It's not hard to match this information against the original plan, budget, and schedule to see if you are on course. But, how do you measure the intangibles? How do you measure how well your team members are getting along? How do you measure whether communication is effective or not? How do you measure the quality of the work that has been completed?

Status reports won't tell you if the work is done poorly. After all, who's going to write down "The new roof is in place, the job is completed . . . but the roof will leak"? So what can you do? Be omnipresent—the more walkthroughs, the better. Walkthroughs are those little strolls you take just to see that all is going well. No, you don't want to appear to be looking over peoples' shoulders, but you do need to know that the person in charge of hiring a stripper to strip the shingles off the roof doesn't hire a stripper in an exotic outfit. You want to remain somewhat unobtrusive, yet approachable; somewhat cheerful, yet businesslike. Don't get sidetracked by lengthy conversations; set up appointments to discuss matters that would slow down your otherwise breezy jaunt.

**FACT**

Depending on the project, your monitoring may end up in the daily newspaper. Yes, the media follows projects. While only large-scale projects will make the larger-market papers, a store moving to a new location after twenty-five years might be a headline in a small-town paper, and you may be managing that move.

Activities not only need to be done on time, they need to be done correctly. Make sure you have a feel for exactly what task members are doing and how they are doing it early on. Then politely set task members back on course if they seem to be going astray. If the first page of the brochure copy makes little sense, it's not likely the next three pages will be any better.

It helps to have examples available of exactly what you want. A picture or video presentation is worth a thousand words. Explaining, "We want the pool to look like this one," as you hold up a photo of an in-ground, kidney-shaped pool will prevent misunderstandings. Since most projects do not create something completely new and original, you can use a model to show both the quality and specifics you are looking for.

As for monitoring morale and cohesiveness, you need to make a concerted effort to note whether people are working well together or just barely tolerating one another. Although you may be tipped off by a slowdown in production or a lack of interest in planned extracurricular activities, this is primarily a judgment call. Encourage people to discuss matters with you, particularly if they are having trouble working with other team members. Never take sides; just try to create a situation in which the two parties can come to common terms on the project and work together. You need not create friendships, just a workable partnership. Spell out what each side should expect from the other, almost like drawing up a contract, as to how they can best respect and work with one another. Keep it informal, unless you see the potential for serious problems. (There's more on resolving conflicts in Chapter 18.)

**QUESTION?**

**How is communication measured?**
If people are asking many questions about your requests and project requirements, you may not be communicating clearly. Measure communication from your office, or easy chair, by how many people are questioning your instructions or the number of errors in the work being turned in.

You can also measure communications by how effective the communications system is that you are using. If no one is getting your e-mails, the system is not working. If everyone is getting your memos but they are using them to shoot baskets, the system is not working. Make sure people are receiving—and reading—your communications.

Your team's communication will affect the ease of transition from one phase of the project to the next, and will be reflected in the quality of the final product. Take active steps to maintain clear expectations throughout the project. Set up meetings to ensure that team members doing task A and team members doing task B know their deliverables are for the team waiting to work on task C. Team-C people should also have some representation at these meetings to address minor issues as they arise.

All parties need to know what is expected of them regarding the flow of information to each other and to you. Facilitate and encourage ongoing communication by having reliable and efficient systems in place—they will show your commitment to the initiative. "Please let shipping know what percentage of widgets are completed by Friday so they can prepare for how many you'll be sending down next week" is a reasonable request.

Yes, you will have to use a combination of good listening, subtle scouting, a keen overall awareness, and a little intuition to monitor all the intangibles of a project that won't show up on status reports or be caught by your software program. Look, listen, and keep your door open.

## CHAPTER 14

# The PMO: Project Management Office

The latest trend in corporations around the world is the Project Management Office (PMO). Just like project management, a PMO is defined in many different ways and rarely follows the same trend. In this chapter, you'll read about the general definitions and trends regarding the PMO.

## What Is a PMO?

The PMO is an ever-evolving concept. Early on, it was thought that project managers could be part of their own department of a corporation. However, once they were situated, they looked at each other and thought, "Now what?"

Just like a great project, a PMO should have a charter and some governing principles. A project charter gives authority to the project manager and recognizes the existence of the project. A PMO charter should do the same for the PMO.

The question is, why even have a PMO? What is the benefit? Depending on which study you read, 70–90 percent of projects fail. This is a shockingly high number. This was before there was so much pressure placed on senior management via laws like Sarbanes Oxley. Now that accountability has reached an all-time high, companies are starting to invest in PMOs to help regulate, document, and control the project environment.

## Types of PMOs

There are several types of PMOs in practice today. They can run the gamut of size, scope, and responsibilities. However, they generally fall into three different styles or roles: the Librarian, the Advisor, and the Partner.

### The Librarian

This type of PMO is used for documentation purposes only. It normally consists of one or two project managers. The organization that uses this type is generally young in their project management maturity or is reluctant to release any control of spending and authority to the PMO. These types of project managers are there to document, observe, and report. They are rarely given any authority on the projects and often exist to ensure that the company is following Sarbanes-Oxley requirements.

### The Advisor

This type of PMO is generally made up of one to three people, and often includes consultants. They are responsible for creating an overall methodology for project management and standardized templates for project use.

There are normally several project managers within the organization, and they do not report to the PMO. Instead, they still report to their respective departments, but will have a dotted-line relationship to the PMO. The PMO will approve project plans, ensure that the methodology is followed, and will be a small part of the management team.

## The Partner

Organizations that have embraced the PMO and see it as a true strategic partner for growth are reaping the benefits of the investment. What many organizations are realizing is that a PMO is much more than creating a methodology or governing project documentation. If used properly, a PMO can help the organization grow and meet their strategic targets. How? When used properly, the PMO should be a major factor in project selection so that projects selected can align to the strategic plan for the organization. This means that projects can be selected by their overall contribution to the company versus whichever division has the most political power.

## Responsibilities of the PMO

Depending on which role is selected for the PMO, the responsibilities differ. The general responsibilities of a PMO are:

- **Methodology Creation:** The PMO can help create the company methodology. The intent is to create successful and repeatable processes.
- **Provide Project Management:** Some PMO structures will house the project managers as a separate department. In these cases, the PMO would supply the project management function to the business units.
- **Resource Planning:** Advanced PMOs can function as a resource manager, forecasting the demand for resources, planning for needs, and maximizing the productivity of project resources.
- **Centralized Reporting:** One of the key functions of PMOs is to provide organization-level reporting. They can provide the complete view of all project activity and summarize cost and progress reporting for the entire company.

- **Knowledge Center:** Some PMOs will act as an advisor and will maintain a knowledge center for project documentation. This includes maintaining historical information on past projects and creating a repository of information for use by the company. The information could be a summarization of the most common risks or issues the company faces or an analysis of the accuracy of project estimates.
- **Project Selection:** The most mature and advanced PMOs are generally involved in creating criteria and methods for project selection. This is designed to help a company pick the right projects and ensure that the project efforts are aligned with the company's objectives. This entails many of the above items, like resource planning and knowledge center, to occur.

This is just a small sample of the responsibilities of a PMO. Most PMOs are undertaken because of a specific need or issue that the company faced. Whatever the cause, be sure to create a charter to clearly define the responsibilities of the PMO.

## Standards for Project Managers

If you gather fifteen project managers in a room and ask for project documentation, you will receive fifteen different ways to do everything. Some project managers combine risk and issue logs. Some have a log for each. Some take meeting minutes that document every word spoken in the meeting. Some take meeting notes that are a documentation of key discussions and decisions. Some track their projects in a project-planning tool. Some track them in a spreadsheet tool. You get the picture.

The number of different ways that you can do the same thing is amazing. This is true of reporting as well. There are many theories about showing task progress. Some believe that you enter a percentage complete by asking the resource what percent they think they have finished. Some use the 20 percent/80 percent rule that says a task is automatically 20 percent complete when a task starts and the other 80 percent is shown when the task is complete. Some use the same logic but call it the 80 percent/20 percent rule. Some, quite frankly, have no method at all. So is it any wonder that sometimes a PMO is needed?

One of the most important functions of a PMO is to help standardize project progress. It is not to state which method is right or wrong; it is to make sure that each project manager is using the same method to report project progress. This will normalize the data across the enterprise and allow for more accuracy and less ambiguity.

## The Collective Group

Another large benefit of a PMO is bringing project managers together to share experiences. Great project managers have a series of past project failures, experiences, and near failures that they draw from. Many risk assessments are simply a collection of past failures to stimulate your thinking process on new projects. Think about your personal life wisdom. You are talking with a friend or colleague and they say that they have just booked a trip to Italy and will see Venice and Rome, and you just came back from the very same trip. Generally, the first thing you do is offer advice and warnings:

- "There is a little restaurant right next to the Pantheon. You can people watch and they have an amazing lunch!"
- "Watch out for crooked taxi drivers; we had one take us two miles without using his meter. He charged us 20 euros!"
- "Once you have seen all of the sites, take a guided tour of all of them at night—it is truly beautiful!"

The advice that you offer your friend is based on actual experiences. You did enjoy the restaurant and the night tour. You did get taken for a real ride in that taxi. These are past successes and failures in your adventure.

Don't be afraid to ask other project managers, both internal and external, for assistance. You may find some time and project-saving tips.

A PMO creates the same atmosphere for project managers. Even if there is no official PMO within your company or organization, a Community of Practice is a great way to share experiences and assist each other in being successful.

One thing to watch out for in the collective group is losing the individuality of each project manager. This becomes the greatest struggle for PMOs: How do you create a standardized environment that still allows project managers the freedom to manage in their own style? A difficult question to answer, but an important one.

## Give Me a "P," Give Me an "M," Give Me an "O!"

The final task of any PMO is to sell, advertise, promote, and encourage project management within the company—they must be the cheerleaders. So much about project management has changed in the last few years, and the PMO must be the champions of why they exist.

This sounds like a self-serving model, and it is. Many companies have to progress through levels of project maturity. There is significant research that shows the growth, profitability, and success of organizations that make investments in their project management processes. However, the move between levels of maturity takes time, effort, and executive-level support to achieve. If you have never played basketball before, it is unlikely that you can start playing for the NBA tomorrow. It takes time, practice, and growth, both physically and mentally, to reach that status. For many, no matter how hard they try, will never play in the NBA. The same is true for PMOs: Some may never reach the top. Some will never reach their potential. To ensure the best chance for success, be out there leading the cheers: "Give me a 'P,' give me an 'M,' give me an 'O!' What's that spell?"

## CHAPTER 15

# Project Management Software

There is an amazing amount of software packages to support your project management efforts. The software ranges from small packages that manage task lists to large-scale enterprise applications. To select the right one, there are many factors to consider. This chapter is designed to assist in your decision making by helping you understand different features and giving some examples of the available packages.

# *Using Software to Facilitate Your Project*

Consider the following questions when determining whether you need project management software:

- How many people are involved in the project?
- About how many tasks are involved?
- To whom are you responsible? (Is the only one involved yourself or does this project affect the entire company?)
- Are tasks being done simultaneously or one at a time?

The key is to know your strengths, and how well you can initiate, organize, schedule, monitor, and complete the project effectively. If a simple to-do list will work, use your word processing program and type it out. If two-dozen people simultaneously handling sixty-five different tasks are involved, it might be easier to invest in a project software package. Keep in mind that many projects were completed well before software packages ever existed. However, there's nothing wrong with making life easier, is there?

Don't make the common mistake of depending too heavily on your software programs. They are there to help you facilitate the process, but they cannot do the project management job for you. Every project needs human input.

Software programs are designed to help, but you are still in the driver's seat, especially when it comes to weighing various options and making decisions. You, not your software, are responsible for maintaining integrity. For example, the software will not tell you that someone has entered brochure copy that they've plagiarized from another brochure. Likewise, your software won't tell you why a key team member missed the morning meeting or that a shipment from a vendor is delayed because someone neglected to order it on time.

Let's look at what you want from a good project-management software package. You want the software to:

- Be user friendly so you don't need to spend an excessive amount of time figuring out the program or entering data. If repeated data entry is slowing you down, then the program may not be beneficial.
- Store, sort, and retrieve all key information on the project
- Assist you in tracking, monitoring, and updating the success of the project
- Provide tips, pointers, warnings, analysis, and other best- or worst-case scenarios based on the data you have input
- Help you by producing charts, graphs, reports, and other project documentation

## Software Shopping

For more complex and larger-scope projects, you may want a program that assists you in all key project areas. Integrated project-management software programs can help you set up your budget, fill in your task list, include all task details, set up schedules, create Gantt Charts and network diagrams (see Chapter 11), and monitor all aspects of the project. From hours put in by team members to expenditures and reaching key milestones, the monitoring process should cover various project areas. In the end, the program can print out a table, graph, chart, report, or whatever project information you need.

For smaller projects, you can use a basic spreadsheet program, a word processing program, or a presentation program. Basic, cross-functional programs can handle the elements of a simple project, and are easier to familiarize yourself with than the more elaborate integrated systems. Of course, if you use several different individual software programs to handle various tasks, you won't have the added feature of integrating them. You'll be re-entering data several times, and that will slow you down.

### Keep It Simple

Don't make a project more complicated than it is by setting up an elaborate software program. Personal projects, home improvements, school projects, neighborhood projects, and smaller-scale business projects generally won't require you to use specialized project management programs. Check out what tools you have available to you on your computer before investing in additional software.

**FACT**

One of the most significant aspects of software programs is that they handle numerous details. On larger, complex programs, this is beneficial from an organizational perspective. The programs allow you to clear your mind of extraneous information. Lower your stress level—let the software program manage the wealth of details so that you can handle the people problems and make the big decisions.

When deciding what software will best suit your needs, consider your own level of comfort and expertise on the computer. Some people can sit down with a complicated program and figure it out in an hour. For such people, the finest software systems are worth their abundance of capabilities. For others, the more intimidating the program, the more reasons there seem to be not to use it. Every year, millions of hours are wasted by team members and project managers staring at computer screens trying to figure out what went wrong. Don't let this happen to you.

Besides data storage and implementation, what do you need from a software program or programs? Use this checklist to help you determine your requirements:

- ❏ Scheduling
- ❏ Task-management listings, skills matrix, and personnel lists
- ❏ Gantt charts and other graphs and diagrams
- ❏ Budgeting capabilities
- ❏ Accounting
- ❏ Calendar
- ❏ Word processing
- ❏ Problem-management solutions
- ❏ Project tracking and monitoring
- ❏ Resource tracking

❏ Tracking multiple projects
❏ Multiple-user capabilities
❏ "What if" risk-management assistance
❏ Communications system (for working with team members on and off site)
❏ Creating reports and presentations
❏ Compatibility with other programs

### Be an Educated Consumer

It's also advantageous to get a thirty-day, money-back guarantee, in case the program isn't delivering what you anticipated or the functions are not user friendly. Allow for a reasonable learning curve, but be realistic. If the package is overwhelming and it isn't making your life and the life of the project easier, then it's not for you.

Look around for various other features, and determine what you need given the scope of the project. Be sure you factor in your computer skills and comfort level. Try to anticipate features you may need as the progress grows and changes. It's better to have an extra feature or two than to not have significant features you may need later on. After evaluating your needs, determine whether you are going to use an integrated project-management program or separate organizational tools. Keep in mind that if you need more than two individual programs, the integrated system may be best. Consider the scope and the costs involved in your project, and remember that the software package should not cost more than the project!

## Popular Favorites

The Internet has presented many more options for project management software than were available in the past. However, ever since Microsoft Project, Primavera, and Open Workbench were released they have been favorites. Many project managers started with the first version of the product (Microsoft Project was first released in 1990), and having learned the program, upgraded to newer versions. The following are brief descriptions of some of the favorites in project-management software titles.

## Microsoft Project

The most popular project software program comes from Microsoft. Designed for the individual user (the project manager), Project 2003 and 2007 let you easily create and categorize a database of information for your entire project. You'll be able to customize the network diagram to fit your project and make adjustments as you go. The software not only provides an overview of all facets of the project and helps you monitor them, it is also designed to help you think through scenarios using what-if situations. Essentially, the software is designed to provide great flexibility while helping you from the start of your project through each of your deliverables. For more details, go to *www.microsoft.com*.

## Open Workbench

From Niku, which was purchased by CA, Open Workbench boasts many of the same features as Microsoft Project. The largest differentiator is the price. Open Workbench is free. It is a very graphics-based application that allows you to manage all aspects of a project. To download a free copy, go to *www.openworkbench.org*.

Make sure the software package that you are interested in is compatible with your existing computer setup. System requirements are usually clearly spelled out on the software package. If you're not sure, ask before you purchase anything.

## SureTrak Project Manager 3.0

From Primavera Systems, SureTrak features a user-friendly KickStart tool that helps you simplify the often intimidating and worrisome initial planning and project-starting phase. Built-in tutorials help guide users through the process of creating project schedules and monitoring the project. PERT and Gantt charts are easy to customize and allow you to clearly examine the relationships between various tasks. You'll find specialized calendars, numerous customizable reports, up-to-the-moment budget-tracking capabilities, team member to-do lists, float calendars, critical path scheduling, baseline comparisons, and an easy manner in which to distribute assignments or reports. An extremely comprehensive program, SureTrak provides tremendous flexibility and assists you from the planning phase through organizing and tracking the project to its completion. SureTrak has proven to be highly effective for beginners as well as advanced project managers. To find out more, go to *www.primavera.com*.

## Other Software Products

The following sections examine several other software packages you might consider for your project.

### AMS REAL TIME

A suite of software products from AMS includes several cross-platform compatible programs designed to let you manage your project more efficiently. REAL TIME Projects includes cost management and critical path method analysis; REAL TIME Resources lets you organize and track all resources; REAL TIME Solo allows for interaction with team members; and REAL TIME Server serves up an overview of the project. For details, go to *www.amsusa.com*.

### Artemis Views, 7000, and Knowledge Plan

Artemis offers three powerful software products. Views handles project planning, cost control, tracking, and analysis; Artemis 7000 provides a sophisticated, customized cost-control system; and Knowledge Plan is a well-stocked resource base to assist with cost estimation. To learn more, go to *www.artemispm.com*.

**FACT**

Often, companies already have software packages or individual programs that they use. If the company already has sufficient project management software to do the job, you probably don't need to buy something new.

## B-Liner Project Outliner

This project organizer from B-Liner provides a flexible, user-friendly system you can use to create your work breakdown structure, estimate costs and time, and set up your project schedule. Project analysis and technical development are included. For details, go to *www.bliner.com.*

## CommonOffice

An easy-to-learn, Web-based management and collaboration tool, CommonOffice helps you save money on IT administrative costs while performing numerous timesaving activities. Some of the possibilities include hiring talent from anywhere in the world, booking boardrooms, and finding rental-car deals for out-of-town stakeholders. The system makes it easy to track and generate reports and coordinate activities with off-site team members and other key players. For more information, go to *www.commonoffice.com.*

## iTeamWork.com

iTeamWork offers a simple system for creating projects and tasks and assigning tasks to team members. You can check out the overall status of the project or use the e-mail notification system to communicate with team members about various tasks as they proceed through the project. For details, go to *www.iteamwork.com.*

## Journyx Timesheet 4.0

A Web-based time-tracking component, Timesheet works with any operating system and browser. Wireless capabilities let you create time records and track time from anywhere. You can also track billing and payroll, or keep tabs on other aspects of your project. Timesheet 4.0 can be customized to integrate and import information to and from other software programs. For more information, go to *www.journyx.com.*

## Micro Planner

Micro Planner offers X-Pert and Manager to support different-sized projects. The programs interface with one another to support all levels of an organization. X-Pert is used by high-level executives and can handle up to 10,000 operations (tasks, milestones, etc.) while reporting on both progress and cost performance of many projects. Manager is an easy-to-use, multifaceted program with up to 1,500 operations and five subprojects per file. Data entry on Gantt charts, spreadsheets, work breakdown structures, and reports are all included. To find out more, go to *www.microplanning.com.*

## onProject.com

The onProject Web-based interactive system is designed to help managers work with their team and allocate resources while bringing team members together from any location. For one low price, you can bring as many as twenty team members together. For details, go to *www.onproject.com.*

**FACT**

Many software packages offer what-if scenarios to help guide you through a variety of events that may take place. The software can provide alternative methods, find resource conflicts, and display the project at any point along the critical path from any of several desired angles.

## OPX2 from Planisware

A Web-based system, OPX2 offers a suite of products for enterprise-wide project management. OPX2 Pro, TimeCard, Server, and Intranet Server will allow you to customize your project planning and reporting based on templates and business rules. Continually refine the process and optimize your production as you work with these fully integrated tools. For more information, go to *www.planisware.com.*

## Plan & Progress Tracker from 4aBetterBusiness, Inc.

A Microsoft Excel–based program, available for one to ten users, P&P provides planning and actual Gantt charts. The software lets you track all the important elements of your project and provides percentage completion data and a visual warning system. For details, go to *www.4abetterbusiness.com.*

## Project KickStart3 from Experienceware

Eight steps in easy-planning icons allow you to quickly start planning your project. Task lists; a library of goals, phases, and obstacles; unlimited report capabilities; sample projects; easy-to-maneuver Gantt charts; and free tech support are features of this comprehensive PM program. To find out more, go to *www.experienceware.com*.

## QuickGantt from Tools-for-Business.com

An easy-to-use software program, QuickGantt includes a pop-up calendar, intuitive worksheet, and, of course, the popular Gantt charts with multiple features and capabilities. QuickGantt allows you to compare actual project data to the original plans, make numerous revisions, and print customized time- and cost-variance reports. For details, go to *www.tools-for-business.com*.

## Task Manager 2000 from Orbisoft

From single- to 100-user versions, this easy-to-use program is designed to help organize any project. Task lists, budgets, instant snapshot overviews of work in progress, user-friendly graphic-interface custom reports, and direct e-mailing features are all included in this highly rated program. For more information, go to *www.orbisoft.com*.

## TeamPlay from Primavera.com

An extensive project, process, and resource management program, TeamPlay was designed as an IT software package to handle numerous projects of varying scopes. A centralized system maintains all project background and data, and can be used with other information systems. For more, go to *www.primavera.com*.

## Time Control 3 from HMS Software

A widely used, state-of-the-art time-management tool, Time Control 3 links with other popular time-management programs and works as a project timekeeping system. Numerous features include a hierarchical data system, preprepared timesheets, and customization of the user interface. For details, go to *www.hmssoftware.ca.*

## Time Tiger from Indigo Technologies, Ltd.

Designed to replace timesheets, Time Tiger easily tracks all time-recording activities. For Workgroups 1.6 and 2.0, the program also includes invoicing and tools for current project analysis, and can support workgroups of up to 150 users. For details, go to *www.indigo1.com.*

## Which One Is Right for You?

Software packages range from $40 or $50 for a simple one-task program to upwards of $60,000 for the top-of-the-line multiuser programs (for high-level project management). Generally speaking, for $350 to $500, you can own a solid software package to handle the majority of your projects.

Look for clear information about all the features of the program and make sure it comes with whatever documentation you will need to learn how to use it. Also, check for a customer service phone number and see if it is a toll-free number. Save all packaging until you are sure everything works. Then save key information.

The capabilities of these and other programs are quite impressive. Customized Gantt charts, histograms, network diagrams, reports, and detailed tracking systems are among the commonly found features. You'll need to look more closely for other features that you feel will help you as the project manager. The goal is to let the program manage the paperwork, provide a clear picture of the overall project at all times, use calculations and formulas to guide you, and provide early warning signs when necessary. In the end, you'll want to combine modern technology with your own ingenuity, decision-making ability, management style, and people skills.

Discuss your potential selections with others who may have purchased similar software. Often, a recommendation is the best way to determine which program is the best. Decide whether there are potential future uses for the software, particularly if you are buying something for a home or personal project. A program with flexibility will be beneficial to you when you embark on your next project.

## High-End Users

While this book is designed primarily for people who manage an occasional project at work, home, or in the community, there are products designed for high-end users. Project management pros often handle numerous projects at once for a major corporation. Software for intensive use needs to meet advanced demands, allocate resources, and track progress on a number of projects simultaneously. As one might expect, this level of software can run thousands of dollars. Cobra, Primavera Project Planner, Clarity, and Micro Planner X-Pert are a few of these high-end software packages.

These packages require a more expert use and understanding. They are designed to help assist and manage the uncertain. For example, think of the Mars Rover project. The project was created to launch a vehicle into space, land it on Mars, send vital information back to Earth, and allow scientists to determine what the vehicle does and where it goes. This is an extremely complex project, with several uncertainties, conflicts, and deadlines that must be managed. Can you imagine trying to keep up with who is supposed to do what and when in a spreadsheet? They require intricate plans that assist in creating risk and cost plans, as well as predicting the likelihood of finishing a project on a specific date or for a specific cost. High-end project managers will use more sophisticated tools as needs warrant.

## Enterprise Project Management Systems

As project management software grew in popularity, so did the overall use. A new problem then arose: How can we see a rollup of all of the projects in the enterprise? The next step was to create a repository of all of the individual projects into an enterprise view. Although many companies offer solutions for this issue, such as IBM and Mercury, there are three market leaders.

- **Clarity by CA:** Clarity is one of the most configurable tools on the market. It provides an easy-to-use configure interface that allows companies to utilize the tool in several ways. It is sold in modules and on the low end can provide project or resource management, and on the high end completely integrate into your financial back-end and ERP systems such as PeopleSoft or SAP. It is completely Web based and can allow you to continue to use Microsoft Project or Open Workbench, as well as use unique "Schedule in Browser" capability. It is the author's opinion that this is the most robust and functional tool on the market. However, it is also one of the more expensive products.
- **Project Server by Microsoft:** Project Server extends the many capabilities of Sharepoint and Microsoft Project. It utilizes a collaboration approach to project management. It has many features of an enterprise system, but still lacks some of the complete integration that many of the other products have. You must have the professional version of Microsoft Project to use this tool. It is a far less expensive option if compared to Clarity.
- **Primavera:** Primavera seems to have had tremendous success in the construction and engineering world. Primavera is a mature product that handles many of the integration and collaborative options that most EPM tools use.

Choosing a tool is extremely important; however, there are many factors. Do not simply purchase a tool because it has the most features or is the most expensive. Determine what you plan to get out of the tool. If you feel your company can close $1,000,000 worth of more business due to better project planning, then a powerful enterprise system is worth the investment. If it will only help a company garner $10,000 of savings, then a lower-end system will suffice. The most crucial point to understand is that no matter what tool you select, it will not solve poor process. If solid processes and good core project practices are followed, then automating them with a tool will dramatically increase business results. Automating poor processes will just be a waste of money. Software does not solve issues; it facilitates great process.

## CHAPTER 16

# Risk Management

The next two chapters look beyond scheduling, budgeting, and progress of the project to what can go wrong. You will read about two very different concerns that can befall any project: risk and conflict. There is much written about risk and how it is assessed and controlled throughout the course of a project. While risk is inherent in any project from the onset, conflict is not. In this chapter, learn how you can manage risks to your project.

## *The Nature of Risk*

To begin looking at risk, you need a workable definition. From a broad-based perspective, risk is the exposure to uncertain, and potentially bad, consequences. In the scope of project management, risks are uncertainties that may negatively affect the project by challenging the project's constraints or parameters. Unforeseen consequences may result in loss of time, money, labor, or the project as a whole. This differs from the financial-planning definition, in which greater risk is seen as potentially promising, with higher potential rewards. The financial planner looks at the risk/reward scenario, whereas the project management considers the completed project without negative risks to be its own reward. Positive outcomes of risk are generally not addressed in project management's definition. One of the reasons for the continuous addition of the positive aspect of risk taking is that it is from taking a calculated risk that new discoveries and new methods of dealing with issues are founded. After all, if Christopher Columbus hadn't defied those who said the earth was flat and that the idea of sailing to discover the Indies was not feasible, he never would have discovered America.

People seeking excitement will often take greater risks. Hang gliding and other extreme sports are very much based on the excitement that accompanies great risk. Projects also take risks that result in positive outcomes, as there are risks inherent in any decision that you make. If you knew you could never be wrong, you would no longer be taking a risk. Even the simplest decision to order software package A over package B has some degree of risk involved. Package A might not work for your particular project. Of course, the other side of the equation is that if you take a chance on a package that you are not sure of, it could prove to be more beneficial than you had hoped and solve other problems for which you had not initially purchased it. Again, I remind you this is a different definition of risk than that usually associated with project management.

Any project is inherently a risk, because you are trying to accomplish a goal without the certainty that you will reach it. One might conclude (fairly) that project management is essentially a form of risk management, in that from the initial plan you are uncertain of the end result. Furthermore, the initial plan contains variables such as time and cost that cannot be set in stone. Despite all the calculations, analysis, and research that you have done to create your initial project plan, the project will proceed without you, or anyone else, knowing exactly what course it will ultimately take.

**FACT**

If projects didn't allow for some degree of risk, great discoveries and inventions would never have been made. The Wright Brothers and Charles Lindbergh took great risks to achieve their projected goals. Risk should be managed with precautions, but it should not stop you from proceeding with your project, unless you determine that the risk is too great or without reward.

Despite the common definition of project risk management—to seek out and avert potentially negative factors that will prevent the project from being completed on time and under budget—risk is actually inherent in many forms throughout the project, and is both positive and negative. For our purposes of understanding project risk management, consider risk a negative factor throughout the chapter. However, this chapter will point out some positive aspects of risk taking from time to time.

## Types of Project Risks

Risks associated with the project itself are termed internal project risks or technical risks. Risks associated with the impact of the project on the rest of the world are termed external risks, and may often include safety risks. Generally, the project focus, at least in the corporate world, is on internal risk, or trying to prevent uncertainties from threatening the life or the direction of the project.

Obviously, the degree of risk, internal or external, will determine the attention such a risk merits. If a new Web site isn't launched on time, the world won't end. However, if a project goes awry that has an effect on the health or safety of individuals or the environment, such as an oil spill, there is greater concern because the effects of that risk are greater.

A project manager must look beyond the internal risks of time and budget on a project with a potentially significant impact in order to see the global picture. A project that might result in the next Three Mile Island disaster takes on a more significant risk than what's involved to bring your office project in under budget.

## Assessing Risks

Assessing both internal and external risks means thinking through the probability of project success or failure and the subsequent results of any or all tasks involved in the project. How likely is it that task A will set you behind schedule? Will the need to add more resources to complete that task put you over budget? How likely is it that task A will be hazardous to the company or the neighborhood?

Risk mitigation is a factor that needs to be included in your budget. Look at all possible repercussions before you make a move. If you find that you have too many areas in the project that call for advance action (or mitigation), you may want to rethink the feasibility of the project.

During the initial planning stage of the project, you are assessing risk each time you assign a completion date or a budget figure. If, for example, you plan to move the office but aren't sure whether to select June or July for the move, you will assess the possibilities of moving in either month and choose the one in which you have the greater likelihood of a successful, cost-efficient, and time-efficient move. From an internal or technical perspective, you need to determine in which month you will have the resources and the budget to complete the project successfully. From an external or safety perspective, you will determine in which month the move will be least likely to interfere with the overall workings of the company and its ability to conduct business. Assessing the risk as you plan your project will add up to this overall determination. Granted, most tasks on most projects have little external risk, but it's well worth keeping such risks in mind.

You may also face a quality risk. The project may be proceeding on schedule and within budgetary constraints, but the product may be inferior to what you were originally seeking. It may not be as easy to determine such risks to the quality of the final deliverables as it is to see what might set you behind schedule or cost more than your budget allows. Inexperienced personnel, poor equipment, dated software products, poor internal communications, and similar factors raise the level of risk that you may not produce the quality that you had hoped for.

For example, a popular freelance writers' Web site has writers bid against one another for writing assignments. The site does not set minimum bids, and ultimately some inexperienced young writer will end up winning a job that should pay $1,000 for a professional writer, because he or she is willing to do it for $100 to get his or her foot in the door. The company accepting an amateur for a job that should have a professional is taking a tremendous quality risk. Often, they find themselves hiring a writer for $1,200 to do a rush-job rewrite because the original work was substandard. Of course, the flip side is that the young new writer could have fresh ideas and this could be his or her big break. The big question: Are you willing to take a risk this big with your project's quality?

## Dealing with Risks

Now that you know what the risks are, what can you do about them? First, you analyze each risk associated with the project. Take all the internal risks, anything that could stand in the way of successfully completing the project (on time and under budget), and prioritize them. Which risks need the most attention because they could shut down the project completely? Consider these your top priorities—risks that, if not addressed, will spell disaster. Next, look at risks that can be monitored closely and managed with some adjustments. Finally, look at low-level risks that can easily be fixed, eliminated, or ignored with no impact on the overall project.

You will then need to respond in one of three manners, as discussed in the following sections.

### Contingency Planning

Have plan B, your backup or contingency plan, in place just in case. Contingency planning is an important safeguard. It can range from a less favored, but perhaps more cost-effective, manner of handling a situation to a backup parachute, which can save the life of the project. The more critical a task or resource is to the outcome of the project, the more you need a backup plan.

If you are prepared with viable contingency plans, you will have already minimized the level of risk. In fact, you may even be able to take greater positive risks. One project manager, knowing that for a yearlong project he had a backup plan that would still keep the project under budget, got management's permission and moved some surplus funding into a CD account. Thus, the funding actually grew during the duration of the project. This was a calculated risk, since he was earning money that had not been earmarked for a specific task or resource. If anything had gone wrong, he might have needed this surplus funding, but his plan B scenario did not utilize the extra funds.

Establish a backup plan for your team members should they become ill or leave the project. Even the President of the United States has a backup, in the form of the Vice President. Cross training your team will enable a current team member to fill in temporarily and keep the project moving.

No one is saying that you need to take such risks. Risk management does not necessarily mean that you have to make proactive decisions in favor of the project. Just be aware that being closed to innovative ideas may limit your opportunity for growth.

Of course, there are also contingency plans that are not simply another way of reaching your project's goal, but are a way of saving anything from a project to a life. Plans that you hope you'll never need must be in place for the safety of individuals first, and the project second. These types of plans aren't usually specific to the typical business or personal project, however. Often, such emergency procedures are already in place, in the form of smoke detectors or alarm systems. Unless you are working with chemicals or dangerous materials, such emergency situations are usually outside of the project scope. The larger safety plan of the environment in which you are working (i.e., the office building, school, community center, etc.) already has procedures for dealing with emergencies.

## Risk Mitigation

When you act in advance—spend the time and money to implement methods of reducing or eliminating the risk ahead of time—you're mitigating risk. This approach requires you to make a judgment call based on the probability that a risk will interfere with the success of the project. Much of the feasibility study, used when you started the project, touches upon risk management or potential risk management. You don't want to start a project that isn't cost effective, nor do you want to start one that is too high risk, unless you have ways of managing that risk.

Sometimes, a degree of risk mitigation is built into the plans by outside forces—such as registering your project with a particular governmental body or taking safety precautions as mandated by government or policy makers. Risk mitigation that comes under your jurisdiction is similar, only you have to make the decisions. How prevalent is the risk? What would happen in the worst-case scenario? Loss of money? Loss of time? Loss of manpower? Before starting out on the project, perhaps you need to settle a labor dispute to avoid a slowdown or work stoppage. You might have to scale down an aspect of the project to mitigate a high-level risk. You will then need to address this mitigation to see the potential effect on various other aspects of the project, as well as on the project overall. Make sure that:

- Other tasks are not adversely affected by mitigating a risk in one area
- The project is still cost effective
- The project will still produce the same quality results

If a potential risk is discovered after the project has already begun, you can still mitigate that risk. Once again, you will have to look at other areas of the project.

## Risk Monitoring

To monitor risks effectively, you must have an adequate system of tracking the probability of a risk occurring, based on reevaluating that probability at various times throughout the project. A long-lasting or complex project will obviously require more monitoring. If there is a delay in starting the project, this will also mean you will need to monitor the project more closely once it gets started. Often, project managers are forced to put a project on hold. They then start it later than expected, changing the due dates, but do not take into account all the added risks that may exist because of the change in starting date. From personnel no longer being able to meet the necessary time commitment to changes in policy or government regulations, risks have to be reevaluated every time a project is delayed.

Monitoring also means knowing when you can accept a level of variance from your original plan. Remember, you should anticipate variance from the start, since very little, if anything, in your original plan is set in stone. Costs, labor hours, and numerous other factors will probably not be the same as what you anticipated in your original plan. As you monitor the project, ask yourself what level of variance is acceptable and what variance between the intended and the actual numbers shows high risk for potential problems. You'll need to make this determination carefully and then act or not. If, for instance, you are looking at the date by which deliverables are due, you need to determine whether or not you can afford a delay from the standpoint of time and money. If you cannot afford such a delay, you may need to pay more money to get the deliverables in your hands on time. Monitoring will keep you abreast of this situation so you can best prepare. A poorly monitored project is in danger of undetected risks that may present you with many unwelcome surprises. (See Chapter 13 for much more on monitoring.)

If you worried about every risk in life, you would probably never leave the house, and certainly not start a project. Risk is inherent in everything. Every time you take on a project, you risk failure. Therefore, it is important not to dwell on risk to the point of being immobilized.

If you had a dollar for every time someone managing a project said, "I don't even want to think about that," you'd be richer than Bill Gates. Most people don't want to face potentially negative risks. This is true in many aspects of life. We've all sidestepped a problem by pretending it wasn't there, but failure to address an issue regarding your project won't make it go away. You must be realistic about potential problems. Of course, on the other hand, if you focus on every little risk, you'll never start the project. You must be ready to take some risks to begin the project. The bottom line is that you need to address all risks and weigh them—not ignore them—then decide what actions you'll take next.

# Prioritizing Risks

You can label them in any manner you like, but it is important to prioritize potential risks. The following shows one way of prioritizing:

- **Four-alarm risks** (****) are those with a high probability of having a major impact on the project.
- **Three-alarm risks** (***) have a lower degree of probability, but still pack a wallop and can have a major impact on the project.
- **Two-alarm risks** (**) are high in probability, but are manageable or controllable with the right degree of attention.
- **One-alarm risks** (*) are low in probability and will not prove harmful, perhaps just a minor nuisance.

Each project is unique, so no boilerplate program can tell you in which category to put each risk. Time and money will factor heavily into the issue, as will the nature of the project itself. Even the same risk in two scenarios can be quite different in scope. For example, a computer problem on a computer-based project is a four-alarm problem. Greater precaution needs to be taken to guard against the system going down, and a full backup plan needs to be in place. The same crash of a computer that is storing information for a small dress shop's upcoming sale is a one-alarm problem because the information can be recreated and the sale can commence regardless of whether the computer is repaired. Perhaps a hard copy of the discount structure would be a simple safeguard against the risk of being incapacitated.

As a project manager, you'll act quickly when you see a three- or four-alarm risk, monitor a two-alarm one, and hopefully handle a one-alarm risk quickly or delegate it to someone else.

**ALERT!**

Backing up all computer programs, files, and data is an easy and essential manner of risk mitigation that can save you hours of time, effort, and money in the event of a power failure or computer mishap. Make it a practice to back up your work regularly.

Knowing how and where you could get your hands on another copy of a software program, or having one installed in a laptop that is not plugged into the same electrical line as your computer system, is a simple way to mitigate some technical problems. People rely too heavily on "the system" when, too often, the system is not up and functioning. Be able to work around it effectively.

## Monitoring Every Step of the Way

While not all risks are substantial enough to require constant monitoring, some level of risk monitoring is necessary throughout the project. The trick is to look ahead as you proceed through the project and see what you can find in advance. Twenty-twenty hindsight would only be valuable if you had a way to go back in time.

If you find risks in your feasibility study and can address them even before starting the project, you will be that much farther ahead. If the risks are too great and the potential for disaster is greater than possible benefits, you won't bother starting—at least under the current circumstances. Only in the movies will you hear, "We may all be killed, but we've got to try it anyway."

### Look Outside

The next place to look for risks is within your resources. Can you hit warp speed without blowing everyone to smithereens? Will the software program accommodate such a big project? If the wood you choose is mahogany, will the kite ever get off the ground?

Look for risks inherent in your resources, including your personnel. Are the people performing the tasks skilled at those tasks? Has she ever flown a plane before? Will he be able to spot an iceberg if you are sailing directly toward one? Giving responsibility to the wrong party can be risky. All resources, including people, need to be accurately assessed in advance, and monitored once selected. Careful monitoring of your resources is very important. A loose cannon on your team can spell disaster just as surely as faulty equipment.

One way to assess risk is to study what went wrong in previous projects that were similar to yours. If you can determine why such errors occurred, you may be able to prevent them from reoccurring in your project.

You need to monitor externally as well as internally. Knowing the exact speed at which the ship is traveling at any given time still does not mean you are monitoring for icebergs. Monitor for all significant details. Usually, this focuses around time, money, and quality in your project.

## Monitor the Variables

Once the project proceeds, new risks can occur with every unknown cause-and-effect relationship. Many projects fail because the project team is not aware of the factors that lead to risks. When the risks become apparent, they are either not detected in time or they are not clearly identified and properly communicated to management or to those that can help avoid or eliminate the risk. Other projects fail because risks were actually detected and communicated but the party on the receiving end did not fully understand the nature of the risk. If one party communicates a four-alarm risk and management perceives a two-alarm risk, it will not be properly resolved.

Risks can also be detected too far into the process to make adjustments. An error in phase two of programming may not be detected until phase five, at which point the project is doomed because it is too late to turn back due to time and cost limitations. You must detect, assess, and monitor risk during every phase of the project, and testing needs to be implemented, especially for technical projects or new product development.

## Risk Hunting

It's easy to say that you must look for risks that jeopardize your project's well-being, but where exactly do you look? The risk is generally associated with the boundaries set forth by the project. If, for example, money were no object, you would never be at risk of going over budget. If the project deadline were open ended, you could never fall behind schedule.

Sometimes, assessing a risk factor and making a decision on how to handle it is a marvelous learning experience. As long as no one's safety is jeopardized, you may let some risks go so your team can learn from trial and error. Newcomers may also benefit from exposure to risks, as long as neither they nor the project are in danger. Step back and see if he or she can find, and deal with, the potential risk that lies ahead.

The parameters that surround the project determine the need to monitor for specific internal risks. You have to assess what can make a project go over budget or fall behind schedule. Do you have proper funding? Are all expenses going through a set accounting system? How carefully have you researched and confirmed all costs, estimates, or quotes?

**The biggest problems in budget management generally stem from:**
- Improper estimates of costs for resources (including manpower)
- Unmonitored or uncontrolled spending
- Not properly estimating the time or scope of the project and needing more money to cover additional time and labor
- Not allocating proper funding for monitoring and testing

**Scheduling risks generally stem from:**

- Poorly estimating the duration of tasks and the overall project
- Not accounting properly for dependency tasks to be completed before other tasks can begin
- Not allowing proper time in your schedule for monitoring and testing

Other key internal risks include having the wrong person doing the task, poor communication between yourself and your team as well as among team members, and the always-prevalent technical glitches and failures.

Numerous other internal factors can present risk, which is why you should plan detail by detail and task by task, then monitor constantly. You must keep your hand on the wheel as you guide a project along its course.

## Making an Educated Guess

External factors can be harder to gauge. The world serves up its own parameters, including the state of the economy, laws, and other external constraints. Depending on the project, you may need to keep tabs on the financial market, industry-specific news, buying trends, competition, legal issues, politics (office or government), and even the weather. External risk factors fall into two categories: those you can foresee and those you can't.

Naturally, you can take precautions against the former, but not the latter. In some cases, however, you can buy insurance to protect larger-scale projects from unforeseen risks.

Evaluating potential external risks will have you following the same logic investors use when they read up on trends, overseas economic conditions, and other factors that could affect their investment. You need to evaluate how external factors could impinge upon your project and take precautionary steps. Often, public relations is used as a risk-management tool against possible negative publicity that could deter customers or clients. When the overall state of Web-based companies began to struggle from a glut of companies jumping on the Internet bandwagon, project managers working on Web sites saw the need to act quickly in order to not lose their funding. Those few that were able to catch this impending risk early broadened their horizons and planned to expand into brick-and-mortar businesses so they were no longer solely dependent upon e-commerce.

What if you know there are risks lurking in your project, but you haven't yet identified what they are? You could call in an expert or even someone who has managed a similar project. You could also call in a consultant to find risks. Be forewarned, however, that there are many so-called consultants out there. Before hiring a consultant:

- Make sure you do not take a consultant at face value. Find out where they have consulted previously.
- Make sure they understand exactly what you need from them. Good communication is essential.
- Make sure the consultant is not using the old trick of telling you what he thinks you want to hear or spreading rhetoric around. If his guidance isn't supported by solid, documented research and findings, be skeptical.

**FACT**

People use many methods of risk avoidance daily—every time you buckle your seat belt in a car or wear a helmet while riding a motorcycle. Whatever the risk of an unplanned event, you take precautions. Other examples of risk-management planning that you are familiar with include fire/emergency exits, rain dates for a scheduled event, sun block, antivirus computer software, and safety goggles.

## Use Your Team

You need not fly solo when risk hunting. Team members, through meetings, questionnaires, and reports, can identify concerns and potential risks to the project that you may not have otherwise been aware of. Brainstorming can provide a marvelous forum for revealing flaws in the underlying plan or risks in the developing project. Effective brainstorming means allowing everyone present to have a chance to chime in. It also requires that you take good notes. After the brainstorming session, you should follow through on all ideas and see if they lead to a risk in the making. The flip side of this is that team members may identify a better course of action or cost-effective method that may be reason to take a calculated positive risk.

# *Worth Your While*

Assessing and managing risk have benefits other than saving the project from impending doom. By monitoring and seeking potential pitfalls—or for that matter, areas of potential strength—you're encouraging forward thinking. Assessing risk and determining how you will get around it, work through it, tackle it, or succumb to it are all processes that encourage communication and analysis. Tasks are not simply being performed; team members are encouraged to look at the big picture. Strategies are emerging. Team members who look for risks as they proceed are thinking beyond their isolated roles. They are also looking at the potential impact of their work and the overall project. Evaluation and decision making become part of the ongoing process and are therefore honed skills.

If the project centers on a product or service for the consumer, a positive step in gaining consumer confidence is to make the process of risk management known. Don't you feel more confident knowing a product was carefully pretested? In any project, there is a higher level of confidence in the final product if you know that a lot of the what-if questions were asked and answered during the development and production process.

Risk management also drives the development of a hands-on approach. A project manager cannot sit back and assume all is well. It necessitates monitoring and facilitates sound decision making based on tracked and recorded results. The need for team-member accountability and accurate reporting of time and money status are elevated. People are responsible for the information they provide regarding their work.

The fewer surprises that occur in a project, the more in control you will stay and the less variance you should have from your original critical path. This can be summed up in the equation: greater degree of risk management = fewer surprises = less need for crisis management.

From a financial perspective, risk management is a sound business practice. You pay little for using logic, analysis, brainstorming, and forward thinking to detect risks. You can pay much more if high-risk situations that could have been avoided suddenly occur late in the project. The majority of negative project risks can be avoided if they are detected soon enough. The more people appreciate and utilize risk-management techniques, the less likely it is that risks will slip through the cracks.

A discussion of the negative impact of risks would be incomplete without noting your stress level as project manager. If you are aware of potential risks as you proceed, you will have alternative strategies. You will have open lines of communication with your team members, who will be following your lead and also thinking ahead. Knowing all of this should reduce your stress level significantly. Having a sense of control and a firm grasp on where the project is at any given time will allow you to feel more comfortable.

## Risk Interactions and Magnification

Have you ever been in a situation where one step in the process goes wrong, and that one disconnect leads to another and then to another, like a domino effect? A late deliverable at stage one of a project leads to a late deliverable at stage two. That leads to a delay in the meeting at stage three, which leads to delayed funding, and so on.

**ALERT!**

The project manager needs to research the capabilities of a technical team closely before hiring it. Be sure the team has done a project of this magnitude before.

Let's look at an example. One of the many dot-coms that did not survive the downsizing of the industry in early 2001 was a real estate Web site that hired content writers, a sales staff, and a technical team. The technical team, however, miscalculated how long it would take to set up the site. The project of building the site fell way behind schedule, causing the content writers to have to rewrite much of their material so that it would be timely, thus adding to the expense of the project. The sales team, meanwhile, had made cobranding deals that had to be delayed because the technical team was not finished with its end of the project. This cost the company a great deal of money, as several of the cobranding deals fell through, which, in turn, cost the company more money and hurt its reputation—no one wanted to make a deal with the uncertainty surrounding the launch of the site. By the time the technical team finally completed their work on the site, the sales team had departed for greener pastures and the project had virtually run out of money to pay the content writers.

The project's phases should have been layered so the content and advertising sales teams did not start their tasks until the technical team was much closer to completion. That simple precaution—waiting to make sure the project was progressing as planned before becoming overcommitted—would have saved the company not only money, but their reputation. The technical aspect of the project should have been monitored more closely and tests should have been run to see what this site could and could not handle. With awareness and knowledge, a more realistic assessment could have been made to determine when this phase of the project would be nearing completion and what needed to be reprogrammed.

## Limit Your Exposure

The bottom line is that risks in one area can affect other areas. Schedule accordingly, and then monitor closely and take necessary precautions from the earliest stages.

A risk can also become more significant as the project increases. When writing a ten-chapter book, not having an antivirus software program running during the writing of Chapter 1 is risky. You could lose an entire chapter, or 10 percent of your book. Writing four more chapters without installing the antivirus software or backing up your work means that 40 percent of the project is now in jeopardy. The longer you work without a safeguard in place, the more you risk losing should something jeopardize the project.

Limit the degree of risk you may face by negotiating various escape clauses in contracts. If the other party does not meet its contractual obligations, you can get out of the contract without any repercussions. In other words, you are sharing the risk rather than taking on all of it yourself.

Here's another example. Let's say you are handling the money at a four-hour book drive (which raises a similar amount of funds every hour) and someone is scheduled to take the collected money to the bank every hour. The risk of that money being lost or stolen is only 25 percent, because that is the amount of money on hand at any given time. If, however, no one picks up the money for two hours, you may have 50 percent of the day's profits in the till, meaning there is more potential loss at stake. Risk increases as you fail to either monitor or take action.

## Sample Risk Analysis

Even the simplest of plans has its tripwires. Ask and answer as many what-ifs as possible before you begin, and remember that anything can disrupt your progress.

| PROJECT DETAILS | |
| --- | --- |
| Location | A small business with twenty employees, occupying an old building. |
| Project | You have an area in your office space with plumbing and a sink that is now used for storage. The facility has windows and ventilation, but very few electrical outlets. You would like to transform the space into a lunchroom facility for your employees. Your employees are willing to help. |
| Goal | Set up a lunchroom where employees can eat. |

Below is a section of your risk management plan.

| RISKS THAT YOU NEED TO CONSIDER | |
| --- | --- |
| **What You Need to Asses** | **Risk Factors** |
| Can the facility be used as a lunchroom | The electrical wiring and outlets won't support a refrigerator, microwave, etc. |
| Amount of time needed by team to complete the job | Taking people away from doing other work. |
| Resource costs | Cost factor will be excessive. High costs for electrician, contractor, etc. if needed. |
| What equipment and other items need to be purchased? | Lack of research |
| Personal safety | Injury to anyone moving or lifting equipment. |

**Priority risks:**
1. Electrical wiring
2. Personal safety
3. Cost factor
4. Researching and pricing materials
5. Number of items to purchase
6. Time factor

**Your preliminary plan of action:**
1. Draw up a rough diagram of the new lunchroom facility. Consider how much space you have and how many people it will service. Determine that it is indeed feasible. (Your feasibility study may require you calling in an electrician to make sure the wiring will support a lunchroom facility. If it would take major rewiring, you might rethink whether or not this plan is feasible.)
2. Put together a team of people who will help you transform the space into a lunchroom, and to discuss what you will need to purchase.
3. Determine who can best do each job and assign tasks.
4. Research the items that will need to be purchased. Have team meetings to discuss what to buy. Use brainstorming and then get a consensus as to what is needed.
5. Research the cost of any outside resources necessary, such as a carpenter, movers, etc. (This will be in conjunction with a need for expertise and to avoid personal injuries to team members.)
6. Draw up a budget.
7. Estimate a time frame for completing the lunchroom.
8. Meet with everyone again to determine what does and does not fit within the budget so you are sure you can afford to embark on this project.
9. Create/post your task breakdown.
10. Set up a preliminary schedule. Review with team before finalizing it.
11. Monitor your progress as you and your team create the new lunchroom space.
12. Look for risks to completing the project that may occur along the way.

Remember, the goal of this project is to transform an unused storage space into a comfortable lunch facility. Your team will determine exactly what needs to be purchased and help make the transformation. This will include clearing out the space, cleaning and painting the area, and purchasing all the necessary items. You may note that the time frame is a low priority on this project since the facility has not had a lunchroom before and there is no one saying it must be ready by a specific date. Therefore, while you are picking a date you'd like to open up the lunchroom, it is not vital that it be completed in $x$ amount of days, making the time aspect of the project less of a headache.

**ALERT!**

Monitor for conflict during projects where people may vary in their opinion of what is and is not necessary. Put people in charge of making certain decisions and have everyone agree to abide by that decision. The person responsible can elect to solicit outside opinions—or not—but ultimately, the decision is his.

And in the end—after much hard work, some conflict, and a few changes to the original plan and budget—a new lunchroom facility is born and the team can take pride in a job well done.

## Common Project Problems

Risks are generally thought of as those things that can go wrong. What about all those common things that are simply defined as project problems? Besides the risk of falling behind schedule, going off budget, or simply producing poor-quality results, here are some common project problems:

- **Too many chefs spoil the project.** One person wants it done by Wednesday, one says make it Tuesday; another wants you to use Microsoft Project, while another hates that program. It's important to establish from the start who is in a position of authority and who is not—and figure out where you come in. If you have to answer to nine people, you'll have a project going in nine directions and none of them will be toward the goal.

- **Dust it off and try again.** Little do you know, but the project you have embarked on has already failed three times, for numerous reasons. Make sure you scout around and do a feasibility study—find out if this project can indeed be done, or if you are in a situation with too little funding, poor resources, and no clear-cut plan of action. If that's the case, run like hell. Old disasters under new names with new leaders do not work unless a key component has been changed.

- **Bad timing.** How many people saw ads for new start-up Internet companies at the time when so many were falling by the wayside? How many people wanted to jump onboard those projects? Many projects fail because there is no market for them at a given time. Check economic factors, industry factors, competition, and other signs that may determine whether or not your project is a good idea at this time.

- **Oops, there goes another one!** Too many people dropping off the team means the incentives are not keeping them on board, they do not have a vested interest in the team, or they have no enthusiasm for the project. Losing a member or two along the way is not uncommon and shouldn't be a major problem, unless it's that one expert you really need. However, if you are losing people left and right, it's time to up the payoff, boost morale, or find out why so many are jumping ship.

- **We'll start tomorrow.** Some projects are constantly delayed. Something is always slowing them down, whether it's funding, permits, inspections, lack of resources, or simply low priority due to other, more demanding projects. This is not generally a good sign. Try to get a firm start date. The longer you delay, the less likely the project will succeed.

- **Nobody speaks to one another.** Sure, there are plenty of documents, reports, and even e-mails, but poor or no communication between people is generally not a good sign. As far as things have progressed technologically, when projects that rely on people have no communication, they generally lose both enthusiasm and the element of creative thinking and planning that comes from such interaction among team members.

- **What a chummy group!** The opposite of no communication is a chummy, enthusiastic team that spends way too much time chatting, lunching, and socializing, but little time working. While camaraderie is great, you'll need to channel such enthusiasm into some productivity. Be tactful and make the work enjoyable, but coax people to get the job done.
- **What are we doing here again?** If there have been so many changes to the project in terms of resources, planning, and primary objectives that you're no longer sure what the goal of the project is, you're in big trouble. After all, how will you know when you've reached the goal if you don't know what it is? Make sure all of the changes fit in with your primary plan and your initial project goal. Don't let changes occur faster than you can comfortably process them into the plan, or things can go spiraling out of control.
- **Naked Thursdays!** If the boss has odd requests, make sure to (tactfully) put them into perspective. You cannot do every offbeat scheme that upper management wants to try. Be very selective and always explain that your decision is based on what's in the best interests of the project.

You're likely nodding your head at this list of common problems. You have probably experienced the same things. It is impossible to plan for all of the potential risks on a project or prevent projects from going off track. However, with a list of common project problems, at least you know where to start the planning process.

## CHAPTER 17

# Communications Management

The Project Management Institute (PMI) states that 90 percent of a project manager's time is spent communicating. You should have seen throughout this book all the different types of communications that are going on. Another key aspect of great communication is to set proper expectations. Communications management is simply a guideline of how you intend to manage the communications on the project.

## *Who's on First?*

Imagine the early days of NASA. President Kennedy promises that the U.S. will land a man on the moon. Everyone looks at each other and says, "Now what do we do?" Communications management is a complex and integral part of project management. A movie that came out in 1998 titled *Armageddon* had a scene where a group of astronauts were about to launch into space. As they were being strapped in, one character said, "Do you know we're sitting on four million pounds of fuel, one nuclear weapon, and a thing that has 270,000 moving parts all built by the lowest bidder? Makes you feel good, doesn't it?"

Think of the amount of communication it took to create a machine like a space shuttle. From inception to fruition, the space-shuttle program contained thousands and thousands of smaller projects. The communication of what was needed when, where things were, and the ongoing status of the project was an enormous undertaking.

Imagine this: You are an off-site project manager and you receive a call from a client stating that one of your contractors just showed up for work, and they did not know that they were coming. You panic, because you scheduled the contractor but failed to communicate that to your client. What is the impact?

- Your client has to either scramble or send the contractor away.
- Your contractor loses a day, maybe two, due to the mistake.
- The relationship between you, your client, and your contractor can become strained.

You could have avoided the issue by simply notifying your client that the contractor was coming.

**ALERT!**

Just because you have sent an e-mail to somebody doesn't mean that you have communicated. For proper communication, there needs to be an acknowledgment back that the intended party received your message.

With the advent of communication technology, communication is supposed to be easier. In many cases, it is. However, there is still the human element that must be involved. Technology may give reach and range to your communications, but it can also create more places to hide.

## Communication Paths

A communication path is an interesting concept that has a simple formula. If you have two people on a project team, you have one communication path. However, if you add one other person to the team, your communication paths grow exponentially. The formula used for communication paths is $(N \times (N-1)) / 2$. This formula identifies the number of communication paths on your project. "N" stands for the number of project participants that will need to be communicated with. Therefore, if you have five people on your team, the formula is $(5 \times (4)) / 2$. For five people, there are ten communication paths; for six people, there are fifteen.

It makes you think about how many paths you have to communicate on to be successful in letting everyone know vital project information. This also means that your grapevine and potential "broken paths" grow exponentially as well. The downfall of many project managers in communication paths is twofold:

1. Failure to understand communication paths
2. Assumption that one communication method will fit all

When there are three people on a project team, it is pretty easy to manage communications. When there are fifty people and ten subteams, it becomes quite difficult. To account for this difficulty, your communications need to be clear, concise, and have their own plan.

## I Have to Plan My Communications Too?

Yes Virginia, you have to plan your communications, too. Well you don't have to, but if you don't, your communications will be managing you. Communication planning can be a complex process.

Ask yourself the following questions:

- Is my whole team physically at one site or multiple sites?
- Does everyone have access to e-mail and have the same version of office products?
- Is everyone in the same time zone?
- Does everyone have to be at every meeting?
- Should there be one big communication meeting or a series of smaller, more concise ones?

These questions are just the tip of the iceberg. We haven't even started talking about document formats.

In communications studies, there are generally two roles: sender and receiver. Each of these roles has 50 percent of the responsibility in the communication process. The sender must send a message in a clear manner and the receiver must receive and understand the message. If the received didn't understand the message, they must let the sender know. Likewise, the sender is responsible for ensuring the receiver at least received the message. The key then becomes whether or not the receiver understands the message. Did the sender send the right kind of message? Would the receiver like the message in a different way? These are all questions that should be asked and answered during the communications planning process.

## Types of Communication Documents

There are several types of communication documents. A description of the document, the purpose, and the frequency of communication should be detailed in a communications plan. During a project kickoff meeting, bring an example of each one of the communication documents so that team members can become familiar with them.

The following tables detail some common project documents. Not all of these documents are required. Many projects may only use one or two. This is a great reason why a project manager should bring examples of these documents to a kickoff meeting to decide what each member would like to see. If nobody signs up to see a specific document, then why take additional time to create it? Unless of course, in your judgment, you need to.

## STATUS UPDATES

| | |
|---|---|
| Audience | Sponsors, stakeholders, project team |
| Frequency | Weekly or bi-weekly |
| Timing | Same time each week (typically on Friday). |
| Method | E-mail, informal document, or formal template |
| Purpose: | Communicate weekly progress of project. |
| Description | The status update is a weekly communication for overall project status. It is intended to inform the team of any progress made on the project. It can be a formal document or an informal bulleted list. It does not have to communicate the five main ideas as required of the status report (discussed in the next section). This is just an informal update of what has occurred on the project. |

## STATUS REPORTS

| | |
|---|---|
| Audience | Sponsors, stakeholders, project team |
| Frequency | Weekly |
| Timing | Same time each week (typically on Friday). |
| Purpose | Communicate weekly progress of project. |
| Method | Status report template or formal document |
| Description | The status report is a snapshot of the project's progress for the prior week. It communicates the issues, risks, deliverables, completed items, and upcoming project tasks. It is intended to show weekly progress as well as serve as a vehicle to bring the core issues of the project to the forefront. |

## MEETING NOTES

| | |
|---|---|
| Audience | Absent team members, project team |
| Frequency | As needed |
| Timing | As soon as possible after the meeting. |
| Purpose | Documentation of what occurred in the meeting. |
| Method | Formal document (status or one-off meetings), or on status report (one-off meetings) |
| Description | Meeting notes are intended to be a snapshot of what occurred in the meeting. They convey what decisions were made and document the discussions that took place. The main audience for this document is the team members that were unable to attend the meeting. Additionally, a historical record is created for reference. Utilizing the PM's best judgment, if it is a highly political or involved meeting, formal notes should be recorded. If it is a one-off meeting, the key points and decisions can either appear in a formal document or in the Notes section of the status report. |

## MEETING AGENDAS

| | |
|---|---|
| Audience | Project Team |
| Frequency | As needed |
| Timing | 1–2 days prior to meeting. |
| Purpose | Prepare team members for which topics will be discussed in the meeting. |
| Description | Agendas are intended to establish the meeting flow and ensure that all items pertinent to the project are discussed. The agenda should give the attendees ample notice of the expected update items and allow them to prepare their responses. |

## ISSUES, RISKS, AND DELIVERABLES LOG

| | |
|---|---|
| Audience | Entire project team |
| Frequency | Weekly |
| Timing | As soon as possible after the weekly status meeting. |
| Purpose | Communicate action items and issues. |
| Description | Issues, risks, and deliverables logs can serve multiple purposes. It is an itemized list of items that require the attention of the project manager. It can help prioritize tasks and help communicate to the team the impact of the items. Logs are not a required communication, but are the most effective at quickly updating status received in weekly status meetings and communicating to the team what needs to be done. |

## PROJECT PLAN

| | |
|---|---|
| Audience | Project team |
| Frequency | Weekly |
| Timing | Normally sent at the time the status report is sent. |
| Purpose | Show current time frames and tasks. |
| Description | Some team members and sponsors like to see the project plan. It is good practice to make it available to the team upon request or based on the communication plan. |

## TO-DO LISTS

| | |
|---|---|
| Audience | Project team |
| Frequency | Weekly |
| Timing | Normally sent at the time the status report is sent. |
| Purpose | Itemized list specifically for each resource. |
| Description | It is good practice to send out the to-do lists to the project team members. It is an effective way to communicate what each resource will need to complete for the project. Many project team members dislike the project plan because it can be difficult to understand and the information is not concise. |

## BUDGET

| | |
|---|---|
| Audience | Project sponsor |
| Frequency | Weekly/monthly |
| Timing | As needed. |
| Purpose | Communicate the financial status of the project. |
| Description | Depending on the project, the project manager may need to keep the financial records of the project. |

# Formal, Informal, Written, Verbal, and Everything Else

There are several categories of information. They can be as formal as a signed scope of work or as informal as a hallway conversation. They can be written in an e-mail or occur on the phone. All types of communications are necessary. The decision becomes what type of method to use.

For instance, if a contractor is about to breach their delivery of services contract on your project, a formal written notice of a breach warning may be necessary. If a team member is running behind on a task, an informal pep talk may be in order. Use the following as a guideline.

## Formal Versus Informal

Formal communication is required if it represents material value to the project. If it is a discussion or agreement on scope, cost, or resources, a formal communication is necessary. If it is of nonmaterial value, then informal communication is acceptable. Asking for a quick update on a task during the middle of the week can be an informal communication. Asking for the official status during a status meeting can be a formal communication.

## Written Versus Verbal

For project managers that have had projects go wrong, there always seems to be that one communication or decision that you wish you had documented. Deciding what should be written and what can stay verbal is a touchy road. You do not want to overdocument so that your written documentation loses effectiveness. However, you do not want to underdocument either. The same keys that applied to formal versus informal apply to written versus verbal. If it effects time, cost, or scope, then it should be written. If it is just a quick update or a status conversation, then it can stay verbal.

It may not always be easy to decide between the exactness of formal writing and the ambiguity of an informal verbal. Knowing the differences and making decisions up front should assist in navigating the communication paths.

## Communications Matrix

A communications matrix can be a tool to facilitate your communications plan or it can be your entire communications plan. The matrix is a simple concept that lists the resource names on one side of a spreadsheet and the communication documents on the other. Then, you mark which resource agreed to which communication. Here is an example:

| COMMUNICATIONS MATRIX | | | | |
| --- | --- | --- | --- | --- |
| **Name** | **Status Report** | **Issue Log** | **Project Plan** | **Budget** |
| Mark | | | X | |
| Cindy | X | X | X | |
| John | X | | | X |
| Carol | X | X | X | X |

Placing this into your overall project plan can clearly state your communication intentions on the project. It can also cut down on unnecessary communications to team members.

## Ensuring Communication

Once you have planned your communications, created the matrix, and have started the project, you have to do what you said you were going to do: You must ensure project communications. They are vital to the success of a project.

A phenomenon on projects is that communications will be created in the absence of official communications. The exponential communication paths grow and grow and the more there are the more complex the network becomes. If you as the project manager are not sending official communications, then the grapevine communications become the official ones. In fact, people tend to communicate more when there is a lack of project communications.

If you ever played the grapevine game as a child, you understand the phenomenon. In the movie *Johnny Dangerously,* the main character in the movie is in jail. Someone wants to send him a message through the jail grapevine. The message starts as, "Vermin is going to kill Johnny's brother at the Savoy Theater. Pass it on." The message gets sent through the grapevine until the final exchange:

**PRISONER:** There's a message through the grapevine, Johnny.
**JOHNNY DANGEROUSLY:** Yeah? What is it?
**PRISONER:** Johnny and the Mothers are playing "Stompin" at the Savoy in Vermont tonight.
**JOHNNY DANGEROUSLY:** Vermin's going to kill my brother at the Savoy Theater tonight!
**PRISONER:** I didn't say that.
**JOHNNY DANGEROUSLY:** No, but I know this grapevine!

Don't let the grapevine run your project. Communicate properly, timely, and efficiently.

## Communicating on All Levels

The last part of communications management is to make sure that your communications are at the right level. You don't necessarily want to send detailed time tests of an application to the CFO of the organization. You also may not want to send detailed cost reports to the project team. For project managers, you must communicate to all levels. This could mean a direct conversation with the CEO of a company, or you can be pushed to the eighteen-year-old mailroom clerk. Whatever the case may be, you must make sure that your message is being sent and received.

One of the greatest things about being a project manager in the company is that you do get exposure and visibility to all levels of an organization. One of the worst things about being a project manager is that you do get exposure and visibility to all levels of an organization. In all seriousness, the project managers that know how to communicate properly and effectively have a shot at moving up the corporate ladder quickly. Those that do not may find that they are reporting to that eighteen-year-old mailroom clerk.

## CHAPTER 18

# Conflict Resolution and Handling Various Personalities

This chapter deals with conflict resolution, which, like risk management, is a method of problem solving within the scope of the overall project. Conflict may be considered by some theorists to be inherent in the course of human interaction. In essence, conflict is a type of risk, because, left unresolved, it could jeopardize the future of your project. Unfortunately, it is not a risk you can usually mitigate in advance since you do not usually know where such conflict will arise. However, if you're putting together a team, you can make an effort to include people who you know generally get along with one another.

## *Cooperative Resolution*

The idea of cooperative conflict behavior suggests that parties work together to resolve their conflict. This, however, assumes that both parties are willing to enter into a cooperative agreement. Getting two sides to sit down and cooperate is easier said than done. In any group situation there is also the potential for competitive conflicts, which perpetuate and lead to greater problems.

As a project manager, you will have to address the need for cooperation while understanding that there may be a degree of competition involved at the root of a conflict. Often, conflict is also the result of attitudes, or a belief system embodied within the individual long before the project was ever initiated. Such prejudgments are often at the root of an impending conflict. There may also be self-doubt and lack of confidence in one's own abilities. Interacting with others who may be more confident or highly skilled can intensify these insecurities.

**QUESTION?**

**What causes conflict?**
Conflict is often the result of uncertainty or miscommunication. Frequently, someone has simply neglected to include all of the details in their communications to another team member, or procedures or even intent was misunderstood.

To nip potential conflicts in the bud, a project manager needs to look for signs that team members:

- Are lacking in self-confidence or displaying uncertainty about tasks or procedures
- Are unsure of what their functions are, which is often the result of miscommunication
- Are predisposed to disregard authority, or have a prejudicial attitude toward others
- Are consumed by a competitive nature (although sometimes a healthy competition can be positive for a project)
- Are motivated by their personal agendas at the expense of the project

## *Identifying Key Characters*

Certain characteristics distinguish different types of individuals. You will likely discover some of these common types on your team:

- **Tigers** intimidate others by holding a degree of power over them. Often insecure about their own role, tigers will use any leverage they can, from a bully threatening to beat up a classmate to a manager who threatens to fire anyone who dares question his or her authority. Watch who you put in positions of authority, and make sure they have the necessary people skills.
- **Prima donnas** display inflated egos and a misguided sense of self-importance. These types can be condescending toward others and are often working with a personal agenda. Your best resource is to let them enjoy a false sense of importance as long as it does not impinge on the project.
- **Passive-aggressive types** operate in a quiet manner, yet communicate calculated or manipulated messages through judgmental comments, body language, well-placed guilt, playing the martyr, or displaying an attitude that often seems aloof or unconcerned. The more aggressive and obvious version of the passive-aggressive is the brown-noser, who is always trying to appease the right person to score points and satisfy his or her own need for importance. Passively try to maintain control with the passive-aggressive and stay a few steps ahead of the brown-noser.
- **People-pleasers** will do whatever is necessary for praise and a much-needed ego boost. They simply have a more basic need for approval than the brown-noser, who has an agenda. Let the people-pleaser know you are pleased with his or her efforts.

And finally, you'll encounter the legitimate team player, who is, at least as far as you're concerned, comfortable with himself or herself and content within the parameters of the project and the people with whom he or she is working. Yes, you'll have team members who will simply come to the project to work hard and interact socially (or not). If you're lucky, this will be the majority of your team—or at least they will appear as such throughout the duration of the project. After all, your primary concern is how they interact with you and the project team. A bully on the ball field or a manipulator at home is not your concern in the project environment.

## Assessing the Conflict Situation

Now you know the characters, so what do you do when conflict rears its ugly head? First, you will need to assess the nature of the conflict and who the featured players are. A conflict can manifest itself at various levels:

- Is it a conflict between two individuals on the project team?
- Is it a conflict between two groups of individuals?
- Is it a conflict between one individual and the rest of the team?
- Is it a conflict between one individual and management, sponsors, stakeholders, or you?
- Is it a conflict of a moral or ethical nature, between one or more team members and their beliefs?
- Is there a conflict between your team and an outside source?

Conflict is not always two team members not getting along. Several variations on the theme of conflict can arise within a project. There are also levels of disagreement, ranging from petty arguments to threats, legal action, or violence.

**ALERT!**

Gathering the necessary facts is essential to successfully resolving a conflict. One side of the story, and sometimes both sides, will not provide the entire picture if the conflict is based on an occurrence or series of activities. Make sure you find out all the details before taking action.

You, therefore, need to assess who the conflict is between and its level of severity. You also need to assess where this conflict fits in the scheme of the project. Does it stem from something internal? Is the argument over the process that the project is following, or is the dispute about politics, parking spaces, or another issue that is external to the actual project but causing friction or tension that is affecting the success of the project?

Conflicts frequently arise during the initiation phase of the project based on scheduling, task assignments, work distribution, and clarity of the tasks to be performed. Often, people disagree about how long a task should take, or because they are being given more of the workload than someone else. As the project progresses, the team generally settles into a comfortable rhythm and adapts to each of the varying personalities, but at the beginning, team members can be resentful if they feel they are carrying more of the weight. This occurs most frequently in volunteer projects when there is nothing personal at stake. In these cases, the best you can do is remind the individual of the value of his own work and diminish the concern about what others are or aren't doing.

Before returning to how to deal with the various configurations of conflicts mentioned earlier, let's look at several ways to successfully manage them.

# Methods of Conflict Resolution

Mediation is an attempt to find a peaceful settlement to resolve a dispute between individuals. The process uses a neutral party to mediate. As a project manager, that often becomes your job.

## Mediation

The underlying principle of mediation lies in the genuine willingness of all disputing parties to participate. As project manager, if the dispute is between team members and does not involve you, then you can act as intermediary (unless there is a clearly defined perception that you are aligned with one of the parties in the dispute). Depending on the nature of the dispute, mediation can present a short-term cure by bringing the project-related arguments from both sides to the forefront and trying to find a middle ground or compromise settlement.

If, however, the conflict stems from underlying, nonproject-related issues, ranging from personal feelings to previous conflicts, the idea of finding a compromise and creating a true win-win situation is less likely. The best you can hope for is to find a temporary short-term solution through which everyone can work. If you are in the position of mediator, you need to hear both sides' arguments. Hopefully, you can find a middle ground that allows each side to walk away satisfied with the outcome. If the situation is a clear-cut, win-lose argument, such as whether to use program A or B, you need to make a clear decision and explain that it is based solely on the factors involved and not the individuals.

**QUESTION?**

**What is mediation?**
Mediation is a method of resolving conflict in which a neutral third party intervenes to try to settle a dispute between two parties.

## *Conflict Transformation*

A more complicated process called conflict transformation uses mediation, but focuses on the attitudes and perceptions of the parties and looks to alter these perceptions. On small-scale or short-term projects, the time frame won't allow this level of resolution to make radical changes in personalities. Long-term, large-scale projects with significant impact on a widespread population may require loftier resolution techniques in which the parties are encouraged to look beyond the project to their feelings and attitudes. Conflict transformation is concerned primarily with changing the attitudes and perceptions the parties have about one another. In the long term, this can be very beneficial, as changed attitudes can result in less conflict moving forward. Television programs designed to teach youngsters how to properly accept and understand other people use the same techniques. Moralistic in nature, they work with adults too, but success is often harder to achieve since attitudes are more firmly embedded within adults.

To achieve such transformation, you may need the help of outside professionals to get to the root of the conflict. Compromise is a key factor in conflict resolution. Once again, as in any mediation, both parties need to be amenable. Parties will need to sit down and negotiate a settlement that is satisfactory to both sides. In a situation that doesn't present a clear-cut decision, a compromise is often the result of mediation.

## Compromise

When both sides have something tangible to bring to the table, compromise can be the fastest and easiest way to resolve difference. For example, if the dispute is over which person will do a specific task the tangible factor is the task, and it can be divided so that both parties will do various aspects of the task. A simple dispute over where to hold a retirement party could end with a third choice that has some of the best aspects of the two previous choices.

If various elements are involved, each party can gain something important to them while conceding something that isn't. Perhaps one individual wants up-tempo music with dancing for the company holiday party while another wants a more reserved, quiet, no-dancing atmosphere. The compromise could be a quiet dinner and a more up-tempo, dance-oriented atmosphere after the meal.

Even disputes between management and team members can offer an opportunity to compromise, show good faith on both sides, and bring different views together. Sometimes scheduling is at the root of the dispute, and the schedule simply needs to be tweaked to meet the needs of both sides. When negotiating a compromise settlement, it is important to have a priority list from each side in advance to know which issues are more important and which can be sacrificed. Then it's a matter of trading off issues.

Compromise, however, won't work if someone is just plain angry that he or she is doing more work than someone else or not being included in the decision-making process. Personal grudges and disenchantment lead to conflict of a less logical method that can't always be solved using tradable tangibles.

## Shift Perspectives

Putting things into perspective is a most interesting method of conflict resolution. If, for example, Fred is furious that Maryanne is not pulling her weight on the project, you need to put the situation into perspective for that individual. You can talk to Maryanne and evaluate why she does not appear to be working as hard as Fred. If she is slacking off or just not trying, then Fred may have alerted you to a potential problem. However, maybe Maryanne is working just as hard as Fred; he may simply not be aware of what she is accomplishing, or perhaps she is slower than he is at producing results. Either way, you need to remind Fred that he is a fast worker and not everyone can maintain his pace. Put into perspective that people work at different speeds, and that as long as they are trying to fulfill their roles as best they can, that's all one can and should expect.

Before approaching Maryanne, you need to assess whether Fred has a valid claim. Maryanne may be doing an excellent job, but because they dated socially and it did not work out, Fred may have approached you for the wrong reasons. This goes back to conflict transformation, in which you need to address the root of the conflict between individuals, which is not always what it appears. The fact that he has ill feelings toward her and needs to address and work through them is an underlying issue—perhaps they were simply not suitable on a social level. Putting that into perspective and moving forward will help change Fred's attitude toward Maryanne's work habits and end potential conflict. For your purposes, you need to find a manner in which they can work together and show each other respect.

Put things into perspective for team members who may be arguing or complaining over issues that, in the grand scheme of things, are unimportant. Try, in a polite manner, to put these issues into proper perspective with the individual or individuals involved. Often, people don't realize when conditions are actually pretty good.

Three other approaches to conflict resolution include a consensus approach, smoothing, and the dictatorial approach. A consensus approach means taking the issue to the people. If the conflict is between two groups with opposing viewpoints, you might—with their consent—bring the issue to a vote. Call a meeting and decide this issue once and for all. Exclude yourself from the voting. Try to find a time when everyone involved can attend the meeting and make sure that everyone understands that this is the final vote on this issue. Let both sides have the same amount of time to voice their issues before calling for the vote. Also, make sure everyone is eligible to vote. In organizations, unions, or associations, check the bylaws. On a project team, you may simply state up front that everyone involved in working on the project can vote. Make sure this is set up clearly before taking a vote.

In other settings, you may informally poll individuals and get a consensus of how they feel the situation should best be resolved. Once again, make it known in advance that you are going to ask all the team participants. You can even do your voting or polling with an anonymous survey. A consensus doesn't necessarily require an actual vote. Informally obtain the opinions of everyone involved and make a decision based on the data you've collected. Make sure everyone understands that your decision is not arbitrary, but is based on the information you've obtained.

Smoothing is essentially sticking with what you do agree on and glossing over or putting aside whatever causes conflict. "Let's table that discussion until the next meeting" is a means of smoothing over a situation for the time being. While this is actually buying time until the conflict situation comes up again, it may provide time to research acceptable solutions, find more money, or utilize better resources to help settle the conflict. If you're lucky, the conflict is not as heated when the issue comes up again, and in some cases the conflict has resolved itself. Smoothing is not an active way of dealing with problems and can only be used with less serious conflicts.

You should have a zero-tolerance policy toward any type of racist, sexist, or violent behavior. Make sure, however, that you are correct before acting or accusing anyone of any such behavior!

When the project is close to the finish line, or time is of the essence, you may be forced to take the dictatorial approach, which doesn't appease many, but keeps the project on course. If the team members have nothing to lose, they could defect; if they are on staff, receiving a salary or compensation, or hope to gain from their experience with the project, they may simply have to buckle down and follow your commands. If the project is seriously threatened and other manners of conflict resolution will take too much time, you may need to take control in this manner. Use this method only as a last resort.

To sum it up, follow these tips when trying to resolve a conflict:

- Carefully assess the nature and severity of the conflict. Do some research. Don't take things at face value.
- If you are not specifically approached to resolve the conflict, decide whether and when you should get involved.
- Make sure you know all the information before trying to mediate or reach any kind of agreement.
- Respect people's wishes about whether to make a conflict known to others.
- Know when a conflict is minor and will either go away or resolve itself without your intervention.
- If you are involved in the conflict and feel that you cannot be objective, or might be perceived as unable to do so, have an outside party mediate or try to solve the conflict.
- If the conflict requires an expert to solve the problem, such as a technical expert who may have the best solution to a dispute over which software to use, seek one out.
- Look for compromise settlements and make sure each side walks away winning something in the negotiations.
- Work to solve problems within the context or the scope of the project. If, for example, you are working with someone who is clearly displaying antisocial behavior, don't expect you will change such behavior developed over twenty-five years. Just find a way in which you and the team can work with this individual. If, however, it is a two-year project, you may need to deal with deeper-rooted problems.
- Take a dictatorial approach only when absolutely necessary because of time or budget constraints, or because the quality of the product or service is poor.
- Mediate, negotiate, and seek solutions that are the byproduct of collective ideas. Encourage positive alternatives to conflicts rather than rehashing and reiterating the conflict situation.
- Do follow-up monitoring to make sure a resolved conflict stays that way.
- Encourage people to use legal action only as a last resort.

- Use a consensus or yield to a higher authority if necessary. Make sure all parties understand that that ruling will be the end result of the conflict and that they can then move on.
- Always use tact, diplomacy, and take the high road.

## *Taking the Initiative*

Knowing how and when to jump in to try to resolve a conflict takes practice and experience. It is not an easy call. Sometimes you may elect to stand back and let team members learn the hard way. People will learn from their mistakes; however, you cannot generally afford to do this if the project will suffer.

Most often, it is up to you to recognize a conflict situation and monitor it closely. If it is brought to you by a team member, stakeholder, or dropped in your lap, you'll have no choice but to get involved. If you see conflict in the making, but it has not yet been brought to your attention, you have a few options. You can alter the schedule, task assignment, or other variables to ease the potential conflict without approaching either party directly.

If you have overheard hostile behavior between two parties or have gotten wind of it through your involvement in the project (or even casual walk throughs), you might simply switch assignments so that these team members will have little or no contact with one another. Anyone planning a party will do this if they are putting together a seating plan and so-and-so should not sit next to so-and-so.

The opposite approach is to bring combative parties together and force the issue, while closely monitoring the situation. Making two children who don't get along partners on the class project may bring out their common concerns, likes, and dislikes, and the conflict may simply disappear when they get to know each other. The same may occur with adults.

The manner in which you approach the conflict depends on numerous variables. When an entire team is unhappy with one person, you need to address its concerns. Talk to the members individually and see if they all have a similar assessment of the situation. A valuable team member with a not-so-valuable attitude might be a pain to work with, but still gets the job done. Therefore, you might try to set up a situation in which the antagonistic party does not interact as often or as closely with other team members.

Sometimes the team mentality becomes a mob mentality. A few people may have legitimate concerns, but others simply jumped onto the bandwagon and created a monster that doesn't really exist. People often direct their own tension and anger toward a scapegoat. A person may not be bothering anyone or causing any problems regarding the project, but the team perception is that the person is a problem.

**ALERT!**

Be wary of letting someone work off site just because the person is difficult to work with. Telecommuting appeals to a lot of workers who would love to forego the morning commute, and it might appear to others that you are rewarding antisocial behavior by letting this person work from home.

For example, in an office setting, Mary was working at a slower pace on a project. Janice, a team member, who never liked Mary personally, kept spreading the word that Mary was so slow that she was holding up production. When the project eventually fell behind based on numerous factors, of which Mary's role was of minimal consequence, the opinion of many team members was that Mary was the cause of the project falling behind. They made her feel like she was to blame, when in reality the perception stemmed from one person's bias and was not a fair assessment of the situation. A simple story, but it illustrates two key points:

1. Groups of any type very often seek out a scapegoat when there is any deviation from the plan.
2. Groups often make judgments based on hearsay. In this case, all anyone really knew was what Janice said about Mary's work.

Once again, people need to be presented with the overall picture, not just one little slice of the pie. In this case, the team members needed to understand that there were many factors that produced the delays in the project—it was not just the fault of one person. Internal conflicts on a project can be dealt with in a number of ways, depending upon the unique circumstances surrounding the project and the participants.

So how should you handle conflict?

- Do your best to handle conflicts early on.
- Take action that suits the particular project and situation.
- Don't act out of anger, panic, or any other emotion. Weigh the conflict and make a decision based on facts.
- When you make a decision, stick to it.
- Make sure you listen to both arguments and address the issues on both sides before making your decision.

## *Other Factors to Keep in Mind*

You will have to be respectful of the attitudes and beliefs of others when dealing with conflicts of an ethical or moral nature. For example, a magazine was putting out a special issue and members of the publication staff were being asked to work on the project. At the request of the publisher, however, the special issue was going to have a more erotic theme than the monthly magazine. A seasoned editor felt she could not work on this project because of the nature of the material. The project manager was obligated to carry out the publisher's wishes and could not compromise the content, but reassured her that leaving the project because of her personal views would have no repercussions on her status or position in the company. Ultimately, the editor did some work on another aspect of the project, but did not work on the rest of the material. Conflicts that arise because of beliefs, views, or personal values can only be resolved by respecting other people.

If external factors are involved, you may have to contact sources outside of the project to handle the conflict. This could be a conflict with a particular vendor, a government agency, or a competitor. In these cases, you represent the good of the project team and the project. You want to stand behind your team members as often as possible. Make sure, however, that you have all the facts in such a situation.

If your team member is clearly at fault or if he or she acted in a manner unbefitting the team and the company or organization, you also need to be able to take the high road and go ahead and apologize on behalf of the team. External conflicts brought about by others within the project team are your conflicts, too. It is important that everyone involved in the project represent himself or herself in a manner that best exemplifies the organization or group.

If the conflict is project or issue oriented, work from the perspective of the project and keep personality issues in perspective. If the conflict is people oriented, be careful to make no judgments and focus on what the individuals have in common. Start working from a people-oriented perspective, then refocus everyone back to the project.

Some good things can come from conflicts. Many new ideas come to the forefront because of an initial conflict. Sometimes, positive competition is the result of two parties not getting along initially. Conflicts can serve to present viewpoints that might not have been expressed otherwise, and such clearing of the air can serve as a catharsis of sorts. Finally, conflicts resolved by a project manager can serve to enhance the respect afforded to that manager.

## Handling Various Personalities

The beginning of this chapter identified some of the key personality types that are probably on your project team. Now you need to figure out how to handle them effectively. Being an effective project leader requires that you hone your people skills, which means being able to work comfortably with various types of personalities. Determine the degree of handholding, praise, or self-reliance each team member requires, and work with them accordingly. Many team members will work best if left alone to complete their tasks. Others will require constant affirmation or direction. In time, you'll learn which method produces the best results from the individuals. Be careful not to be misunderstood yourself. You don't want to appear to be favoring one individual over another.

As a leader, you may need to spend more time with a team member who simply requires closer attention because he or she has less confidence in his or her abilities. Someone else, who you believe works well on her own, may misread the attention you are giving to another team member and feel that you are showing favoritism. Just because someone works better without constant supervision doesn't mean there is no need to check in with this person as well. You may simply spend a few moments chatting, and mention that she works so well on her own that you don't want to crowd her. Remind her, however, that you're interested in her work and that you are as accessible to her as you are to the rest of the team.

The scope of the project, as well as the length and the setting, will determine how well you will need to get to know the personalities involved. Naturally, if you are working on a weeklong project by telecommunications with someone 3,000 miles away, you probably won't get to know his or her personality very well. On the other hand, if you are one of three individuals spending day and night in a cramped office space for three weeks, you will most likely become quite familiar with the others in your group. The nature of the project and amount of work involved will also factor into how well you will need to know the personalities involved. There will be instances when you will work on a project for three days and can read someone like a book. On the flip side, there are people you can work with on a month-long project who never reveal very much about themselves. As long as the work gets done and conflicts are minimal, it doesn't really matter how well your team members get to know each other. As a leader, you cannot push people to divulge more of themselves than they choose any more than you can tell people who wear their emotions on their sleeve to hold it all inside.

## *Other Characters*

You'll find those who are competitive, those who are quiet or reclusive, and even the occasional slacker. You will also come across people who can't take criticism and others who think they are always right. There will be whiners and complainers as well as gossips. Jokers and crowd pleasers will also be on your payroll. Keep in mind that the less your team has a personal stake in the project, the more you will have to be everyone's pal. After all, if Fred has nothing significant to gain by helping you move your furniture, there's no reason for Fred to stick around if he feels unwanted, uncomfortable, or unappreciated.

So how do you do it? How do you work with all these personality types? When working with competitive individuals, it's best to channel their competitive spirit into something that benefits the project. Can they sell the most widgets? Move the most office furniture? Write the most new programs? Let them compete, whether you or anyone else is actually competing with them. As long as the competition remains friendly and does not impact the project, let it be a motivating force.

If repeated warnings and attempts to increase someone's work are not improving his performance, you may have to let the person go. Keeping someone who isn't doing his share is detrimental to the team and the project. It may be better to lose one person than to risk resentment and lowered morale among other team members.

The quiet, secretive, reclusive team members often simply come and go without any fanfare; often they want it to be that way. You should make an effort to determine whether the individual is comfortable with this arrangement. If he or she is quiet because he is intimidated or uncomfortable, you may need to modify the situation so the person can feel more a part of the team. However, if someone is quiet or introverted by choice, let him be who he is.

Slackers need a proverbial kick in the butt. If someone will only do the minimum to get by, you'll have to make sure that the minimum is sufficient for the project's success. Someone who's not committed to moving the project forward should not be in a high-level role, and you may have to take corrective action to get the team member focused and the project back on track. Within reason, find out what motivates your team—what you can wave at the finish line that will get them off their slacker routine.

If you're dealing with someone who doesn't take criticism well, start off with praise and highlight all that they do well before pointing out anything that is wrong. Acknowledge that everyone makes mistakes, and emphasize the importance of learning and applying new skills in the future. Avoid blame in any victimless situation, and keep your feedback constructive and positive.

If you are trying to work with someone who feels he or she is always right, let him or her be right in all the insignificant areas. On those where the individual just happens to be wrong, let him discover the right answer by laying out pieces of the puzzle in a way that he can find the right answer. This way, while he may be wrong, he will still save face by thinking he discovered the error. You are not out to say, "I told you so." Instead, you should skillfully point your team in the right direction for the sake of the project.

Whiners and complainers require a patient ear and an occasional reality check in which you point out some of the positives of the situation. As mentioned earlier, often people don't realize that, comparatively speaking, conditions are not really so bad. Grin and bear some of the griping and complaining, but encourage anyone who is dissatisfied to make proposals or suggestions on how things could work better. In many cases, people complain because they don't believe they'll be heard any other way. Once you establish that you welcome contributions from all sources, use their negative energy to achieve positive results. If rabble-rousers are not willing to be constructive or positive, they will undermine the team, and you do need to intercede.

**FACT**

When going into negotiations, the more you have to give, the greater strength and bargaining power you have. If you have nothing to give, then obviously you can't expect much in return. Determine what the other side needs the most—that is your bargaining chip. Prioritize your own needs, and you're ready to negotiate.

Jokers can be listened to and may even be entertaining. If and when such clowning interferes with the flow of the team's work, or if they are insulting or offending others, you will have to gently but firmly explain that they need to tone it down.

A good project manager is a good people manager, which requires knowing and understanding all the players and what makes them tick. Obviously, on very large-scale projects with hundreds of team members, you won't get to know everyone involved. You will need to set up managers who are as skilled in managing people as they are the tasks you've delegated. Meet with your key managers to discuss ways of working with people. Make sure that they have the same understanding as you do.

As you assess the personalities of the people working with you, try to see their strengths, not their weaknesses. If, for example, someone is very outspoken and has an aggressive personality, see if that fits into a role in which you need someone outspoken and aggressive. Embrace the differences people have to offer, and never discuss one person's personality quirks with others.

## The Art of Negotiating

Negotiating is a method of reaching a compromise settlement. As a project leader, you may find yourself in the middle, playing go-between in negotiations to end conflicts. Be fair, listen to each side, make sure both sides walk away with something of value—including their pride—and don't be hasty in making a judgment. But being the middle person is no fun. The art of negotiating goes a lot further than just that of arbitrator in a conflict.

Negotiating is a skill that will come into play at various stages of the project, and is useful in making numerous types of agreements with other parties. Many areas will require basic negotiating skills, some you may not even recognize. You may need to make special arrangements to have a key player join your team, or work out arrangements to have special speakers, hosts, or sponsors support your project. Then, of course, you have the standard negotiable issues: contracts, rates, and deadlines.

From the outset, you need to assess exactly what it is you want. If you are not clear in your ultimate objective, your negotiations may go off course in the middle and you could end up with nothing. While working toward your objective, you will have a series of end results that you want, ranging from the ideal to the very least that would be acceptable. If you were negotiating with management for additional employees to put on your team, you might consider an ideal number to be ten employees. However, you know you could do the job with six or seven if you absolutely had to, and would keep this in mind as you negotiate. For example, a team member may want to have one day a week to telecommute. Whether this person telecommutes one day may be inconsequential to you, but you might take that opportunity to ask the potential team member if he or she could be available once a month on Thursdays to stay late for important meetings with the sponsors. This can be an even exchange: the person works one day a week at home, and in return is willing to stay late one Thursday a month. After this simple agreement sets the tone of reasonable cooperation, you can get down to the nitty-gritty: hours and compensation.

Start by making reasonable offers. You do not request everything, nor do you offer everything. Give something the other side wants in exchange for something you want, and build from there. Starting with smaller points allows both parties to feel comfortable.

Look at the following tips for effective negotiating:

- Concede on points that are low on your list of priorities in exchange for points that are high on your list of wants.
- Save their top offer for your top priority. If a ball club trades away their best pitcher, it will become that much harder to acquire the other team's best hitter.
- Keep in mind that things need not be exchanged one for one. If you have two lesser items that are not as significant to your needs and they have one biggie, consider trading two or three for one.
- Don't offer too much up front—give yourself room to build. Not unlike a game of poker, you don't want to throw in all your money on the first wager.

- If you win big, give back some concessions. It may be something of no great significance to you, but it's an act of good character and good business to say, "Listen, we really don't need this, why don't you keep it." Next time you negotiate, this gesture may be remembered.
- Do not be adversarial or put the other side on the defensive. When the other side talks, listen and work together in good faith to try to settle on something that makes both sides walk away from the table feeling good.
- If things are not working out and neither side is happy, stop talking and take a break. Try again later, possibly with a neutral third party to break the stalemate.
- Take time to think about offers before making a final decision. Let the other person know that you will get back to them promptly. Evaluate the offer and even get a second opinion or compare the offer to the rates of others. Then make and communicate your decision within the time frame that you set.

Effective negotiating will come up during crisis intervention and conflict management, but it will also come up throughout the entire project. In fact, negotiation is a good skill to have in life, and any combination of the above tactics will work for most situations. Give a little, get a little—that's what it's all about. Above all, have patience.

## CHAPTER 19

# Motivational Skills

To motivate is to stimulate to action by providing an incentive or a motive. Real motivation, however, is more than just action; it is based on an attitude. The drive to succeed, learn, grow, and attain a goal is motivation. Personal investment in a product, activity, or outcome will motivate individuals also. As a project manager, you need to keep your team motivated, focused on completing the project, and achieving the team goal. From wise words to cash rewards, motivation comes in many forms. You can use several techniques with your team, but the best two come from you: be creative and be sincere.

## What Motivates Us?

For people to feel vested in a project, they need to see the big picture and look at the project from a global perspective. This big-picture view needs to be established from the onset. Unlike a Woody Allen film, where most of the actors never get to see the complete script (just the scenes in which they appear), projects are not usually successful if the people involved are not aware of the ultimate goal. The more a person is attached to—or feels involved with—the overall project, the more motivated he or she will be to work harder.

Motivation is not something you use only when the project is going downhill or has fallen behind schedule. Proper motivation should be established from the start of the project. You want to put together a championship team from the beginning. To do this you need to:

- Seek out personalities that work well with others.
- Bring everyone together in an introductory meeting.
- Present the broad picture of the project and the impact it will have on other people.
- Establish a team identity.
- Let others know what this team plans to accomplish on the project. Spread the word—present the team and their mission to the larger group, be it the company, the whole organization, the school board, or the world.

## Motivational Theories

Motivation takes on various forms. Internal motivation could be satisfaction from a job well done, an inner sense of fulfillment, or the sense of doing for others. External motivation includes material goods, awards, recognition, and of course, money. The nature of the project, the sponsor, and the setting of the project will dictate which, if any, external motivating factors you can offer. On every project, you can try to inspire team members to seek internal rewards along with the external rewards.

To motivate others to perform, you need a basic understanding of human nature. Many people in leadership positions do not fully understand the basic elements of motivational thinking as it pertains to others. Motivation can be an individual factor. Although a desire for monetary rewards is somewhat common, one person may be motivated by a possible new title or promotion while another may simply want more time to spend at home with the family. Unfortunately, an enthusiastic leader often assumes that the motivating factors that propelled him to his level of success are the same for everyone else. It's as if they think, "I became a manager, so why shouldn't everyone else be trying to work their way up to the same lofty position?" This is not a broad-based view of what motivates others.

A winning sports team believes that it is going to be the champion. The players tell everyone that they are intent upon winning the title. They have individual identities, as well as an awareness of what everyone is doing in the game. Loyalty, identity, and pride are great motivators.

Any team or group is made up of people who have different levels of self-motivation. Someone who grew up in a very wealthy family may not be as motivated to earn money as someone who grew up in poverty. However, the person from a wealthy background may never have experienced the satisfaction that comes from overcoming obstacles.

People at any level want to feel good about themselves and what they produce. It has long been debated whether or not people are born motivated, and if so, to what degree that may vary between individuals. Freud saw people as inherently lazy, not motivated, and wanting only security or gratification. Maslow embraced neither the behaviorist nor psychoanalytical approaches popular at the time. Instead, he believed that man strives to reach his highest level of capabilities. He believed that people were born inherently good and that among the basic human needs were self-esteem and self-actualization, both of which can only be achieved with motivation. Maslow concluded that for human salvation, one must indulge in "hard work and total commitment to doing well the job that fate or personal destiny calls you to do, or any important job that calls for doing."

Maslow's "self-actualized" needs are those needs of people involved in "a cause outside their own skin." He felt that self-actualizers are devoted people who work at something precious to them. Although an individual project will not usually take on that level of significance, the process of striving for self-actualization can be a strong motivating force.

Typically, studies in human behavior regarding motivation show us that if a person feels gratified, they will seek out, or return, to the source of that gratification. Conversely, there is the motivation to avoid danger or situations that a person is fearful about. At any level of development, a person will be motivated to protect himself from impending harm. In society, motivation to avoid negative consequences can be seen in staying out of jail or not getting fired.

When it comes to committing to a project, rarely is someone involved for absolutely no discernable reason. In these cases, motivation comes from several factors, including:

- A need to be part of a team or group—to work with others
- A need to be recognized and acknowledged
- Awards or merit
- An innate desire to produce a worthy product or accomplish a task for self-gratification or self-fulfillment
- Desire to make a social or cultural change or contribution
- Monetary rewards or bonuses
- Potentially greater responsibilities or a promotion in rank or stature

Most team workers will put forth a greater effort if there are tangible rewards such as money or a prize to be won. The trick is to get the team to work hard when the motivation is not as clear-cut as a shiny bicycle for the child who sells the most cookies. You need to tap into what motivates each individual. Unfortunately, all you may have to work with is the motivation to avoid getting in trouble or fired or being alienated.

**ALERT!**

Working only to avoid punishment does not lead to productive results, and this kind of motivation can produce discontentment and conflict. Negative motivational factors need to be counterbalanced with positive rewards in order for someone to give you her best effort.

Working for seven hours a day so as not to lose or fail is far less productive than working for seven hours a day to win and succeed. Same time frame, opposite motivation. Two classmates can do the same work and both will get a "C." The student who is motivated by simply passing will be quite happy with a "C," whereas the one who was trying to excel and earn an "A" will surely be disappointed. Because different things motivate the students, the next test may produce different results. The "passing" motivator knows he has done enough work to achieve his goal. The "excelling" motivator has not achieved his goal, and will therefore apply greater effort moving forward.

## *Lighting Their Fire*

When it comes to motivating a team, you need to reach both the individuals and the group as a whole. Your project plan may include incremental bonuses or incentives for the team. As a leader, you may have to take responsibility for the more personal motivation.

Here are some do's and don'ts for motivating your team:

- **Do** help the individual to identify what is in the project for them. Yes, it sounds like a selfish motivational factor, but no matter how team oriented a person is, there will be something that inherently drives that person to succeed. Find out what that is.
- **Do** provide praise, recognition, and approval. Some people are driven by that, and everyone deserves it.
- **Do** offer incentives, if possible.
- **Do** allow team members to feel empowered and invested in the outcome of the project.
- **Do** accentuate the positives and point out possible rewards other than money or a pending raise, particularly if those don't factor into the equation.
- **Don't** assume that everyone has the same level of interest or initial commitment to the project.
- **Don't** offer rewards or incentives for some team members and not for others.

- **Don't** assume that the same things motivate everyone—people have different needs.
- **Don't** give people fluff when they need substance.
- **Don't** bring in preconceived attitudes or opinions about people. Try to start each project with a clean slate.

The last point is particularly significant. If John Doe didn't give 100 percent on previous projects, that simply tells you how he has acted in the past. You need to start this project with the assumption that Mr. Doe will be as motivated as anyone else. If you see otherwise, you can respond by trying to find out what motivates him. Start out assuming everyone is on the project and ready to go, seeking a personal goal as well as the project goal.

There will be instances when you will be able to motivate by competition. Certainly, a sports franchise is motivated by the desire to win. Rival companies, or even a friendly competition between schools, neighborhoods, families, small businesses, or any such groups, can also provide a motivational force for participants. Sometimes the "Us versus Them" attitude is the impetus for motivating the team.

**FACT**

A good leader acknowledges the contributions made by team members and even sets up situations for team members to offer new ideas. Encourage your team to find the answer, even if you already know it. A good leader can take a backseat to his or her team and still be a strong and effective leader. Good leaders can step away from the need for individual accolades and let others take the credit.

Friendly internal competition can sometimes be a motivator, provided the stakes do not make for a blood-sport event. Keep the stakes enticing, but not worth battle. Internal competition should be based on a good-natured spirit and fun—anything beyond that can lead to trouble and conflict.

The best you can hope to do, once the project is under way, is continue to promote whatever it is that keeps your team members motivated. Whether it's looking forward to the upcoming rest and relaxation of a vacation or a trip to Las Vegas for the top sales rep, it's up to you to keep the motivational forces intact. Remember, it's always much easier when money or material goods are at the end of the tunnel. Also, compensation in the form of vacation days, time off, or a shorter workweek is high on the priority list of many employees. Offering comp time can benefit a company because it won't cost more in actual funds. Always be creative in offering incentives, and solicit the opinion of your team—remember that people are motivated by different factors.

## *Motivational Seminars*

Motivational seminars must fit the tone and nature of the group. Make sure the speaker is accustomed to talking to the type of group he or she is addressing. A corporate group needs a trained corporate motivational speaker. Sales teams need someone who can motivate people to be better salespersons. Artists need a speaker who is familiar with creative vision. A corporate executive and a fiction writer probably won't benefit from the same motivational speaker unless the speaker has a wide-ranging bag of tricks.

First, assess how your group would welcome an outside source, then search for one that can address the needs of the group and tailor their presentation accordingly. Some groups might respond to humor, others are dealing in areas where that might not be appropriate.

People tend to meet high expectations. If you tell someone who is doing a fair job that he is doing a good job, he will do a good job. The opposite theory, practiced by many parents, suggests that you should never give too much praise, always saying, "That's good, but you can do better." This has led to a generation of self-doubters who need constant encouragement as adults, since they believe that nothing they could ever do is good enough.

If you choose to bring in a motivational speaker, make sure you've done your homework. Look at the backgrounds and previous speaking engagements of several motivational speakers. Compare rates. You don't want to waste your team's valuable time or your company or organization's money.

You can evaluate a speaker based on a video or audiotape, or, if possible, attend a seminar given by that speaker. Find out his or her credentials, what associations he or she belongs to, and whether or not he or she can provide an interactive presentation.

According to Rosita Hall (*www.rositahall.com*), a Canada-based motivational speaker in Canadian and U.S. companies, "One of the mistakes commonly made is that companies wait until they are at a critical juncture and then call someone in to save them. They believe that someone can come in like a messiah, and in one afternoon change everything that's taken place for the last six months or a year. It would be more beneficial for companies to work in such a speaker from the beginning, knowing that at some point people will need to be motivated. I can't think of anyone who doesn't need motivation at some point in their life."

It's beneficial to all concerned that management be involved in any motivational speech or seminar. Don't make it just for the team, or you are separating yourself from the group. This is like saying, "The team needs to be motivated, but management is always motivated." Not true.

Motivational speakers are used (and needed) the most during periods of change. Hall, like many speakers, focuses on making change less stressful. Instead of focusing on the change itself, she concentrates on providing people with an overall awareness of the self—encouraging people to feel comfortable with themselves before worrying about organizational change.

Consider the motivational needs you anticipate throughout the life of the project. The longer the project, the more likely it is that you will need to include a motivational speaker, especially if you expect changes to the project or the company.

## It's the Little Things

Doing lots of little things can motivate your team to make big things happen. Set the tone, lead by example, and be a consistent and positive force. After all, if the leader doesn't believe the project will be a success, why should anyone else?

Don't pat yourself on the back or gloat about your own triumphs along the way. Lead with humility. It has been said that, "Upon reaching the summit, you should turn around and offer a hand to the person behind you." That philosophy holds true with your project team. If you are praised for the work done so far, turn around and pass that praise on to your team.

Little things that help motivate a team include a group lunch outing, a card and cake for a team member's birthday, an upbeat cartoon posted on the bulletin board, a funny story or tasteful joke, a saying—anything that gets people smiling or thinking positively. Some projects have even had slogans, such as the '73 Mets, who coined "Ya Gotta Believe."

**FACT**

The idea of motivating a team by making a project enjoyable goes back to what we try to teach children through learning games: If you enjoy what you are doing, you are more likely to do a better job.

Establish this fun principle early on. Roger Reece, a motivational consultant who runs Fuddwhacker Consulting, establishes a fun quotient from the outset of the project. Reece believes that the stress level and intensity of a project will build as the project progresses, so it is very important to start out with the project and its goals in proper perspective.

"Motivation really is a function of attitude adjustment," says Reece. "If you aren't encouraging positive attitudes, you'll have marginal results." He also introduces Buford Fuddwhacker (Reece's alter ego), a character to enlighten, entertain, and loosen up the often tense team members.

## Bridging the Gap

There is a fine line between conflict and motivation. If people are not happy with each other, or if they are unhappy with the overall structure of the corporation, organization, or management, they will not be motivated to work at their peak level of efficiency.

In business, schools, or other situations in which there is a hierarchical structure, there is a tendency for people to regard upper management as the enemy. A team may feel helpless against the management, school board, local governing body, or other authority figure. You may hear responses like, "Oh, we've tried that before" or "Management will never let us do that" from disgruntled team members. As the leader or project manager, you must break through that barrier that separates the "us" from the "them" and gain trust and respect from the team. If you can win points with management on their behalf, you can show the team that their efforts can make a difference. Winning even the smallest of battles shows that you can make things happen, and your team will respect you for it. Bridging the gap between your team and management, or authority, goes a long way toward motivation.

## What Will It Take?

Besides money, some of the most important motivational elements expressed by people working on projects include:

- Time off, vacation, compensation, or personal time
- The option to work from home (telecommuting)
- Better working conditions, such as a larger office or an assistant
- Greater authority and decision-making capabilities (this can even be found on a home-based project, where children do such a fine job on a family project that they are given greater responsibilities and are allowed to make some of their own decisions)
- Acknowledgment that they are appreciated for their contributions

Beyond these wants, people expect to be treated with respect. Remember, the project is only as successful as the people behind it. Success is a byproduct of self-confidence, and that comes from being treated well.

If the well-intentioned company dinner to boost team spirit has a "must attend or else" tone about it, you're not helping matters. Likewise, if a consultant comes in and makes new demands that don't sit well with the team, the exercise will be ineffective. Motivation comes about through respect, openness, good communication, and understanding of individual needs. You cannot force inspiration, and you cannot force positive motivation.

Roger Reece points out that in companies, individuals often see dealing with management as an "us" against "them" situation. It's important, according to Reece, to set up circles of "we." Blending the hierarchy will create overall company unity and a feeling that "we are all in this together."

## *Keeping Yourself Motivated*

As project manager, you may need a kick in the proverbial butt on occasion to keep your own level of motivation high. It's easy to lose your drive and desire if all around you team motivation is crumbling. In that case, it's time to take one step back before taking three steps forward. Sometimes the best thing you can do as leader is take a day away from the project, physically and, more importantly, mentally. Remind yourself of your personal goal in this project. Look at your own vested interest in the project, and look at your goals and interests away from the project.

As you proceed through your career and work on various projects, you will be able to fairly assess what does and does not motivate you best. For some people, competition provides the shot in the arm; perhaps knowing that another team is developing their software at a faster rate. For someone else it might be a setback. While some people see a setback as a time to throw in the towel, others see it as the impetus to buckle down and work harder. When you feel motivated to get out there and double your effort, know what motivates you and use that to get yourself going.

One project manager, who was feeling burned out after working ten-hour days to get the project finished, said he simply went home one night and watched his two young children sleep for about two hours. He reminded himself that when the project was over, he would be getting an extra two weeks off to take them to Disney World. The time to spend with his family was his motivation to get the project finished on time, and his personal motivation is what kept him on track.

## CHAPTER 20

# What Happens If
# My Plans Fail?

All project managers have experienced a failure in one form or another. If anyone says otherwise, they are not being honest. By their nature, projects will fail at one point or another. Your well-thought-out and documented project plan will fail as well. What is important is that you understand why and act upon it. Killing a project that is bound to fail can actually be a success. If you know why projects or plans are likely to fail, then you will be better equipped to deal with potential project roadblocks.

**20**

## *The Inevitable Project Roadblock*

If you recall from Chapter 7, 2 percent of your project will fail no matter how good you are. It can be said that a project isn't really a project unless something goes wrong. It is going to happen. You will not know where, you will not know how, but it is going to happen—be ready for it.

Conflict, roadblocks, or project issues are not always negative. They can have positive impacts on the project or your relationship with a client. Just like when you and a friend have a disagreement, talk it through, and then know each other better than ever. The same is true for projects. Just because something went wrong doesn't mean you should panic, throw your hands up, or quit. It just means that now you are earning your stripes.

Project management is a series of scars. When you read about PMOs and their merit, one of them was the sharing of experiences. Here is where you develop those experiences.

## *Why Plans Fail*

Plans can fail for many reasons, but they almost always come down to some common misunderstanding or failure to communicate. You didn't understand what you were estimating or you didn't get all of the information from the client or you misjudged how many people were showing up to the party—plans can just fail. If you are following the cycle within the cycle, then you know that you can adjust your plan based on the information that you received from the controlling phase. Too many people at the party? Let's open the patio doors and let them mingle outside.

Some of the key reasons that plans can fail are:

- **Lack of Executive Support:** Your boss or sponsor didn't give you everything that you needed: the resources you needed; the money to purchase all of the materials; or they didn't support your plan. This is one of the biggest reasons your plan can fail.
- **Users Were Not Involved:** Have you ever been on a project where it was supposed to improve the livelihood of employees or make them more productive, but it didn't involve them at all? It is an absolute

mess. Projects that involve adjusting the workflow of an employee without the employee's involvement is a good way to promote project failure.

- **Lack of Clear Direction:** Sometimes, "Go over yonder and build me a house" needs to be a bit more defined for a successful project.
- **Project Manager Experience:** Many times, your experience or lack thereof may be the cause of a project failure. Failure to recognize a major roadblock or delaying a decision based on indecisiveness are areas where your experience could be the catalyst.

The thing to remember is that at least 2 percent of a project is going to fail. However, because a small percentage of a project fails doesn't mean the whole project will be a failure. Just be ready to help course correct it when problems arise, and you can still have a successful project.

## How to Course Correct

So, your project has hit a roadblock or is about to fail. What next? First, don't panic. You have read this many times, but it is important: As project manager, you are the project leader. When things go wrong, the team will look to the leader for guidance. If the leader is confused and panicked, then everyone else will go that route as well. If you are calm and composed, then the team can take guidance from you, calm down, and help work to find a resolution.

When bad things happen, people look to their leaders. In the context of a project, you have to be the one that they look to. Although every situation is different, there are some things that you can do to help course correct:

- **Remove Blame:** It is not important who is at fault or how the project got to this point. It will be later, but in the context of crisis containment, remove the blame. Don't let it become a finger-pointing session. Identify the issue and move forward.
- **Look Forward:** Plan the next steps; don't dwell on what just occurred. Whatever happened has happened. Look forward to how it will be resolved.

- **Go to Your Team:** Your team is your panel of experts. Rally around your team and let the creative juices flow for unique approaches to solving your issue.
- **Instill Confidence:** Let your team know that you are confident in whatever approach you agree too. They just took a hit to their egos because of where the project is; let them know that you are confident that they can fix this.

Once you have your team settled and some options on what the next steps may be, your job is 50 percent complete. Now, you have to go to your sponsor and/or client and get them on board with the new plan.

## How to Garner New Support

Feeling confident in your new plan? Ready to sell it to the higher powers? Your confidence will be the make or break point of garnering support for the new plan. Just like the session with your team, do not allow this to turn into a bashing session. The project is where it is. No amount of dwelling on it or discussing it will fix the issue, only new plans will.

**QUESTION?**

**What if you are not confident in your plan?**
Do not present it then, or at the very least, don't lie. It is much better to look a sponsor in the eye and state that you don't know how to fix an issue versus setting a false hope that you can, and then letting them down again.

To garner new support, show all of the options. Talk through the issue with your sponsor, the path you'll use to reach the current decision, and how you plan to manage the new plan. Projects are full of mistakes—just don't make the same ones over and over.

Sponsors, clients, and executives are all just people in the end. They may not be happy with your progress. They may be upset at the current state of the project. But at the end of the day, it is what it is. Presenting the options, keeping them informed, and staying honest with them is where you will garner your new support. Lie to them, make and break too many promises, or shield them from all of the information, and you will most likely lose more than their trust.

## Where Did All of My Resources Go?

A great dilemma for project managers is the missing-sock syndrome. You know that you put three pairs of socks in the dryer, yet only five socks came back out. Is there a fairy in the dryer stealing socks?

You will feel that way with your disappearing resources. It starts with needing Johnny for a quick meeting. Then Carol has to have surgery. Joan is called out to deal with a production issue. This leaves you and your plan. Maybe you have experienced this when several parents have decided to throw a party for the PTA. Ten parents signed up to help. You all agreed to decorate the gym at 8:00 P.M. on Friday. At 9:00 P.M., when you and your streamers are still the only one there, you realize you are on your own.

Disappearing resources is a caveat for project failure. If you have learned nothing else in this book, keep this with you. Report the facts and all of the facts in your project statuses and two things can happen. Nothing, which means nobody really cares, which removes the burden from you. Or, the problem will become visible because someone does care, and you will start finding the missing socks.

How do you report the facts? Following your communication plan, send out your status report moving all project deliverables to red, calling attention to the fact that they are about to fail. Then wait for the reactions. Here are two scenarios:

### Scenario 1: Nobody Cares

**Problem:** You are working on a project and, one by one, your project team has found other, more critical work to be done. You have talked to their managers and find that they are really busy and will get to it when they can. You have reported in your status report for the last two weeks that nothing was being completed. Nobody has responded or has seemed concerned.

**Potential Solution:** Go ahead and send a project-closure or project-cancellation form to the sponsor. The sponsor will then be forced to make a decision. They can cancel the project, commit resources to finish the project, or put the project on hold until a later date. Whichever they choose, you have your directions. If you want to ensure something gets looked at, ask someone to sign off!

### Scenario 2: They Do Care!

Due to the reporting of the status, the sponsor steps in to find out what has been happening. From your standpoint, issue resolved. You have escalated properly and now have the attention of someone who can assist.

These are simple fixes, but the honesty approach tied with reporting what is really happening will get you results.

## This Project Has No Risk, Because It HAS to Finish On Time!

This is a real quote from a real sponsor on a real project that involved inconveniencing thousands of customers. A company announced a plan to make a major change to their operations, sent customer notifications, and committed to government agencies before ever talking to their internal team about the feasibility of the change.

The project manager received this project and immediately asked for a risk session so that the project could have a chance at being successful. The sponsor declined the risk session and said, "This project has no risk, because it has to finish on time." Of course, this project was full of risk, because it had to finish on time. Sliding the production date simply wasn't an option.

Sometimes, projects are doomed to fail before they even begin.

## CHAPTER 21

# Finishing the Project and Evaluating the Results

Some projects end with a bang and others a whimper. This chapter addresses several methods of wrapping up a project, whether it is presenting the final product or transitioning it to its next phase. The end of a project will also impact the team, which may take pride in its success, be uncertain of what comes next, and have mixed emotions about breaking up as members move on to new jobs. Depending on their personal interest in the ensuing tasks that await them, this can be exciting, depressing, or frightening—or a little of all three.

## The End Is Near

While you may find it a bit presumptuous to start planning for the end of your project before you start (and some people focus too much attention on this), you should have some plans for a smooth closing that are in place from the outset. For example, do you have a file for each person who leaves the project? Invariably, someone will leave along the way. You need to have information available should you need to contact this person when the project ends, for any reason from missing a report to sending a 1099 form. Make sure from day one that you have files on all vendors you use and anyone else who may only be involved with the project for a short time. You also need to make arrangements for:

- Returning items borrowed from other departments or from friends or neighbors
- Accounting for leased or rented equipment
- Cleanup after a conference, party, or banquet
- Presenting the final product or finished project to stakeholders

Final phase and end plans need to be in place from the start. There must also be a discussion of postproject evaluations so the team knows to expect them. Evaluations will provide a forum for team members to give and receive feedback on several aspects of the project, including its organization and leadership, as well as their own performance.

## Beyond the End

If the project is one in which you are creating a product or service that will be sold or distributed to the public, you also need to set a time to start planning your postproject marketing strategy. One of the biggest mistakes a company can make is not looking beyond the actual project. For example, a project to make a Web guidebook was set to take three months. The project was completed and the books were printed and ready to go. However, no one took the time to put together a marketing plan. Thus, the project team was asked to scramble and try to start selling the book. They sold a few, but the results of this successful project were unsuccessful book sales. Why? Because the handoff was not addressed during the project phase. Set the wheels in motion during the creation of a project so that the product or services have a life after the creation.

How many people have built something and never bothered to use it, or written something they meant to send to magazines or publishers but never did? There are many unfinished projects, but there are also many finished ones that never got beyond their creation.

## Learn from the Past

Although you may not be doing this exact project again, you may find yourself doing one that is similar in the future. You will want to learn from your experiences on the project. Make sure you are documenting what you do as you proceed for the sake of your own future projects and those of the group, company, or organization who will benefit from them. Even in a family project, it's a good idea to save the plans of your trip to France just in case you decide to travel to Italy in a couple of years. Half of your research will be done, and you'll be able to learn from what you needed to do for your previous long-distance vacation.

Taking good notes for the duration of a project can benefit future projects. Documentation on research and initial planning is important, but don't forget the second half of the project. Information on what could, and did, go wrong and your solutions are critical in helping the next team create a better plan from the outset.

## The Carrot

You might also consider doing some motivational advance planning. If you're building a patio for the backyard and have a pretty good idea that you will be finished by June 23, why not plan a July 4 party to christen the new patio and show it off to all of your neighbors? Likewise, if you are moving to a new office space, plan a big office-warming party. Anything you can imagine that will help encourage everyone to keep plugging away is worth considering. Many filmmakers look forward to their big opening night even before the final editing. While a project launch can be motivational, it is important not to think too long about the end results before you get down into the trenches and do the work.

**ALERT!**

If you're planning a conference, party, book sale, auction, picnic, or seminar, make sure you include the cleanup process. It's important to plan for cleanup, breakdown, or disassembly in the end. Put this in your initial plan along with other closing activities such as final evaluations and reporting.

## Final Phase Responsibilities

Okay, so what do you have to do to properly end the project? The following checklist will get you on track for closing the books.

❏ **Make sure all unfinished project activities are completed.** Many project managers drop the ball at this point, assuming everything is done because most tasks are completed. Assume nothing—do a thorough review. Sometimes people cut corners to move on to their next project or operations. Don't let this happen to you. Set up a task list of final items and review it to ensure that everything is completed and the quality of the work is satisfactory.

❏ **Have a team meeting to evaluate the project.** You may do one meeting with your team to prepare a wrap-up presentation for stakeholders. Determine how you got where you are, and what you might do differently in the future. Review your documentation to be sure it's complete for the next project team. Include a thorough review of the budget, your resources, and barriers. Share what you learned the hard way to save the next team time and money.

❏ **Meet with stakeholders, sponsors, and anyone else who needs to approve or sign off on the project.** Make sure that everyone with final authority agrees that the project has concluded.

❏ **Finish off all accounting procedures including paying final bills and fulfilling all contracts.** Make sure all bookkeeping is up to date and all information for team members is accessible, including personal information needed for 1099s or other tax-related documents. Your goal is to close the books on the project before shutting off the lights.

❏ **Make sure all documentation lands in the hands of those who will need it in the future.** If you have created a new product or started a new service that the sales team will now be selling, make sure the sales force has all the information (such as product specifications, user tools, or plans for future development) they require.

❏ **Meet with team members and thank them for their efforts.** Let them know that the stakeholder, sponsors, and others are pleased with the job they have done. Also, thank vendors and others who were integral to the success of your project. Make sure everyone knows the project is indeed officially over, for better or worse.

❏ **Reassign team members.** If you own your own business and the team was made up of employees, you will need to either assign them to a new project, move them into operations resulting from the project, or have them return to doing their original jobs. Let people know what they should do next.

❏ **Return all tools, equipment, or anything you borrowed to its rightful owner.** If you purchased equipment for the project, decide what to do with it. Often, when people leave a project, a lot of "stuff" is left behind. You need to clean up the mess and determine what is necessary for project maintenance and standard operations, and what was part of the project phase only. Can this equipment be used on future projects? On occasion, tools and equipment have been known to "grow legs" as the project winds down—keep tabs on resources and equipment. If you do have some dispensable goods, give them away to team members.

❏ **If the project was a success, celebrate!** Sometimes, even a failed project is cause for celebration, recognition, and appreciation.

Successful and unsuccessful projects need to shut down in a similar manner; however, on projects that have failed, there are a few additional considerations:

- You may have a hard time convincing stakeholders that the project is indeed over. Many hopeless projects linger on indefinitely because one or more of the stakeholders do not want to accept that the end has come.
- You will have less celebrating and more consoling to do, since team members may feel frustrated or disappointed. You need to encourage team members to focus on how much was accomplished and what everyone learned. Do not rehash mistakes or lay blame; acknowledge that sometimes that's the way things work out.
- It may take longer to close the books, since there may be outstanding or irreconcilable bills. Set up a time frame in which to try to close the books.
- Depending on the project and the attitude of the team members, you may need to pay special attention to security issues.

A project may fail for many reasons. It is important that at some point the project failure is realized and accepted, and there is an official shutdown. This can take a long time if there are legal entanglements, but in most projects there is a need to acknowledge that, at some point, it may indeed be over, even if you believe in your heart it shouldn't be.

Be sure to get necessary information from temporary or contracted team members, including their computer passwords and file locations. If team members will no longer be around after the project ends, don't forget company badges, security cards, and office keys. If you don't have a formal exit interview process, arrange an informal meeting to give and receive feedback and collect company property.

And then there are projects that end while you're still going strong. All appears to be going well, but management, for whatever reason, decides to pull the plug. Team members are especially let down when a project ends abruptly, because it means the rug is pulled out from under them. Sometimes there are warning signs, but not always. Businesses move quickly and changes are made in the course of a few days or even a few hours.

A sudden shutdown is never easy, and sometimes the only way to deal with it is to pick yourself up as soon as possible and move on. Console and comfort others who are likely as shocked and angered as you are. Even in this scenario, you are often expected to tidy up a bit. The team will be gone, but as a leader, you may have to straighten out loose ends. If you are no longer on the payroll, you are in a good position to negotiate a deal to do whatever is asked of you at this point, but be sure to get it in writing.

# Postproject Evaluations

In your postproject evaluations (sometimes called postmortems), you will want to document in writing which methods worked and why. You will be able to look at how tasks were completed, and determine whether the best methods were used. If the process was one that the team found to be effective, you will want to carefully review the process so that it can be duplicated in future projects. If a task was accomplished but the method could have been improved upon, you will want to list exactly what aspects of this process should be analyzed and revamped for future projects. Determine why the revised method would be more effective and what the implications would be if you used it on the next project.

## Circle Back

Naturally, it's important to look at the big picture to determine how close the final result was to the original plan. A completed project is rarely identical to that original concept. Trial and feedback throughout, plus testing, tinkering, and confronting numerous obstacles along the way, will change the course and alter the outcome of any project—sometimes for better and sometimes for worse.

You want to have preset levels of what is considered acceptable. Perhaps the new marketing campaign resulting from the project is effective, but the message is not exactly what you envisioned when you started the project. Now is the time to evaluate what is different and discuss whether you sacrificed aspects of the original idea to complete the project, or simply found an easier way to reach comparable results. Quite often, the new approach works very well without all of the details of the original plan. Sometimes, the act of planning a project takes on a larger scope than necessary, and too many details are added simply because everyone wants to have some input. Simple solutions can sometimes be the most effective.

## Revisit the Detours

You should also review the changes and decisions that were made along the way. Obviously, if the project came in below budget, some decisions were made that worked in your favor. Hold a team-review meeting and invite everyone in attendance to participate and describe how they succeeded at their various tasks. The learning process is twofold: Not only will future project teams learn from your detailed accounts, you will also improve your skills for your next assignment. In the end, you and your team can have a strong impact on future projects, but only if you carefully retrace the steps you took and the alterations and decisions you made along the way.

If you are asking team members for their evaluations in written form, make sure your questions are simple and to the point. Ask for direct feedback to specific aspects of the project. If you are holding a meeting to get final evaluations (and you should), ask the team whether or not they felt the project really met the intended goals. Find out whether they agreed with how you approached issues that arose throughout the project. Look for constructive criticism. Ask team members to point out what could have been done in a different way, then ask them for suggestions for an alternative approach. You know where the project ended up, now review how it got there and how it might have gotten there in a better, more efficient manner.

**QUESTION?**

**What is a PIR?**

The Project Issues Review (PIR) is a document that includes survey results, often featuring graphs or charts, that helps the team determine what was done well and what could be improved upon in the future. Survey participants are asked to complete the review in a specified amount of time.

## *The Nitty-Gritty*

Let the team know at the onset that when the project is deemed complete, there will be a postproject evaluation meeting. When you are ready for such a meeting, make sure all key personnel have advance notice. Request that they bring as much documentation as they have of their work on the project. Naturally, on large-scale projects, you can't expect people to carry in files of reports, but key information that helps define what they did and how they did it will be useful.

You also need to have your own project records and documentation on hand. Include the original and final schedules, original budget and final expenditures, progress reports, updates, and correspondence, along with other key information that helps you recount the course of the project.

To review your records effectively, consolidate all of your materials down to the key information. Highlight specific documents as you proceed through the project, making a clear notation of when critical decisions were made and what processes were enacted.

Many aspects are involved in a project's success or failure. The environment, the economic climate, the schedule, the budget, the resources, or the organizational structure could be at the source. You need to differentiate between factors that were within your control and those that were not. If the project failed because of flooding or a hurricane, it obviously was out of your hands. Try to pinpoint each source of success or failure within the project. Ask yourself and team members to think through the various elements that made up the overall project. Consider the following:

- Was the initial plan too complex or too simple to attain the desired results?
- Were the best resources used?
- Was the team missing certain expertise?
- Were there too many or too few people involved?
- Was the communication system effective?

- Was there a conflict that went unresolved and slowed down the project?
- Were there risks that went undetected and caused large-scale problems?
- Were previous projects reviewed and evaluated properly?
- Were the outside experts or consultants effective?
- Did management change the rules, and subsequently the project goals, along the way?
- Did outside agencies, policies, or other political factors impinge on the project's progress?
- Were there external factors that could not be avoided? What were they?
- Should key decisions have been made sooner?
- Should the contingency plan have been implemented at some point?

You should look for ways to improve on the things that did not work toward the best execution of the project and ways to optimize those aspects that did.

## *Setting Up the Next One*

Quite often, people have an easier time finding fault with something they were dissatisfied with than they do in noting positive accomplishments and achievements. Success is often hard for people to grasp, especially when they are busily testing, evaluating, retesting, and reporting on each phase of a project. At some point, however, the actual project ends and the resulting product, service, or ongoing activity goes forth into the world.

Naturally, it is hard to judge the real success of a project until there has been some impact outside of the project environment. Does the new system enhance service for real customers? Can people actually play in the reopened park? Are people able to apply what they learned at the seminar? These questions will take time to answer as the project results meet the world. For your purposes, you can look at what you did in accordance with the initial plan and goals set forth at the onset of the project. If the initiator of the project, manager, or others involved have deemed the project completed, then somehow you have succeeded in reaching that step.

Here are some of the most common evaluation errors:

- Only evaluating the final results, not how they were achieved or how they differ from the original plans.
- Not getting a broad view. If the project is going to affect thousands of people, three people's evaluations may not be enough.
- Not taking good notes. If you don't document the results of feedback, what good is receiving it?
- Evaluating the work but not the team or evaluating the team but not the work. If the team worked on the project, then both should receive evaluations.
- Working with evaluations that are too complicated. If you've ever been handed a ten-page form to evaluate a twenty-minute lecture, you'll understand the need to keep evaluations within the scope of the project.
- Only looking at the errors and neglecting to review and leverage what went right on the project.
- Waiting too long between project end and review. Don't expect everyone to remember all the important details if you don't get around to the postproject evaluation until three months have gone by.

## *What Did You Learn?*

This isn't necessarily "Where did we go wrong?" because sometimes even a successfully completed task could be the starting point for a new and improved method of doing a particular job. Trial and error often produce positive results. These results, however, are sometimes overlooked because everyone involved is preoccupied with looking for negative factors. Wally Bock, a consultant, speaker, and publisher whose helpful ideas are found at *www.mondaymemo.net*, says that he prefers to call it "Trial and Feedback." Says Bock, "You don't just want to analyze that which doesn't work, but you want to look at what did work well so you can find a way to leverage it."

The end product can be, and often is, run through a series of tests and analyses. Even after the product or service hits the market, there will be a great deal of evaluation and reviews. Today, a successful company is one that continually plans ahead. As soon as a new product is created, the next new one is in the planning stages, particularly in the technology field. Project feedback and evaluation will guide the company into improvements on existing products and services as well as guidelines or suggestions for handling future endeavors.

The team can provide initial feedback. Feedback will also come from stakeholders, customers, clients, the media, and other sources. If the team's initial reaction is similar to the external feedback, then the team was very well aware of how it could improve upon a successful product and has made a good assessment of its work.

Identify the positives, even on a project that failed. Look for constructive suggestions on how a task might evolve from the project and be used more effectively in the future. A company may fail with its initial e-commerce business plan, but still learn enough about the potential power of the Web to produce a successful strategy for its next venture. You can have very successful battles even while losing the war.

Let's say that a team was pulled together to research and produce a new soft drink. The team successfully produced a new drink that satisfied the management and sponsors; however, the team still thought that the drink could be less dry. The product was a success and customers enjoyed it, but the comment the company received most often was that the soda was a little too dry. In this case, the team itself knew what would have improved the product.

Internal changes are easier to identify than external changes because they directly affect the project. External changes, those that affect the stakeholders, customers, and others associated with the project, will require outside evaluation and feedback. Aspects of the final product connect with the external world and need evaluation on several levels. When the project is to create something brand-new, there is a risk that others won't be as satisfied with the product or service as the sponsors or management. No matter how much test marketing is done, there is still the chance that the project champion's idea will not be embraced by the intended market. Focus groups are essential for gauging the possible success of a new product or service.

It is always in your best interest to get outside feedback at various stages of production. Unless it's a top-secret project, it is usually beneficial to get feedback from people who are familiar with the project but not involved with the day-to-day process. Sometimes, an outside contractor who has been involved with the project can also provide good feedback along the way. He or she can see it from a different perspective. One of the most common postproject determinations is that there was a need for more testing. Ongoing tests, reviews, and evaluations are critical.

## Now What?

While evaluations are important, they need to be used effectively. At the end of a major adoption conference in New York City, with some 125 workshops, an event coordinator asked, "Who collected the speaker evaluation forms so we'll know who to invite back at future conferences?" Everyone looked at each other. Sure, forms had been distributed to evaluate speakers, but no one had bothered to collect them at the end of the day and the feedback was lost.

Therefore, you need to:

❏ Save postproject evaluations
❏ Discuss and document the findings, including which methods you want to maintain and which ones need to be changed in the future
❏ Document suggested changes
❏ Create a final report, book, or file as a means of saving the information for future use

The last item should be a review of the project that traces the steps taken from the original plan to the end product. Show how the project reached anticipated milestones or why it failed to do so. Point out changes made to the original plan and key decisions made by you or management that impacted the project. Note the testing that was done throughout the project and how such tests helped the decision-making process. List the key successes in the project, such as new or improved ways of completing certain tasks. Also, list those things that can be improved in the future, using some suggestions from your postproject meeting.

**FACT**

Wally Bock explains, "Most projects only have guidelines and not recipes. Therefore, in the end they will come out differently than you envisioned in your original plan." The hope is that the goal is reached in one manner or another and that the project guidelines are followed. But, he adds, "If a project has a set recipe, you shouldn't have any problem following it to completion."

You want to take what you have gained from the postproject meetings and put together a guide or template for the next team. Your report will also serve as a guide for the future of what came out of the project (whatever it is that you produced, planned, etc.). For example, if the project was to create a new automated filing system, besides providing instructions on how to create such a system, you will have information on how the automated filing system works. Having created and tested the system, you'll have the initial user guide ready for the people who will now be using this automated system on a regular basis.

# CHAPTER 22

# Project Training
# and Certifications

The project management profession continues to grow at an extremely rapid pace. There are many certifications that attempt to establish your level of knowledge and status as a project manager. This chapter discusses the most popular certifications and what is involved in achieving them.

## Project Management Institute (PMI)

Founded in 1969, the Project Management Institute (PMI) is the de facto standard for project management. A nonprofit organization, PMI is a membership community that is focused on the understanding and advancement of the profession of project management. PMI has members in 164 countries with 251 chapters and 30 special-interest groups. Membership has risen more than 1,000 percent over the last decade and continues to have double-digit growth in membership year over year.

PMI is also the largest provider of project management knowledge in the world. The Project Management Body of Knowledge (PMBOK) is in its third edition and is the only published standards guide for project management. Based on the PMBOK, there are certifications managed and monitored by PMI. They are the CAPM and the PMP.

## Certified Associate in Project Management (CAPM)

The CAPM is designed for entry-level project managers, project team members, and college graduates that are looking to show their value as a project leader. The requirements for this certification are:

- High school diploma or equivalent
- 1,500 hours of work on a project team or twenty-three hours of formal education

Candidates fill out an application and send it to PMI. PMI will review the application and then send the candidate an Authorization to Test (ATT) letter. Candidates can then schedule and take a 150-question multiple-choice exam based on the candidates understanding of the PMBOK. If the candidate passes the exam, they will attain the CAPM certification.

# *Project Management Professional (PMP)*

A far more advanced and coveted certification is the Project Management Professional (PMP). This certification is designed to establish your credibility as a project manager. In addition to verifiable experience, the exam is one of the harder certification exams to pass. The qualifications needed to take this exam are:

- High school diploma or equivalent
- 7,500 hours (4,500 hours with a college degree) in a position of responsibility leading and directing specific tasks and sixty months (thirty-six with a college degree) of project management experience
- Thirty-five hours of project management education

Candidates will fill out an application detailing their experience and qualifications. Upon acceptance, the candidate will receive a letter of acceptance with a voucher allowing them to schedule their exam.

The PMP Exam is a 200-question multiple-choice exam that will truly test the candidate's knowledge of project management. There are very few if any definition or general-knowledge questions on the exam. It is all situational based, forcing the candidate to apply their project management knowledge.

On the PMI Web page (*www.pmi.org*) they list sample questions and answers. Here is one of those listed:

You are employing Earned Value Management on your project. You wish to avoid the subjective determination of performance as reported by the work package owners in your weekly status meetings. The following table describes three of your work packages:

| WORK PACKAGES | | |
| --- | --- | --- |
| Work Package | Description of the Work | Estimated Duration |
| 2.2.1 | Create RFP for subcomponent parts | 4 weeks |
| 2.2.3 | Purchase subcomponent parts | 2 weeks |
| 2.2.5 | Assemble subcomponent | 2 weeks |

*(continued)*

Which of the following methods of measuring earned value works BEST for work package 2.2.1?

A. Fixed Formula
B. Weighted milestones
C. Percent complete
D. Equivalent completed units

The _____ evaluation method works BEST for work package 2.2.3.

A. Fixed Formula
B. Weighted milestones
C. Percent complete
D. Equivalent completed units

This is not intended to scare anyone or overhype this exam. It is merely put here as a reference of what the exam will be like. Incidentally, the answers for this question are B and A respectively.

**QUESTION?**

**Are there classes that will help me pass the PMP exam?**
Yes, there are many options. Many organizations have exam-preparation courses, but be sure to do your homework; you will get what you pay for.

The PMP is the most recognized certification for project managers. At the time of this writing, there are over 225,000 PMPs worldwide.

## Other Certifications

Although PMI is the most recognized as the standard of project management, there are a few other organizations that certify project managers.

### International Project Management Association (IPMA)

The IPMA was founded four years (1965) before PMI, which makes it the oldest project management association in the world. Even though it is older, it has not garnered the same acceptance as PMI, with roughly 40,000 members in forty different countries. The IPMA certification system features four levels:

- **Level D:** Certified Project Management Associate—The lowest level of certification. The candidate completes an exam to receive the certificate. This certification is equivalent to the CAPM.
- **Level C:** Certified Project Manager—The level C is also attained by taking an exam and generally also requires some validation of current experience. The candidate should be able to manage noncomplex projects. This level is in between the CAPM and the PMP.
- **Level B:** Certified Senior Project Manager—The candidate looking for the Level B should be able to manage complex projects without assistance. The process to attain this certification is to submit a self-assessment of project management knowledge and experience. The second step is to create a report based on a project that was discussed in the application. The final step is a professional interview with two trained assessors. Upon completion of the steps, the candidate becomes certified. This certification is equivalent to the PMP.
- **Level A:** Certified Project Director—The highest level of certification in the IPMA is the Certified Projects Director. The candidate for this certification must have a minimum of five years experience in project portfolio management, in which three years are in the responsible leadership of the portfolio management of a company. The certification process is the same process steps as Level B.

Recently, the American Society for the Advancement of Project Management became the governing body to represent the IPMA in the United States. They offer the ACPP (Level D), ACPM (Level C), ACSPM (Level B), and the ACPD (Level A).

Another organization that is closely aligned with IPMA is the Association of Project Management (APM). The APM is a European organization focused on project and program management. Their certifications align with the IPMA's in offering four levels of certification.

## Australian Institute of Project Management (AIPM)

The AIPM governs the RegPM (Registered Project Manager) certification program. Candidates are required to show their competence in project management to achieve one of the three levels of certification:

- Qualified Project Practitioner (QPP)
- Registered Project Manager (RPM)
- Master Project Director (MPD)

The levels and certifications are comparable to the IPMA and PMI.

### Rounding Out the List

In addition to the certifications outlined above, the following certifications are also available:

- **CompTIA Project+:** CompTIA offers a certification based on the fundamentals of project management. This requires an exam to complete.
- **Projects in Controlled Environments (PRINCE 2):** PRINCE 2 was created in the UK and is used extensively in the UK Government and throughout the world. PRINCE 2 is a structured method and process that is learned. Candidates study and take an exam for certification. There are two levels of certification—foundation and practitioner.
- **American Academy of Project Management:** The AAPM offers project management training and certification. They have three different certifications—Master Project Manager (MPM), Project Manager E-Business (PME), and Certified International Project Manager (CIPM).

## Other Training

As you can see, there are plenty of certifications and training to assist you in your growth as a project manager. Other training avenues include many universities; there are several degree programs that are incorporating or centering on project management. In addition to universities, there are many organizations that focus on project management. Some of these are:

- ESI International
- RMC Project Management
- Cheetah Learning
- New Horizons

If you do a search on the Internet, you will find hundreds of options for project management training. Find which ones you are the most comfortable with and start there. However, project management is a constantly evolving trade that requires constant education. Do not think that you can attend a course, or read this book, and instantly become a great project manager. It is trial and error and consistent education that will make good project managers great project managers.

## Local Involvement

The final way to expose yourself to project management training as well as the community of project managers is to get involved locally. As discussed earlier, there are many local chapters and special-interest groups that are affiliated with PMI. Many of these chapters have monthly meetings and activities to advance the profession of project management. They also allow guests to attend so that they can experience the local meeting before officially joining the chapter. It is a great way to meet other project managers and to get some education as well. Also, many of the chapters have a mentoring program that will allow you to work with a more experienced project manager and have them take you under their wing.

Many new project managers also tend to struggle with amassing experience in the field. They want to be project managers, but everyone wants to hire somebody with experience. To obtain that experience, look to your local United Way or any other charity or church. They are always looking for volunteers and event managers to assist with a fundraiser, local event, or any number of activities. Talk with them and explain that you are a project manager that wants to build some experience. They will be more than happy to assist you in finding a project that you can run, gaining experience for yourself and helping your community as well.

# Tales from the Other Side: Pitfalls to Avoid

**23**

Throughout this book, you have discovered the basics of the project management process, the inner workings, and how to achieve certifications. You have even read about conflict and turning around failing projects. This last chapter is reserved for the other side of project management. It's now time to categorize some of the types of project managers out there. A great project manager can create a leadership style that benefits his or her team. Some project managers can alienate the team. Here are a few examples of the attitudes that can drive away a project team.

## The Ego

"All this project needs is three more of me!" Ah, the egotistical project manager. The power went straight to the head. Now everyone else is a complete idiot. They work off of the "Do it because I said so" mentality. This attitude type is generally found in new project managers that were recently promoted through the halo effect.

**QUESTION?**

**What is the halo effect?**
The halo effect is when you make a logical leap about a person because of his or her success in a particular skill. "You are a great programmer, which must mean you will make a great manager of programmers."

This behavior normally occurs when new managers are promoted within their own sphere of influence. They also have a tendency to want to do everything themselves, thinking that they are the only one to trust when it comes to doing it right. Hopefully, this is not a role that you aspire to. The important thing to remember is that the only way for you to be successful as a project manager is to ensure that your team is successful. This means getting them what they need, making sure that they are appreciated, and letting them get the glory for a job well done. Remember, if you push people down to climb the ladder, you get pushed down with them.

## The Procrastinator

"I will get that plan out to you tomorrow." However, tomorrow never comes. The procrastinator is one of the worst of the behaviors. Project management is about anticipating, planning, and communicating. Procrastination is not one of the skills listed. There is an old saying: "A lack of planning on your part does not constitute an emergency on my part." Inevitably, whoever wrote that saying was tired of the procrastinating project manager asking for things at the last minute.

Procrastination breeds laziness. Laziness breeds unpreparedness. Unpreparedness breeds project disaster. Don't let "trust in your team" lead to or be an excuse for procrastination either. Earlier in the book, you read about diligently following up on your plans, controlling them, and replanning them. If you procrastinate on these functions, you will be unable to recover a project deviation until it is too late.

## The Noncommunicator

The noncommunicator is the most dangerous kind of project manager. This is because you usually will not see this coming. In the early stages of a project, things generally go as planned, maybe even better than planned. However, you haven't experienced that 2 percent yet. When that bomb drops, the noncommunicator strikes.

As project progress is good, the noncommunicator is more than happy to discuss that you are under budget or ahead of schedule. When things go bad, they crawl back into their shell for protection. They don't want to communicate bad things; they feel that it is a reflection on them when the project is behind. So, they hide and pray that the project fixes itself or that they can recover the plan before anyone finds out. Sadly, it rarely happens that way. Then, when the truth does come out, it is beyond the point where anything can be done about it.

This communication type is also found throughout your team members. If all of a sudden communication stops, you better find out what is happening.

## The Hoarder

"Everyone must give me all of the updates, do not communicate among yourselves." Another term for this type is Glory Hound. This personality type likes to get all of the information and then proudly display it for the entire world to see. They like to be the ones in front of senior management telling them what a wonderful job the project manager is doing managing all of these resources.

Hand in hand with Egos, Hoarders like to funnel all information through them so they can effectively spin it. This personality type goes against the "It is what it is" methodology. They want it to be as they spin it. However, this creates a dangerous and slippery slope. They effectively spin minitruths, then can't remember all of the spins they have created. The project then begins to unravel.

If you know of any Hoarders, be careful if they invite you to copresent at a senior management meeting. You will not see the bus coming. What bus? The one that they are about to throw you under. This allows them to spin the negative news, but it's not their fault—they will pin it on you.

## The Blamer

"We would have been done on time, except Tommy blew his estimates." Everyone else is at fault. "I tried to update the plan, but Jimmy wouldn't return my phone call." The Blamer is going to take everyone else down so that he or she doesn't have to be the one failing. The truth is, the Blamer is the one that failed.

As discussed, communication is a 50-50 road. The sender sends a message and the receiver receives it. The Blamers can easily be confused with the Egos or Hoarders, but they are subtler. Instead of only dealing with big project failures, this personality type tends to plan where to blame much further in advance. For instance, if they usually call you to discuss status, then suddenly ask you out of nowhere for an e-mail or written document, be warned: The Blamer may be setting you up for the fall. A quick forward of the e-mail to the boss, and you are toast.

This personality type generally gets found out quickly, though. They have burned enough team members in the past so that many will find excuses not to be on their project. That is one thing to remember throughout your project management career: Team members have their own lessons learned. Don't let their lesson be that they never want to work on a project with you again.

## The Traitor

"The project team let me down, madam CEO." If this were a movie, this project manager would be dressed in all black and wearing a black cape. This personality type is one of the worst. Rob Thomsett, international author and speaker, stated in his book *Radical Project Management* that projects fail because of context, not content. If this is true, then it is how the project manager managed the information and not necessarily how the team performed. A team can be performing poorly, but the project manager could head that off with proper communication. To let the project fail overall, and then to blame the team, is the villainy of this role.

> As a project manager, you own 100 percent of project failure, yet only 10 percent of project success. What this means is that if a project fails, ultimately it is on the project manager. If it is a success, the team gets the rewards.

Traitors believe that if they blame the team, then they will get off without a warning. The truth is, this makes them look much worse. The executive managers know who or what failed, and by blaming the team, the executives also know that they can no longer trust him or her. Traitors think that they are protected as they throw team members to the flames of blame. This personality type generally only happens once. The team members will take care of the rest.

## The Apathy Machine

"Why are you working so hard? We will never finish this on time." Imagine this being said in the voice of the famed cartoon character Droopy. Projects often require intense effort. As projects are temporary by their nature, most project team members have other responsibilities on top of their project duties. If the project manager is apathetic toward the project, why would the team members be motivated to complete it?

The Apathy Machine also tends to expand at a rapid rate. This attitude is spread much as a designer creates a tie-dyed shirt. They put the shirt on a platform, spin it quickly, and then spill paint in the center and let it flow very quickly to the outside. When the core of the team is apathetic, this spreads very quickly to the outside team members, essentially causing the project to fail before it has a chance to succeed.

## The Yes Person

"You want us to open a branch office on Mars in four weeks with a $50 budget? Yes sir!" Even though the Yes Person is generally a sales person turning over this project to a project manager, there are those project managers out there that fall into this personality type as well.

These are the project managers that run a planning meeting like this:

**PROJECT MANAGER (PM):** I have committed us to building a branch office on Mars in four weeks with a $50 budget. Now how much will it cost and when do you think you can be done?

**TEAM MEMBER (TM):** We need a bigger budget!

**PM:** Gee, I have already committed to $50. I can't go back and ask for more money.

**TM:** We need more time!

**PM:** The boss is already expecting four weeks. Can't we do it by then?

**DEJECTED TM:** I guess it will take four weeks and $50.

**PM:** Great, I will write the project plan!

By now, hopefully, the "It is what it is" methodology is sinking in. The Yes Person project manager should be the one challenging the sponsor and bringing in some realism. A quick statement like, 'Wow, four weeks and $50? Let me take that to the team and see what we can come up with" can allow you proper planning time. Don't just automatically agree; if you do, you might become the Yes Person to another company.

## Closing Thoughts

In closing, remember that your project team is ultimately what will make you successful or unsuccessful. As you read through these personality types, think about projects that you were on or managers that you worked for. Ever have anyone steal your idea and present it as his or her own? Have you ever seen someone blame you even though it wasn't your fault? Take these experiences and don't forget them.

Great project managers have had significant project failures. Just because you have had a project failure does not mean that you are not a good project manager. It means that you missed something that you won't miss the next time. Don't panic if things go wrong—they are supposed to. If they didn't, you most likely wouldn't be reading a book about this profession.

Project management is not for everyone, but if it is for you, it can be one of the most exciting and rewarding jobs. You are in charge of doing something that has never been done before. Not only that, but you have to say when you will be done and how much it will cost!

Embrace the challenge. Have fun with your teams. Enjoy the highs and lows. Project management can be a challenge, but it is also some of the most fun that you can have. Now, go forth and manage!

# Glossary

**budget**
A detailed list of costs for the resources necessary to complete the project within the anticipated time frame.

**contingency plan**
An alternative strategy predeveloped to avoid or reduce a potential risk that could jeopardize the successful completion of the project.

**cost-benefit analysis**
Many companies determine the overall value of the project using this formal method of analysis. The process factors in all aspects of the project, including finances, manpower, and time, to determine whether or not the benefits outweigh the costs.

**critical path**
A full sequence of activities that span the distance of the project and would take the most time to complete.

**deliverables**
The defined end products, results, or services produced during the project. A project goal can also be a deliverable.

**earned value analysis**
The process in which you analyze the progress of the project, comparing the money budgeted with the money spent and the work achieved. You can then determine whether you are ahead of or behind your projected budget.

**feasibility study**
A study that takes into account all the variables of the project, including budget, resources, and time constraints, and determines the likelihood that it can or cannot be done.

**Gantt chart**
A chart that puts tasks on a series of horizontal timelines, allowing you to track a project.

**mediation**
A method of resolving conflict in which a neutral third party intervenes to try and settle a dispute between two parties.

**milestone**
Checkpoint that you can look at to see whether you are on schedule in a project.

**network diagram**
A diagram that indicates the order and interrelationship of tasks in a logical sequence.

**PIR (Project Issues Review)**

A document that includes survey results, often featuring graphs or charts, which helps the team determine what was done well and what could be improved upon in the future. Survey participants are asked to complete the review in a specified amount of time.

**project**

A plan, proposal, or scheme that requires a concerted effort within a specified amount of time. It involves a task that is undertaken by a group of people, such as updating software and training employees in its use; or one person, such as learning a language.

**resource directory**

An organized listing of resources, including names and numbers, for ordering materials and contacting contractors, vendors, and all human resources for this and future projects.

**risk**

The chance that some activity or event will occur to prevent or delay you in your efforts to complete your project in the projected time frame. Look to assess and minimize risk.

**skills roster**

A roster of potential team members that illustrates their individual skills and knowledge in specific areas.

**stakeholders**

People who have an interest—from a personal, monetary, or business standpoint—in the success of the project. A stakeholder list or matrix includes the names of these people.

**task schedule or assignment matrix**

A listing of who will be doing which task or tasks on a particular project.

**team roster**

A listing of who made the project team, plus contact information and possibly other data.

**work breakdown structure**

An organized list, made early on, that includes all of the tasks that need to be accomplished for the project to be completed. This may be used to formulate a budget or network diagram, build a team, acquire resources, and so on.

# Resources

Numerous Web sites, newsletters, and courses are available for those interested in learning more about project management. From basic information and answers to certificate and master's programs, you can find a great deal of additional information on all facets of project management. Following are some resources for expanding your project management skills and knowledge.

## Web Sites

### The Project Management Site

This site provides listings and links to a variety of resources for project managers. The "Tools" section includes companion products for Microsoft Project, and the "News" section has the latest information from the companies making Project Management (PM) software. The "Online" section also provides useful questions and answers, but the font is a bit small.

*www.projectmanagement.com*

### The Project Management Center

This is a comprehensive portal site providing a wealth of resources and information. Seminars, software, organizations, links, news, articles, and even project manager jobs are part of this massive site. Numerous services are offered, including consulting and training, as well as listings of leading trainers and speakers in the field.

*www.infogoal.com/pmc/pmchome.htm*

### 4PM.com

This site is home to a 5,400 page Web site that is a yearlong project unto itself to explore. From online distance-learning courses to project management certifications to tools, software, and even a newsletter, plenty of information is available for the serious project manager. Courses are offered at all levels, and training seminars (in-person or on WEB CD) can also be found. And, if you want to converse with or hear from other project managers, there is a discussion board.

*www.4pm.com*

### AllPM.com

This site is designed to provide IT project managers with all the resources and information they should need. Hardware and software are available in the Project Manager's Store, and resource links include articles, reports, services, training, products, and project managers for hire. There is a bulletin board for posting as well as several discussion forums and an ALLPM newsletter.

*www.allpm.com*

## PM Forum

This site is a global project management site that includes numerous resources. You can find a directory of regional and international professional PM organizations, a PM library, globally accepted practices, and a wide range of services including a virtual office and currency converter. You will also find *Project Manager World Today*, a comprehensive online magazine dedicated to news and events in the PM industry.

*www.pmforum.org*

## Gantthead.com

This is a user-friendly PM site with articles, expert advice, discussions, industry news, templates, tools, and books. Professionals in the field will also find an upcoming events schedule. The comprehensive site is straightforward and offers guidance for all levels.

*www.gantthead.com*

## Max's Project Management

This site presents news, checklists, and the most comprehensive and extensive glossary of project management terms you could possibly imagine—if the term is not found here, it probably doesn't exist.

*www.maxwideman.com*

# Associations and Organizations

## The Project Management Institute

This is a nonprofit, professional membership association with over 70,000 members worldwide. In existence since 1969, PMI offers seminars, symposiums, training, career services, and resources. The institute offers certificate programs and awards for top achievers in the profession. The PMI guidebook is considered the industry standard.

*www.pmi.org* 📞*610-356-4600*

# Newsletters

## EIS Horizons Newsletter

This newsletter provides monthly articles and updates (which you can view online) on project management issues. All aspects of project management are touched upon in the informative newsletter.

*www.esi.intl.com*

## Project Management Insight

This is a newsletter published by Osprey PMI in England, which features PM themes and articles by experts on worldwide project management issues and information.

*www.ospreypmi.com*

# Courses/Distance Learning

## The University of Washington Project Management Certificate Program

The University of Washington offers courses covering the basics of project management from work breakdown structure to closing the project. Through the use of distance-learning modules, you can participate in courses with Internet access, a CD-Rom drive, or high-density disk drive and 28.8-speed modem.

*www.outreach.washington.edu*
📞*1-800-543-2320*

### IBM Learning Services

IBM Learning Services offers a course called Principles of Project Management, which covers the project scope from initiating and project planning to managing a project within budget to closing. The five-day course is offered at various U.S. locations. For information, go to their Web address and click on the course name.

✎*www-3.ibm.com/services/learning/spotlight/ project.html*

### ESI International

ESI International has a course called Managing Projects with Microsoft Project. The online lecture course is available twenty-four hours a day in text or Real Audio formats. Case studies, quizzes, and chats are available.

✆*1-888-ESI-8884*
✎*www.esi-intl.com*

### The University of Wisconsin-Platteville

This school has established a three-course certificate distance-learning program. The program is designed to set a solid foundation for project managers.

✆*1-800-362-5460*
✎*www.uwplatt.edu*

### The American Graduate University

Located in Covina, California, this school offers accredited distance-learning programs with an MA in project management. Individual courses (nondegree) can also be taken.

✆*626-966-4576*
✎*www.agu.edu*

### Western Carolina University

Western Carolina University features a fully accredited distance-learning project management program and master's degree program.

✆*828-227-7398*
✎*www.wcu.edu*

### The International School of Information Management

This school offers a certificate program in project management. The forty-year-old, Denver-based institution has a three-course certificate curriculum. The Web site has a FAQ page with helpful answers about courses.

✆*303-333-4224 or 800-441-ISIM*
✎*www.isimu.edu*

## Project Management Events

### Project World Global

Project World Global offers worldwide events regarding project management. Details on worldwide PM events, along with industry news, can be found on their Web site. You can register online or call for more information on upcoming conferences and expositions near you.

✆*1-888-827-6699*
✎*www.projectworld.com*

# Index

Acceptance, 51–52
Agreements, 90–92, 135, 211.
    *See also* Contracts
American Academy of
    Project Management, 272
"Apathy Machine," 279
Associations, 285
Australian Institute of Project
    Management (AIPM),
    271–72
Authority, 94–96

Baselines, 53–54
Blamers, 278
Budget
    changes in, 134–36
    determining, 125–38
    elements of, 126–27
    juggling, 136–37
    monitoring, 152–55
    sample of, 133
"Budget busters," 137–38

Calendar schedules, 123–24
Certifications, 267–73
Certified Associate in Project
    Management (CAPM), 268
Closing project, 69–80
Closure documentation,
    72–73
Commitment, building,
    96–97
Communication documents,
    208–11
Communication matrix, 212
Communications
    management, 205–13
Communications plan, 121,
    208, 212
Competition, 19–20
Completion of project, 69–
    80, 117–18, 253–66. *See also*
    End dates
CompTIA Project+, 272
Conflict assessment, 218–19
Conflict resolution, 215–34
Consistency, 104–5

Contracts, 18, 135, 199, 232.
    *See also* Agreements
Controlling project, 61–68
Cooperative conflict, 216–17
Cost-benefit analysis, 10–11
Critical Path Method (CPM),
    119
"Cycle within cycle," 63–64,
    248

Deadlines, 40, 48, 117. *See
    also* Due dates; End dates
Delegation, 49, 95–96, 106
Deliverables, 20
Disassembling team, 76–77
Due dates, 51, 59–60, 116. *See
    also* Deadlines; End dates

Earned Value Analysis,
    154–55
Ego, 276
End dates, 46, 52, 59–60, 117–
    18, 146, 253–66. *See also*
    Deadlines; Due dates

Estimating tasks, 116–17

Evaluating results, 253–66

Expenditures, monitoring, 152–55. *See also* Budget

Failure, avoiding, 246–52. *See also* Pitfalls, avoiding

Final phase, 256–59

Float time, 118

Gantt chart, 119–20, 171–72, 174, 177–78

Glossary, 282–83

Halo effect, 276

Handoff, 73–74

Hoarders, 277–78

Incentives, 26, 239–41

Initiation phase, 35–42

Intangibles, monitoring, 159–61

International Project Management Association (IPMA), 270–71

Leadership, 101–8

Leadership styles, 102–6

Learning from project, 263–65

Life cycles, 29–34

List of tasks, 44–45

Mediation, 220

Methodologies, 33–34

Microsoft Project, 174

Milestones, 115, 119, 124

Mistakes, 24–26

Monitoring progress, 139–61

Monitoring risk, 189–96

Motivational seminars, 241–42

Motivational skills, 235–45

Motivational theories, 236–39

Negotiating, 232–34

Network diagram, 110–15

Noncommunicators, 277

Open Workbench, 174

Passive-aggressive types, 217

People-pleasers, 217

Performance Evaluation and Review Technique (PERT), 116, 119, 174

Performance periods, 145–47

Personalities, blend of, 97–100

Personalities, handling, 215–34

Personality traits, 217–18

Pitfalls, anticipating, 122–23

Pitfalls, avoiding, 275–81. *See also* Failure, avoiding

Planning, 43–54

Postproject evaluations, 254, 259–62

Prima donnas, 217

Prioritizing risks, 191–92

Prioritizing tasks, 27

Procrastinators, 276

Progress, monitoring, 139–61

Progress, tracking, 56–59

Project. *See also* Project plan

closure of, 69–80

completion of, 69–80, 253–66

control of, 61–68

evaluation of, 18–19

evolution of, 155–56

execution of, 55–60

goals for, 18–20

learning from, 263–65

life cycle of, 29–34

managing, 1–15

phases of, 29–34, 44–54, 56–60, 62–68

problems with, 202–4

schedule for, 44–45

selecting, 28

success of, 262

vision of, 18

Project Issues Review (PIR), 260

Project Management Body of Knowledge (PMBOK), 268

Project Management Institute (PMI), 206, 268, 269, 270, 272

Project Management Office (PMO), 163–68

Project Management Professional (PMP), 269

Project management software, 169–81

Project manager standards, 36, 37, 111, 166–67

Project manager tips, 18, 106, 163–68

Project plan. *See also* Project
baseline for, 53–54
elements of, 46–51
myths about, 44
selling, 52–53
task list for, 44–45

Projects in Controlled Environments (PRINCE 2), 272

Project sponsor, 31, 38, 58

Research, 21–23

Resource assignment matrix, 120–21

Resources, 284–86

Respect, 86–87

Results, evaluating, 253–66

Risk
analyzing, 200–202
levels of, 144–45
managing, 183–204
mitigating, 186, 189, 192
monitoring, 189–96
of new methods, 19
prioritizing, 191–92

Schedule
creating, 109–24
monitoring, 56–57, 143
for tasks, 120–21

Scheduling rules, 45–46

Scheduling tools, 44–45

Self-monitoring, 156–58

Self-motivation, 245

Selling plan, 52–53

Senior management reporting, 107

Sign-off, 74–75

Skill/Personality Assessment Matrix, 99

Skills chart, 92

Slack time, 118

Software programs, 169–81

Staff coordination, 93

Success, 262

SureTrak Project Manager, 174–75

Tasks
charts for, 91
estimating, 116–17
list of, 44–45
prioritizing, 27
relationships of, 45
schedule for, 120–21

Team
assembling, 81–100
disassembling, 76–77
members of, 82, 147–52, 198–99
personalities of, 97–100
selecting, 82–89
team huddle, 102

Technical team, 151–52, 198–99

Tigers, 217

Tracking progress, 56–59

Training, 267–73

Traitors, 278–79

Transitions, 73–74

Trial-and-error, 263–64, 273

Web sites, 284–85

"Yes" person, 280

# THE EVERYTHING SERIES!

## BUSINESS & PERSONAL FINANCE

Everything® Accounting Book
Everything® Budgeting Book, 2nd Ed.
Everything® Business Planning Book
Everything® Coaching and Mentoring Book, 2nd Ed.
Everything® Fundraising Book
Everything® Get Out of Debt Book
Everything® Grant Writing Book, 2nd Ed.
Everything® Guide to Buying Foreclosures
**Everything® Guide to Fundraising, $15.95**
Everything® Guide to Mortgages
Everything® Guide to Personal Finance for Single Mothers
Everything® Home-Based Business Book, 2nd Ed.
**Everything® Homebuying Book, 3rd Ed., $15.95**
Everything® Homeselling Book, 2nd Ed.
Everything® Human Resource Management Book
Everything® Improve Your Credit Book
Everything® Investing Book, 2nd Ed.
Everything® Landlording Book
Everything® Leadership Book, 2nd Ed.
Everything® Managing People Book, 2nd Ed.
Everything® Negotiating Book
Everything® Online Auctions Book
Everything® Online Business Book
Everything® Personal Finance Book
Everything® Personal Finance in Your 20s & 30s Book, 2nd Ed.
**Everything® Personal Finance in Your 40s & 50s Book, $15.95**
Everything® Project Management Book, 2nd Ed.
Everything® Real Estate Investing Book
Everything® Retirement Planning Book
Everything® Robert's Rules Book, $7.95
Everything® Selling Book
Everything® Start Your Own Business Book, 2nd Ed.
Everything® Wills & Estate Planning Book

## COOKING

Everything® Barbecue Cookbook
Everything® Bartender's Book, 2nd Ed., $9.95
Everything® Calorie Counting Cookbook
Everything® Cheese Book
Everything® Chinese Cookbook
Everything® Classic Recipes Book
Everything® Cocktail Parties & Drinks Book
Everything® College Cookbook
Everything® Cooking for Baby and Toddler Book
Everything® Diabetes Cookbook
Everything® Easy Gourmet Cookbook
Everything® Fondue Cookbook
**Everything® Food Allergy Cookbook, $15.95**
Everything® Fondue Party Book
Everything® Gluten-Free Cookbook
Everything® Glycemic Index Cookbook
Everything® Grilling Cookbook
**Everything® Healthy Cooking for Parties Book, $15.95**
Everything® Holiday Cookbook
Everything® Indian Cookbook
Everything® Lactose-Free Cookbook
Everything® Low-Cholesterol Cookbook

**Everything® Low-Fat High-Flavor Cookbook, 2nd Ed., $15.95**
Everything® Low-Salt Cookbook
Everything® Meals for a Month Cookbook
Everything® Meals on a Budget Cookbook
Everything® Mediterranean Cookbook
Everything® Mexican Cookbook
Everything® No Trans Fat Cookbook
**Everything® One-Pot Cookbook, 2nd Ed., $15.95**
**Everything® Organic Cooking for Baby & Toddler Book, $15.95**
Everything® Pizza Cookbook
**Everything® Quick Meals Cookbook, 2nd Ed., $15.95**
Everything® Slow Cooker Cookbook
Everything® Slow Cooking for a Crowd Cookbook
Everything® Soup Cookbook
Everything® Stir-Fry Cookbook
Everything® Sugar-Free Cookbook
Everything® Tapas and Small Plates Cookbook
Everything® Tex-Mex Cookbook
Everything® Thai Cookbook
Everything® Vegetarian Cookbook
Everything® Whole-Grain, High-Fiber Cookbook
Everything® Wild Game Cookbook
Everything® Wine Book, 2nd Ed.

## GAMES

Everything® 15-Minute Sudoku Book, $9.95
Everything® 30-Minute Sudoku Book, $9.95
Everything® Bible Crosswords Book, $9.95
Everything® Blackjack Strategy Book
Everything® Brain Strain Book, $9.95
Everything® Bridge Book
Everything® Card Games Book
Everything® Card Tricks Book, $9.95
Everything® Casino Gambling Book, 2nd Ed.
Everything® Chess Basics Book
**Everything® Christmas Crosswords Book, $9.95**
Everything® Craps Strategy Book
Everything® Crossword and Puzzle Book
**Everything® Crosswords and Puzzles for Quote Lovers Book, $9.95**
Everything® Crossword Challenge Book
Everything® Crosswords for the Beach Book, $9.95
Everything® Cryptic Crosswords Book, $9.95
Everything® Cryptograms Book, $9.95
Everything® Easy Crosswords Book
Everything® Easy Kakuro Book, $9.95
Everything® Easy Large-Print Crosswords Book
Everything® Games Book, 2nd Ed.
**Everything® Giant Book of Crosswords**
Everything® Giant Sudoku Book, $9.95
Everything® Giant Word Search Book
Everything® Kakuro Challenge Book, $9.95
Everything® Large-Print Crossword Challenge Book
Everything® Large-Print Crosswords Book
**Everything® Large-Print Travel Crosswords Book**
Everything® Lateral Thinking Puzzles Book, $9.95
Everything® Literary Crosswords Book, $9.95
Everything® Mazes Book
Everything® Memory Booster Puzzles Book, $9.95

Everything® Movie Crosswords Book, $9.95
Everything® Music Crosswords Book, $9.95
Everything® Online Poker Book
Everything® Pencil Puzzles Book, $9.95
Everything® Poker Strategy Book
Everything® Pool & Billiards Book
Everything® Puzzles for Commuters Book, $9.95
Everything® Puzzles for Dog Lovers Book, $9.95
Everything® Sports Crosswords Book, $9.95
Everything® Test Your IQ Book, $9.95
Everything® Texas Hold 'Em Book, $9.95
Everything® Travel Crosswords Book, $9.95
**Everything® Travel Mazes Book, $9.95**
**Everything® Travel Word Search Book, $9.95**
Everything® TV Crosswords Book, $9.95
Everything® Word Games Challenge Book
Everything® Word Scramble Book
Everything® Word Search Book

## HEALTH

Everything® Alzheimer's Book
Everything® Diabetes Book
Everything® First Aid Book, $9.95
**Everything® Green Living Book**
**Everything® Health Guide to Addiction and Recovery**
Everything® Health Guide to Adult Bipolar Disorder
Everything® Health Guide to Arthritis
Everything® Health Guide to Controlling Anxiety
Everything® Health Guide to Depression
**Everything® Health Guide to Diabetes, 2nd Ed.**
Everything® Health Guide to Fibromyalgia
Everything® Health Guide to Menopause, 2nd Ed.
Everything® Health Guide to Migraines
**Everything® Health Guide to Multiple Sclerosis**
Everything® Health Guide to OCD
Everything® Health Guide to PMS
Everything® Health Guide to Postpartum Care
Everything® Health Guide to Thyroid Disease
Everything® Hypnosis Book
Everything® Low Cholesterol Book
Everything® Menopause Book
Everything® Nutrition Book
Everything® Reflexology Book
Everything® Stress Management Book
**Everything® Superfoods Book, $15.95**

## HISTORY

Everything® American Government Book
Everything® American History Book, 2nd Ed.
**Everything® American Revolution Book, $15.95**
Everything® Civil War Book
Everything® Freemasons Book
Everything® Irish History & Heritage Book
Everything® World War II Book, 2nd Ed.

## HOBBIES

Everything® Candlemaking Book
Everything® Cartooning Book
Everything® Coin Collecting Book
Everything® Digital Photography Book, 2nd Ed.

Everything® Drawing Book
Everything® Family Tree Book, 2nd Ed.
**Everything® Guide to Online Genealogy, $15.95**
Everything® Knitting Book
Everything® Knots Book
Everything® Photography Book
Everything® Quilting Book
Everything® Sewing Book
Everything® Soapmaking Book, 2nd Ed.
Everything® Woodworking Book

## HOME IMPROVEMENT

Everything® Feng Shui Book
Everything® Feng Shui Decluttering Book, $9.95
Everything® Fix-It Book
Everything® Green Living Book
Everything® Home Decorating Book
Everything® Home Storage Solutions Book
Everything® Homebuilding Book
Everything® Organize Your Home Book, 2nd Ed.

## KIDS' BOOKS

All titles are $7.95
Everything® Fairy Tales Book, $14.95
Everything® Kids' Animal Puzzle & Activity Book
Everything® Kids' Astronomy Book
Everything® Kids' Baseball Book, 5th Ed.
Everything® Kids' Bible Trivia Book
Everything® Kids' Bugs Book
Everything® Kids' Cars and Trucks Puzzle and Activity Book
Everything® Kids' Christmas Puzzle & Activity Book
Everything® Kids' Connect the Dots
    Puzzle and Activity Book
**Everything® Kids' Cookbook, 2nd Ed.**
Everything® Kids' Crazy Puzzles Book
Everything® Kids' Dinosaurs Book
**Everything® Kids' Dragons Puzzle and Activity Book**
Everything® Kids' Environment Book $7.95
Everything® Kids' Fairies Puzzle and Activity Book
Everything® Kids' First Spanish Puzzle and Activity Book
Everything® Kids' Football Book
**Everything® Kids' Geography Book**
Everything® Kids' Gross Cookbook
Everything® Kids' Gross Hidden Pictures Book
Everything® Kids' Gross Jokes Book
Everything® Kids' Gross Mazes Book
Everything® Kids' Gross Puzzle & Activity Book
Everything® Kids' Halloween Puzzle & Activity Book
**Everything® Kids' Hanukkah Puzzle and Activity Book**
Everything® Kids' Hidden Pictures Book
Everything® Kids' Horses Book
Everything® Kids' Joke Book
Everything® Kids' Knock Knock Book
Everything® Kids' Learning French Book
Everything® Kids' Learning Spanish Book
Everything® Kids' Magical Science Experiments Book
Everything® Kids' Math Puzzles Book
Everything® Kids' Mazes Book
**Everything® Kids' Money Book, 2nd Ed.**
**Everything® Kids' Mummies, Pharaoh's, and Pyramids**
    **Puzzle and Activity Book**
Everything® Kids' Nature Book
Everything® Kids' Pirates Puzzle and Activity Book
Everything® Kids' Presidents Book
Everything® Kids' Princess Puzzle and Activity Book
Everything® Kids' Puzzle Book

Everything® Kids' Racecars Puzzle and Activity Book
Everything® Kids' Riddles & Brain Teasers Book
Everything® Kids' Science Experiments Book
Everything® Kids' Sharks Book
Everything® Kids' Soccer Book
**Everything® Kids' Spelling Book**
Everything® Kids' Spies Puzzle and Activity Book
Everything® Kids' States Book
Everything® Kids' Travel Activity Book
Everything® Kids' Word Search Puzzle and Activity Book

## LANGUAGE

Everything® Conversational Japanese Book with CD, $19.95
Everything® French Grammar Book
Everything® French Phrase Book, $9.95
Everything® French Verb Book, $9.95
**Everything® German Phrase Book, $9.95**
Everything® German Practice Book with CD, $19.95
Everything® Inglés Book
Everything® Intermediate Spanish Book with CD, $19.95
**Everything® Italian Phrase Book, $9.95**
Everything® Italian Practice Book with CD, $19.95
Everything® Learning Brazilian Portuguese Book with CD, $19.95
Everything® Learning French Book with CD, 2nd Ed., $19.95
Everything® Learning German Book
Everything® Learning Italian Book
Everything® Learning Latin Book
Everything® Learning Russian Book with CD, $19.95
Everything® Learning Spanish Book
Everything® Learning Spanish Book with CD, 2nd Ed., $19.95
Everything® Russian Practice Book with CD, $19.95
**Everything® Sign Language Book, $15.95**
Everything® Spanish Grammar Book
Everything® Spanish Phrase Book, $9.95
Everything® Spanish Practice Book with CD, $19.95
Everything® Spanish Verb Book, $9.95
Everything® Speaking Mandarin Chinese Book with CD, $19.95

## MUSIC

Everything® Bass Guitar Book with CD, $19.95
Everything® Drums Book with CD, $19.95
Everything® Guitar Book with CD, 2nd Ed., $19.95
Everything® Guitar Chords Book with CD, $19.95
**Everything® Guitar Scales Book with CD, $19.95**
Everything® Harmonica Book with CD, $15.95
Everything® Home Recording Book
Everything® Music Theory Book with CD, $19.95
Everything® Reading Music Book with CD, $19.95
Everything® Rock & Blues Guitar Book with CD, $19.95
Everything® Rock & Blues Piano Book with CD, $19.95
**Everything® Rock Drums Book with CD, $19.95**
**Everything® Singing Book with CD, $19.95**
Everything® Songwriting Book

## NEW AGE

Everything® Astrology Book, 2nd Ed.
Everything® Birthday Personology Book
**Everything® Celtic Wisdom Book, $15.95**
Everything® Dreams Book, 2nd Ed.
**Everything® Law of Attraction Book, $15.95**
Everything® Love Signs Book, $9.95
Everything® Love Spells Book, $9.95
Everything® Palmistry Book
Everything® Psychic Book
Everything® Reiki Book

Everything® Sex Signs Book, $9.95
Everything® Spells & Charms Book, 2nd Ed.
Everything® Tarot Book, 2nd Ed.
Everything® Toltec Wisdom Book
Everything® Wicca & Witchcraft Book, 2nd Ed.

## PARENTING

Everything® Baby Names Book, 2nd Ed.
Everything® Baby Shower Book, 2nd Ed.
Everything® Baby Sign Language Book with DVD
Everything® Baby's First Year Book
Everything® Birthing Book
Everything® Breastfeeding Book
Everything® Father-to-Be Book
Everything® Father's First Year Book
Everything® Get Ready for Baby Book, 2nd Ed.
Everything® Get Your Baby to Sleep Book, $9.95
Everything® Getting Pregnant Book
Everything® Guide to Pregnancy Over 35
Everything® Guide to Raising a One-Year-Old
Everything® Guide to Raising a Two-Year-Old
Everything® Guide to Raising Adolescent Boys
Everything® Guide to Raising Adolescent Girls
Everything® Mother's First Year Book
Everything® Parent's Guide to Childhood Illnesses
Everything® Parent's Guide to Children and Divorce
Everything® Parent's Guide to Children with ADD/ADHD
Everything® Parent's Guide to Children with Asperger's
    Syndrome
**Everything® Parent's Guide to Children with Anxiety**
Everything® Parent's Guide to Children with Asthma
Everything® Parent's Guide to Children with Autism
Everything® Parent's Guide to Children with Bipolar Disorder
Everything® Parent's Guide to Children with Depression
Everything® Parent's Guide to Children with Dyslexia
Everything® Parent's Guide to Children with Juvenile Diabetes
**Everything® Parent's Guide to Children with OCD**
Everything® Parent's Guide to Positive Discipline
Everything® Parent's Guide to Raising Boys
Everything® Parent's Guide to Raising Girls
Everything® Parent's Guide to Raising Siblings
**Everything® Parent's Guide to Raising Your**
    **Adopted Child**
Everything® Parent's Guide to Sensory Integration Disorder
Everything® Parent's Guide to Tantrums
Everything® Parent's Guide to the Strong-Willed Child
Everything® Parenting a Teenager Book
Everything® Potty Training Book, $9.95
Everything® Pregnancy Book, 3rd Ed.
Everything® Pregnancy Fitness Book
Everything® Pregnancy Nutrition Book
Everything® Pregnancy Organizer, 2nd Ed., $16.95
Everything® Toddler Activities Book
Everything® Toddler Book
Everything® Tween Book
Everything® Twins, Triplets, and More Book

## PETS

Everything® Aquarium Book
Everything® Boxer Book
Everything® Cat Book, 2nd Ed.
Everything® Chihuahua Book
Everything® Cooking for Dogs Book
Everything® Dachshund Book
Everything® Dog Book, 2nd Ed.
Everything® Dog Grooming Book

Everything® Dog Obedience Book
Everything® Dog Owner's Organizer, $16.95
Everything® Dog Training and Tricks Book
Everything® German Shepherd Book
Everything® Golden Retriever Book
**Everything® Horse Book, 2nd Ed., $15.95**
Everything® Horse Care Book
Everything® Horseback Riding Book
Everything® Labrador Retriever Book
Everything® Poodle Book
Everything® Pug Book
Everything® Puppy Book
Everything® Small Dogs Book
Everything® Tropical Fish Book
Everything® Yorkshire Terrier Book

## REFERENCE

Everything® American Presidents Book
Everything® Blogging Book
Everything® Build Your Vocabulary Book, $9.95
Everything® Car Care Book
Everything® Classical Mythology Book
Everything® Da Vinci Book
Everything® Einstein Book
Everything® Enneagram Book
Everything® Etiquette Book, 2nd Ed.
**Everything® Family Christmas Book, $15.95**
Everything® Guide to C. S. Lewis & Narnia
**Everything® Guide to Divorce, 2nd Ed., $15.95**
Everything® Guide to Edgar Allan Poe
Everything® Guide to Understanding Philosophy
Everything® Inventions and Patents Book
Everything® Jacqueline Kennedy Onassis Book
Everything® John F. Kennedy Book
Everything® Mafia Book
Everything® Martin Luther King Jr. Book
Everything® Pirates Book
Everything® Private Investigation Book
Everything® Psychology Book
Everything® Public Speaking Book, $9.95
Everything® Shakespeare Book, 2nd Ed.

## RELIGION

Everything® Angels Book
Everything® Bible Book
Everything® Bible Study Book with CD, $19.95
Everything® Buddhism Book
Everything® Catholicism Book
Everything® Christianity Book
Everything® Gnostic Gospels Book
**Everything® Hinduism Book, $15.95**
Everything® History of the Bible Book
Everything® Jesus Book
Everything® Jewish History & Heritage Book
Everything® Judaism Book
Everything® Kabbalah Book
Everything® Koran Book
Everything® Mary Book
Everything® Mary Magdalene Book
Everything® Prayer Book

Everything® Saints Book, 2nd Ed.
Everything® Torah Book
Everything® Understanding Islam Book
Everything® Women of the Bible Book
Everything® World's Religions Book

## SCHOOL & CAREERS

Everything® Career Tests Book
Everything® College Major Test Book
Everything® College Survival Book, 2nd Ed.
Everything® Cover Letter Book, 2nd Ed.
Everything® Filmmaking Book
Everything® Get-a-Job Book, 2nd Ed.
Everything® Guide to Being a Paralegal
Everything® Guide to Being a Personal Trainer
Everything® Guide to Being a Real Estate Agent
Everything® Guide to Being a Sales Rep
Everything® Guide to Being an Event Planner
Everything® Guide to Careers in Health Care
Everything® Guide to Careers in Law Enforcement
Everything® Guide to Government Jobs
Everything® Guide to Starting and Running a Catering
    Business
Everything® Guide to Starting and Running a Restaurant
**Everything® Guide to Starting and Running
    a Retail Store**
Everything® Job Interview Book, 2nd Ed.
Everything® New Nurse Book
Everything® New Teacher Book
Everything® Paying for College Book
Everything® Practice Interview Book
Everything® Resume Book, 3rd Ed.
Everything® Study Book

## SELF-HELP

Everything® Body Language Book
Everything® Dating Book, 2nd Ed.
Everything® Great Sex Book
**Everything® Guide to Caring for Aging Parents,
    $15.95**
Everything® Self-Esteem Book
**Everything® Self-Hypnosis Book, $9.95**
Everything® Tantric Sex Book

## SPORTS & FITNESS

Everything® Easy Fitness Book
Everything® Fishing Book
**Everything® Guide to Weight Training, $15.95**
Everything® Krav Maga for Fitness Book
Everything® Running Book, 2nd Ed.
**Everything® Triathlon Training Book, $15.95**

## TRAVEL

Everything® Family Guide to Coastal Florida
Everything® Family Guide to Cruise Vacations
Everything® Family Guide to Hawaii
Everything® Family Guide to Las Vegas, 2nd Ed.
Everything® Family Guide to Mexico
Everything® Family Guide to New England, 2nd Ed.

Everything® Family Guide to New York City, 3rd Ed.
**Everything® Family Guide to Northern California
    and Lake Tahoe**
Everything® Family Guide to RV Travel & Campgrounds
Everything® Family Guide to the Caribbean
Everything® Family Guide to the Disneyland® Resort, California
    Adventure®, Universal Studios®, and the Anaheim
    Area, 2nd Ed.
Everything® Family Guide to the Walt Disney World Resort®,
    Universal Studios®, and Greater Orlando, 5th Ed.
Everything® Family Guide to Timeshares
Everything® Family Guide to Washington D.C., 2nd Ed.

## WEDDINGS

Everything® Bachelorette Party Book, $9.95
Everything® Bridesmaid Book, $9.95
Everything® Destination Wedding Book
Everything® Father of the Bride Book, $9.95
**Everything® Green Wedding Book, $15.95**
Everything® Groom Book, $9.95
**Everything® Jewish Wedding Book, 2nd Ed., $15.95**
Everything® Mother of the Bride Book, $9.95
Everything® Outdoor Wedding Book
Everything® Wedding Book, 3rd Ed.
Everything® Wedding Checklist, $9.95
Everything® Wedding Etiquette Book, $9.95
Everything® Wedding Organizer, 2nd Ed., $16.95
Everything® Wedding Shower Book, $9.95
**Everything® Wedding Vows Book, 3rd Ed., $9.95**
Everything® Wedding Workout Book
Everything® Weddings on a Budget Book, 2nd Ed., $9.95

## WRITING

Everything® Creative Writing Book
Everything® Get Published Book, 2nd Ed.
Everything® Grammar and Style Book, 2nd Ed.
Everything® Guide to Magazine Writing
Everything® Guide to Writing a Book Proposal
Everything® Guide to Writing a Novel
Everything® Guide to Writing Children's Books
Everything® Guide to Writing Copy
Everything® Guide to Writing Graphic Novels
Everything® Guide to Writing Research Papers
**Everything® Guide to Writing a Romance Novel, $15.95**
Everything® Improve Your Writing Book, 2nd Ed.
Everything® Writing Poetry Book